BEST WISHES,

Ian Woodall

Just for the love of it

Just for the love of it

The first woman to climb
Mount Everest from both sides

Cathy O'Dowd

FREE TO DECIDE

PUBLISHING

To Pemba Tenging Sherpa and Jangbu Sherpa

without whose contribution none of this would have been possible

Pemba and Jangbu on the slopes of Everest.

FREE TO DECIDE PUBLISHING

Suite 501, 223 Regent Street, London, W1R 8QD, UK
Email: freetodecide@btinternet.com

First published in October 1999
Reprinted 2003, 2004

Poem on page 185 © Mike Thexton

Text: Cathy O'Dowd
www.cathyodowd.com

Photographs: Free To Decide

Research: Elizabeth Hawley

Administration: Maureen Nkomo
Charmine Naidu
Wimpie Carstens

Production: Clare Ellis
Ian Woodall
Cathy O'Dowd

Proof-reading: Erica Davies
Cover design: Nadine Kloppers of Vasoline Advertising
Design and layout: Dinki Vergottini
Map design: Milton Wasserman

Reproduction and printing: The Bath Press (CPI Group)

ISBN 0-620-24782-7

Contents

Foreword

"It is one of the symptoms of this age of nerves and hysteria that we magnify everything, that our boasts are frantic and our scares pitiable, that we call a man who plays well at football a hero and that all successes are triumphs."

I quoted this cutting from the Sketch newspaper, which followed Shackleton's return from Antartica in June 1909, in my book *Mind over matter* published in 1993 on my return from the world's first unassisted crossing of the Antartic cotinent.

Although written in 1909 it is astonishing how appropriate it still is today when attitudes to human endeavour are measured largely in terms of success or failure, or the number of points put on the scoreboard, with very little in between. Just 'playing the game' or 'having a go' doesn't seem a good enough reason to challenge oneself anymore and increasingly in our technological age, the value, logic and reasoning behind feats of human endurance and courage are being questioned.

How refreshing therefore, when there are still so many challenges left in the world, and at a time when these very qualities need to be developed in our youth, to find a young modern explorer in Cathy O"Dowd pushing her limits 'just for the love of it'. A reason that seems as good as any, and probably better than most.

Sir Ranulph Fiennes

The Himalaya seen from the Nepal side. Everest is on the left, with Lhotse next to it, and Makalu on the far right. Everest, at 29 028 feet high, is nearly at the altitude at which jumbo jets cruise.

Aerial map of the Everest massif

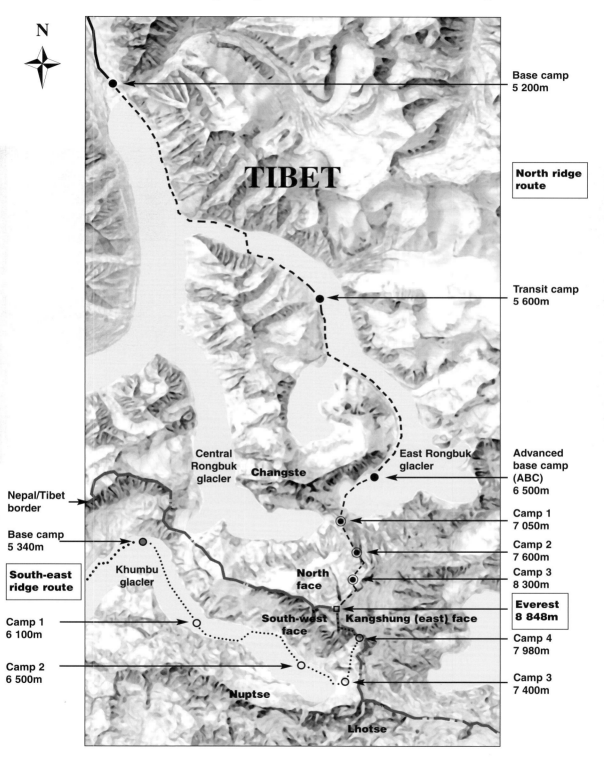

N

Base camp
5 200m

**North ridge
route**

TIBET

Transit camp
5 600m

Central
Rongbuk
glacier

Changste

East Rongbuk
glacier

Advanced
base camp
(ABC)
6 500m

Nepal/Tibet
border

Camp 1
7 050m

Base camp
5 340m

Camp 2
7 600m

**South-east
ridge route**

Khumbu
glacier

North
face

Camp 3
8 300m

Camp 1
6 100m

South-west
face

**Everest
8 848m**

Kangshung (east) face

Camp 4
7 980m

Camp 2
6 500m

Camp 3
7 400m

Nuptse

Lhotse

North Ridge Route

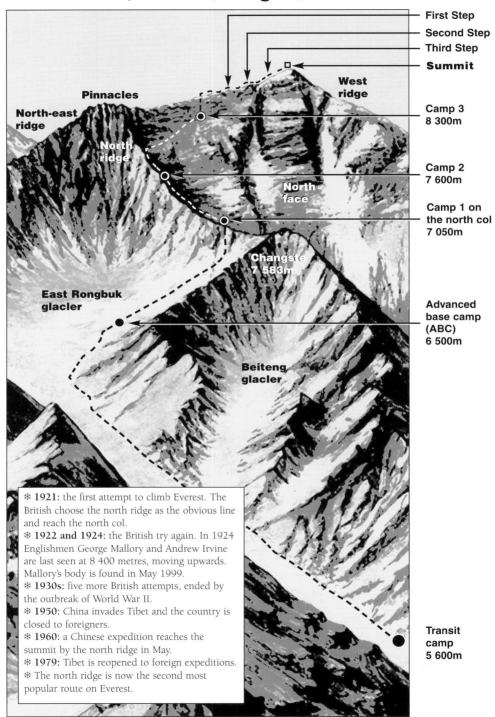

First Step
Second Step
Third Step
Summit

West ridge

Camp 3
8 300m

Camp 2
7 600m

Camp 1 on
the north col
7 050m

Advanced
base camp
(ABC)
6 500m

Transit
camp
5 600m

Pinnacles

North-east
ridge

North
ridge

North
face

Changste
7 583m

East Rongbuk
glacier

Beiteng
glacier

❈ **1921:** the first attempt to climb Everest. The British choose the north ridge as the obvious line and reach the north col.
❈ **1922 and 1924:** the British try again. In 1924 Englishmen George Mallory and Andrew Irvine are last seen at 8 400 metres, moving upwards. Mallory's body is found in May 1999.
❈ **1930s:** five more British attempts, ended by the outbreak of World War II.
❈ **1950:** China invades Tibet and the country is closed to foreigners.
❈ **1960:** a Chinese expedition reaches the summit by the north ridge in May.
❈ **1979:** Tibet is reopened to foreign expeditions.
❈ The north ridge is now the second most popular route on Everest.

South-east Ridge Route

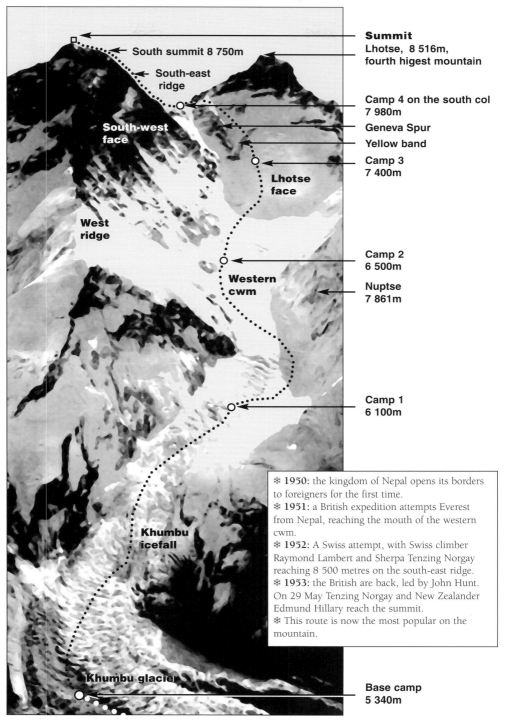

Summit

South summit 8 750m

South-east ridge

South-west face

West ridge

Khumbu icefall

Khumbu glacier

Lhotse, 8 516m, fourth higest mountain

Camp 4 on the south col 7 980m

Geneva Spur

Yellow band

Camp 3 7 400m

Lhotse face

Camp 2 6 500m

Nuptse 7 861m

Camp 1 6 100m

Western cwm

Base camp 5 340m

✽ **1950**: the kingdom of Nepal opens its borders to foreigners for the first time.
✽ **1951**: a British expedition attempts Everest from Nepal, reaching the mouth of the western cwm.
✽ **1952**: A Swiss attempt, with Swiss climber Raymond Lambert and Sherpa Tenzing Norgay reaching 8 500 metres on the south-east ridge.
✽ **1953**: the British are back, led by John Hunt. On 29 May Tenzing Norgay and New Zealander Edmund Hillary reach the summit.
✽ This route is now the most popular on the mountain.

Prologue

I dumped the Sunday paper on the table and went into the kitchen to make myself coffee. I had promised myself a leisurely start to the day before getting back to work writing up my Masters thesis. I would sit in the sun, which was streaming in through the bay windows, read the paper, and then return to my computer. I would rather have spent the day rock-climbing, but it was November, time of end-of-year exams, and there was no one available to join me on the rock.

I lived in Grahamstown, a small town hanging onto vestiges of its British past in the middle of the great sun-baked plains of the Eastern Cape in South Africa. The town centred on a university and a few elite schools. I had been in Grahamstown for nearly three years and was in the final months of my Masters degree in Media Studies.

I was a Johannesburg girl, born and bred in the great city where all South Africa's wealth and industry is concentrated. Johannesburg is not a pretty city, nor a very safe one, but it is vibrant. I found the isolated, small-town atmosphere of Grahamstown alternately soothing and stifling.

As I spread the newspaper on the table I cast my eye over the headlines. One struck me immediately: 'Sunday Times Everest Expedition. We take the South African flag to the top of the world'. Under it was a picture of three men standing on top of Table Mountain. Table Mountain is South Africa's pride and joy, all of 1 000 metres high. It was going to be quite a leap from there to 8 848 metres, the summit of the world. I read on, most interested. I had been rock-climbing for nine years, ever since leaving school, and I was passionate about the sport. For six of those years, I had also been mountaineering, a sport more difficult to indulge in as a South African. The highest mountain at our end of the African continent is Thabana Ntlenyana, which, being all of 3 482 metres high, receives little more than a smattering of snow each year. I had travelled to the Ruwenzori in Central Africa, to the Bolivian Andes, to the Alps. However, the man I had done most of my mountaineering with had been killed in Peru 18 months previously, and I had done nothing since then.

The Sunday Times team was to attempt the classic south route up Everest in May of 1996. It would be the first ever attempt by South Africans. Before the fall of apartheid, we had not been able to get permits for the world's biggest mountains. The expedition leader was Ian Woodall. I had never heard of him. I looked at his photograph - dark-blonde curly hair, small in stature, in his late thirties or early forties. It made little impression on me.

Then the third paragraph jumped out and almost grabbed me by the throat.

'The other male members have been selected, but Woodall is still looking for a South African woman climber.' Women who were interested were asked to send in a written motivation. A short-list of six would be drawn up, and they would accompany Ian on an expedition to Kilimanjaro, Africa's highest mountain. One would then be invited to join the Everest team.

The climbing of Everest had never entered my mind before. It was not a childhood dream, not a life-long ambition. If I had ever thought of it, I had dismissed the idea instantly, as Everest was too big, too far away, too expensive. However, I certainly was desperate to visit the Himalaya. I had been looking around for ways of doing that for over a year.

My first thought was that the woman thing was a sham, a publicity stunt drummed up by the newspaper. I started phoning around until I found someone with a telephone number for Ian. I rang the number and got him on the other end. It was a confident, precise voice, giving nothing away. He assured me the selection was 'for real'.

'You are not going to have us in bikinis at Sun City, parading for the television cameras?'

He laughed. 'That sounds like a good idea. But no, all I want is your application and motivation.'

He would tell me nothing more.

I put down the phone and began to walk distractedly through my flat. I could think of a thousand reasons not to apply. I wasn't experienced enough. I wouldn't be chosen, anyway. It was a publicity stunt. It was sexist to select the women and invite the men.

I could think of a thousand reasons to apply. I was one of the most experienced women climbers in South Africa. I might well be chosen. Who cared if it was sexist? It would be worth it just to get to the Himalaya. It would be worth it for a free trip to Kilimanjaro. The application required no more effort than writing a motivation, and posting it.

One reason prevailed over all others. If I did not apply, for the rest of my life I would wonder what would have happened if I had done so. Another woman would go and I would be thinking, could that have been me? What might have been?

This book is the story of what happened because I chose to apply. Within the next three-and-a-half years I was to become the first woman in the world to climb Everest from both its south and north sides. I was to encounter death on the mountain in its most traumatic forms. I was to become both famous and notorious in South Africa and beyond. I was to give up my planned career as an academic to go into expedition and adventure work full-time. I was to fall in love with the expedition leader. And it was all for the sake of one decision on 19 November 1995.

1

A man and a mountain

I agonised for over a week over the writing of my motivation. It seemed incredibly difficult to express all of myself in a few pages of black-and-white text. I started off with a dry and business-like summary of my climbing experience. I discarded it as lifeless. I wrote a passionate, romantic account of my love for mountains. I discarded that as mushy slop. Then I painstakingly wove the two together.

'Eight years ago, I read my first book about mountaineering. It was called *Annapurna: a woman's place*. It was the story of the first all-woman expedition to this peak. Their motto was, "A woman's place is on top". That inspired me.'

I went on to say that I had done 'enough 18-hour days to have a reasonable idea of just how cold, uncomfortable, and exhausting mountaineering could be,' but that, 'I climb for the challenge of the route, for the satisfaction of the summit, for the pleasure of the surroundings and for the love of mountains.'

Finally I could stand it no more. I put the motivation in an envelope, posted it and tried to focus once more on my thesis. However, I also immediately began a training programme to increase my fitness. If I did make the Kilimanjaro selection, I intended to do as well as I possibly could.

Over 200 women had applied for the team. It was three long weeks before Ian phoned to tell me I was on the short-list. I was to meet him and the five other women in Johannesburg a few days before New Year. I had just turned 27. It was the birthday present of a lifetime. I spent a restless Christmas at the coast with my parents, wondering what on earth I was getting myself into. My parents were totally supportive. Ever since I had come home from university and told them that I had joined the rock-climbing club they had gradually been getting used to my odd interests.

I had been their unplanned after-thought, the menopause that turned out to be pregnancy. My two brothers were much older than I was and for most of my childhood I grew up alone. I did not live near the school I attended and had few local friends. However, my parents had a huge garden, tidy in the middle but bordered by exciting tangles of shrubbery. I disappeared into the bushes each afternoon and constructed elaborate adventure fantasies, casting myself as heroine. In time, books became another source of adventure.

I was a quiet, obedient girl, academically talented but useless at sport. I hated the 'rah-rah' of school teams, the 'I win, you lose' basis of competitive sport. Besides, I couldn't hit a ball straight to save my life. I remember the ignominy of being the only girl in my year to fail junior life-saving. It had taken enormous effort to overcome my fear of heights and do the required jump off the high diving board, but despite that effort I still couldn't swim the required distance.

I lacked confidence but had considerable discipline and determination. I also had a sense of myself as different, although I couldn't have explained why. I preferred to be alone rather than to try and conform to the interests of my fellow pupils. I had little interest in make-up, in night-clubs, in boys, in alcohol.

At university in Johannesburg I was painfully shy, a quiet shadow hanging out in the background. Rock-climbing provided an escape from the city over weekends, a way into the wilderness that I loved. It provided the first physical activity I had ever been any good at. It provided a challenge that was totally personal, your skill and courage matched against a rock wall. It also provided a new group of friends.

I still did not know what I wanted to do with my life, only that I did not fancy the conventional choices my school proposed for middle-class girls. I took refuge in prolonged university studies and found myself drifting towards a career in academia. My mother was a housewife, my father a prominent businessman. I was frustrated by my mother's extensive talents, which seemed to me to have been rather wasted in running a household. I was intimidated by my father's immense intellectual ability and his unapproachable demeanour. All my life I had been asked if I was related to the well-known Michael O'Dowd. Now I told him that if I made the Everest team, people would be asking him if he was the father of Cathy O'Dowd. Neither of us knew then how right I was to be.

On 28 December I met the expedition leader Ian Woodall for the first time. He was a small, fair-skinned man, looking as if he had had too little sleep for quite some time. He was talkative, but in a factual way. I sensed a closed individual, intensely private. He had been an officer in the British Army for a number of years, and it showed. I had spent too much time at university with male friends trying to dodge conscription and military service in the name of the apartheid government to like men who liked armies. I watched him carefully. As much as he might be selecting me, I had to decide whether I wanted to risk tackling something as committing as Everest under the leader-ship of this man. I could always step down.

I also met the five other women with whom I would be sharing the next two weeks. Nandi Scorer, an advertising executive, was bubbly, outgoing, down-to-earth, intelligent. I liked her immediately. Cynthia Anthony-Maistry was a quiet, determined woman who worked in banking. She was a tiny thing, who

Expedition leader Ian Woodall.

looked as if she would snap in a strong wind. Deshun Deysel was a schoolteacher from a coloured township. She seemed friendly but nervous. Anneli Norval was a thin blonde, a farmer's wife from the Eastern Cape. She talked far too much for my liking, always dominating the conversation. Jackie Stein was a young adventurer, recently returned from the United States. She had a pseudo-American attitude that riled me immediately. She was cocky, domineering, keen to impress on us her wealth of experience.

A lovely film crew from the SABC joined us. The cameraman, Ivan Oberholzer, and the producer, Jan Horn, were both older men of immense experience and great empathy. All of us women found in them a neutral haven, someone to talk to about the strains of the trip, occasionally a shoulder to cry on.

What they all made of me I have no idea. Although less shy than I used to be, I was still an introverted person, speaking little, taking a long time to be comfortable with new people. They probably found me as difficult to assess as we all found Ian to be. Ian described me to a journalist as 'difficult to crack through'.

It was an impressive group. Despite the many differences, I could see a common trait in all of us - a determination and focus that we applied to whatever dominated our lives. Where a similar group of men might have been more inclined to posture, to try and top each other with stories of how far they'd run, how high they'd climbed, we pulled together as a group. There was a lot of mutual support. However, under all that lay an intensely competitive spirit. For Ian this might be a selection, but for us it was competition. All six of us desperately wanted to go.

The challenge was that we did not know what Ian was looking for. He was not simply after the most experienced person. In that case it would be a straight race between Jackie and myself. Ian briefed us as to what he was after on the second night. His main point was compatibility. He got Jackie's back up by saying he that he didn't need any of us on his team and that he wouldn't climb with someone he considered a fool, whatever their potential. She thought that was unfair. However, the months ahead were to prove that personality conflict was virtually the most damaging thing that could happen to an expedition.

He then went on to stress more abstract qualities like mental strength and determination. The main point was that we were just to be ourselves. There was nothing extra we could do to improve our chances. That left me with a horrible thought: what if just being myself was simply not good enough?

In fact Ian envisaged the woman's place on the Everest team as a chance for someone to be part of a life-changing experience, rather than as an attempt to find a sixth Everest climber with summit aspirations. The woman was being invited to do something radically different with her life for a few months. She was not going to be dragged to the top and planted there like a flag. The media missed the point completely and called it a search for a woman with 'the balls' for the summit. The public, not surprisingly, became somewhat confused.

We flew up to Tanzania and began the expedition with an ascent of Mount Meru. The mountain was in a setting out of a movie. It looked more like Hollywood Africa than real Africa. Green grassland spread out to every horizon, dotted with small trees and grazing giraffe. Meru lay to the west, rising out of deep green tropical forest. Two magnificent rock ridges formed a horseshoe of huge cliffs, encircling what remained of an ancient volcanic crater. Kilimanjaro lay on the horizon to the east, a great swelling rising out of the plateau. Across its broad summit lay a mantle of snow and glacier. At times it seemed to float above the heat haze of the plain, an incredibly unlikely vision rising above tropical Africa. At dawn Kilimanjaro was hovering in front of a curtain of pink cloud, while honey-coloured light was sliding down the cliffs of Meru. I could imagine no better place to be on New Year's Day, 1996.

The organisation of the expedition was immaculate, and I was impressed by Ian's ability. Talking to him gave me some idea of the far greater challenge of organising Everest. The South African Everest idea had been Ian's. Only once he knew it could be done, that he could get a permit and could raise the considerable amount of finance needed, had he invited the other team members. The result was that the full burden of organisation fell on him. But, as I was to learn, he loved a logistical challenge, the planning and listing and arranging.

However, I was making no progress in getting to know him better. He kept himself to himself. Perhaps he felt that too much friendliness would interfere with his role as leader and selector. Perhaps he was just shy. There were glimpses of a nice person in there somewhere, but just glimpses.

Once we had left the grass plains filled with buffalo and warthog, we entered the forests. Huge trees created a giant green canopy over our heads. Creeper wove from branch to branch, creating an almost impenetrable cover. We walked through great

The team walking across the plains towards Mount Meru.

vaults of cool still air. On the second day we left the forest to enter
a land of tall heather. The mud path had worn a gorge between the
heather plants and it was almost like walking inside the hillside.
On the third day we woke up at 3 a.m. and walked on through the
heather by the light of head torches. It was bitterly cold and there
was little conversation. Dawn came, with Kilimanjaro on the
horizon, silhouetted against a pale pink sky. That was where our
next challenge lay. We moved on to steep gravel slopes, traversing
along the edge of the ancient crater. It was like climbing a cinder
dune, very loose in places. The path undulated upward, revealing
summit after summit. Anneli kept our minds off the slog with a
detailed and very funny description of stud breeding horses. We
reached the summit together, all light-headed and giggly with the
altitude. We stood on the highest point, watching mist come
washing up the crater below us.

As we all became more used to the expedition conditions, the group became less cohesive. Ian made it clear that any of us could withdraw from selection at any time, in complete confidentiality. Indeed he expected that some of us would. He emphasised the difficulties of the Everest challenge, from extreme weather to rough living conditions. We would be away for over two months, away from hot showers, flush toilets, beds, choice of food. It was all good and fun for a week, but did we really want two months of this?

Jackie was constantly needling the rest of us, going on about the selection, speculating about Ian. She walked behind me for some time, expounding on how being quiet was a sign of insecurity. I ignored her. When not talking selection, she was mostly rabbiting on about sex. All the quiet ones - Cynthia, Deshun and myself - were repressed. What we needed was 'a good screw'. It was funny listening to her for a while but Jackie hammered on endlessly. Increasingly we split into pairs, myself and Nandi, Cynthia and Deshun, Jackie and Anneli.

We spent two nights at a hotel before driving out to the foot of Kilimanjaro. As we bumped along the dirt road in the early hours of the morning, the media crew announced us to be 'contemplative of the challenge ahead'. I think we were all just still asleep. We walked up a dirt road between giant banana palms and tiny houses, getting sprayed with dust by each passing vehicle. Then we plunged into lush forest, very green and very wet. The path was an ongoing mud pool, the damp heat baked down on us. It was a relief to emerge from the forest into the heather belt and to find our camp nestled among the giant plants. We had gained 1 200 metres in five hours, and were all exhausted. I shared a tent with Jackie. We had a friendly evening, my irritation with her beginning to diminish.

The next day Ian, Cynthia, Nandi and I pulled away from the main group. It was great to be moving as a small group, rather than as part of a huge party. Although the big mix of people could be fun, on the whole I preferred the cohesion and flexibility of smaller groups. We were climbing through a landscape of scattered heather among rock and moss slopes. Mist swirled in the distance, obscuring the main bulk of the mountain. As we neared the top of the slope, the rain came down in earnest. Cynthia and I raced for the camp through the icy deluge, dived for the nearest tent, and stripped down to change into dry clothes. As the mist lifted beautiful views were briefly visible between banks of cloud, with rock peaks hovering above us. By nightfall it was completely clear. We sat round a campfire, huddled together against the intense cold, and told jokes. A vast black sky studded with stars arched over us.

The next day was to be something of a triumph in my quest for a conversation with Ian. We were traversing around the side of the mountain, on top of the plateau from which the central cone of Kilimanjaro rose. We were in a brown, semi-desert country of rock and shale. Since Meru I had begun a deliberate campaign to extract information from Ian. He always walked at the back, and I would drop back and walk with him. Asking questions was about the easiest way to get him talking, and there was so much I was curious about, about Everest, about the Himalaya.

One of his questions to me concerned what I planned to do after university. Would I move into mountaineering more seriously? That led into a discussion of the kind of trip I could put together if I wasn't selected for Everest. We approached the top of a pass, in the middle of a shower of frozen rain. Looking down the other side, we could see a greener, more welcoming countryside below us.

'Just because I'll get myself to the Himalaya anyway is no reason not to select me,' I told Ian. He just grinned at me.

Descending into the valley, I felt immensely light of heart. We were camped in a lovely valley by a river. Just beyond it, the river plunged into a rock canyon, cascading down a series of falls. Glimpses of ice-white glaciers were visible through the mist far above us. The setting sun filled the valley with liquid gold light. It was all worth it just to be there to see that.

The next afternoon we had a long talk about the risks of climbing Everest, the fact that one in three climbers who goes above 8 000 metres becomes a casualty in some way. This was most poignant to those with partners and children. Did they have the right to risk their lives in such a personal quest? Not having husband or children myself, I had yet, indeed have yet, to be faced with answering that question.

Much later I read the remainder of the 200 applications. Most were not from young adventurers but from women in early middle age. A common thread ran through many of them. The women filled their roles in life well. They were good wives, mothers, employees. Many were clearly outstanding at what they did. However, they felt a need for something more, a need to do something just for themselves, just about themselves. There was an unspoken question in their applications: was this all there was to life? Everest seemed to be a symbol of challenge, of adventure, a dream of achievement.

As I was to discover over the next few years, some of the climbers who reach the foot of Everest come to grief finding that the reality does not match the dream. Everest does not provide answers to life's problems. It is just a very high lump of rock. Our answers have to come from within us.

Of our group, Anneli and Jackie seemed to me best to fit into this category. Jackie, young, restless, foot-loose, had little idea what she wanted to do with her life. Being the woman to go to Everest seemed to provide a short-term solution, and a justification of her worth. Anneli, having long ago made a life commitment to being a farm wife and a mother, felt her potential leaking away, unused. She was looking for a dramatic way out, if only for a little while.

The debate continued around the issue of risk. I had learnt much of my mountaineering from Stephen Kelsey. We had climbed together in Africa, Bolivia and Europe. While living in London I had shared a flat with him and another friend, a climbing partner of his, Graham Wittaker. Stephen and Graham had died falling off the west face of Salcante in Peru in 1992.

I had considered giving up the riskier aspects of climbing then. There seemed no way to justify senseless waste of life. But gradually I had come to feel that it wasn't senseless. Stephen and Graham were so attractive because of their love of life, their readiness for challenge. That was what had led them to mountaineering. You couldn't have the one without the other. I didn't want them to be different, so I couldn't ask for their lives to have ended differently. I believed we take the span allotted to us, and make the most of it.

Ian asked what we would do if a team-mate died. Would we climb on or give up? Jackie took the hard line. You left him in a tent and forged ahead. Ian challenged her on that and she, feeling mocked by him, attacked him. Ian constantly pushed all of us, looking for prejudices, weaknesses that might flare up on the mountain.

On a mountain there is nowhere to go when tempers get raw. You cannot escape your team-mates. You are trapped with them, 24 hours a day, week after week, often in tents smaller than a double bed. Conditions are harsh, at times dangerous. Small issues can flare up to major controversies in the time it takes to make a cup of coffee. You need compatibility and you need tolerance. There are times when you need the discipline to bite your lip and just keep quiet. The long-term goal is worth the immediate inconvenience.

Ian set Jackie off like a match put to fire crackers. Everything he said she had to challenge. Ian had a certain way of stating his opinion as if it was a fundamental planetary law. He could be very blunt, not wrapping his opinions up in rose petals. As long as he talked sense, which he did, the lack of accompanying

A team discussion - left to right: Cathy, Anneli, Nandi, Cynthia, Jackie and Deshun.

pleasantries did not worry me. Jackie couldn't take it. She was desperate to be chosen and even as she was talking, she knew she was diminishing her chances of selection. However, she simply could not keep her mouth shut.

I spent much of my time with Nandi. She was beginning to have second thoughts about the enterprise. She was a 25-hours-a-day woman, always on the go. She loved the frenetic atmosphere of advertising, the short deadlines, the constant pressure. She loved her running, with its immediate, continuous physical demand.

Mountaineering requires a strange combination of drive and patience and she was short on the patience. She was more concerned about the boredom of being tent-bound through a storm that about the risks of the climbing.

I was most concerned about the hardship and the discomfort. On our summit day for Kilimanjaro we left camp at about 1 a.m. The climb started out as unpleasant and got steadily worse. The long, dark hours of early morning are the worst of the day. I felt stiff and uncoordinated, stumbling on the loose scree slopes. It soon became a relentlessly steep slog. I was sliding with each step on the broken rock. I avoided looking at my watch, not wanting to know how slowly time was passing. It was getting steadily colder and I was falling back in the queue. I plodded on, exhausted, icy cold, demoralised. Jackie and Nandi were up in front and seemed to be moving so effortlessly.

I was desperate to stop for a rest and huddled down behind a rock to seek protection from the wind. I rapidly realised that the only way to keep warm was to keep moving. It was a devil's bargain, with rest and warmth incompatible. Somewhere in those long hours, when it seemed as if the sun would never rise again, I decided to withdraw from selection for the Everest team. If Kilimanjaro could be this unpleasant, Everest had to be worse. Without enjoyment, I couldn't see the point of it all.

Then the first glimmer of dawn appeared, a slim line of red on the horizon. I immediately felt better and stronger. All

Kilimanjaro, the highest mountain in Africa.

thoughts of giving up dissipated with the darkness. As others moved ever more slowly I began to pass them, working my way towards the front. I found Jackie huddled down, looking awful. She was nauseous with altitude.

'Bitch,' she whispered, as I passed her.

Nandi and I reached the crater edge together. I hugged our guide, Joachim, and then turned left. We worked our way around the crater rim, towards the highest point. On our left were great slabs of glacier, lying on the rock like massive chunks of wedding cake. I pulled my down jacket around me, but the wind howled on. There was no escape from the cold.

We reached the top of the dome at 5.17 a.m. As I was taking pictures of the summit, Ian arrived, grabbed me and stared deep into my eyes. He asked if I was okay. I was a bit taken aback but then realised he was checking for signs of acute mountain sickness, brought on by the lack of oxygen at over 5 800 metres. He shook my hand and moved off.

As soon as the summit footage was shot, we started back down.

Both Jackie and Deshun were feeling sick. I walked down on my own, enjoying setting my own pace, not being part of the crocodile for a while. The summit had been something of an anticlimax. However, it often is on mountains. For climbing mountains to make any sense at all, it has to be about appreciating the journey, rather than investing all your hopes in the summit.

Back in the hotel, we all met in the garden to find out what would happen next. Up until this point I had felt fairly calm about the selection. I had felt I would be happy for whoever was chosen. I thought I was the best choice and that I had a good chance. However, I didn't want to be too confident for fear of being wrong. Now the tension started to mount. I realised that I desperately wanted to be selected.

By and large the six of us got on well. There was a kind of tense camaraderie among us as we waited. Jackie joked that if I was chosen, she would kill me. If anyone else was chosen, we would kill her together. The whole proceeding was drawn out to provide drama for the television cameras. Ian called us together. We stood in a semi-circle. Jackie was standing on my right, her breathing ragged and shallow. Ian announced he would be inviting two women to come to Nepal on the three week trek to base camp. Only at base camp would one of the two be selected to go onto the permit. Jackie and I immediately stared at each other. I was horrified. I could imagine nothing worse than our rivalry continuing for another month through Nepal.

Ian went off to ponder life. We speculated about this new turn of events. We were standing near a slide. A small blonde girl of about three was perched on top of it, with her nanny behind her. Jackie turned on her.

'Don't ever try to do anything with your life,' Jackie said to the little girl. 'Don't ever try to climb mountains. Just grow up nice and pretty and pleasing to men.'

The little girl stared at her with huge, round eyes. She slowly climbed back down the slide's stairs and into her nanny's arms, where she burst into tears.

Ian finally informed us one by one of his choice. All the while we were being filmed. By now I felt like a piece of putty that had been stretched out way too thin. He rambled on about how difficult the selection had been, and how sorry he was he could not take everyone. My heart sank. Then he invited me to join the team to Nepal. Initially I just felt overwhelming relief. Then the excitement welled up.

The other selection was Deshun. That came as something of a surprise on the face of it, but made sense on reflection. Jackie was simply incompatible with Ian. Anneli wanted Everest for the wrong reasons. Nandi's heart was not in it. Cynthia, although determined and game, was physically tiny. Ian did not think she had the bodily strength. That left Deshun and me.

I had found Deshun quiet, friendly, efficient, determined. I thought we would get on well. Ian's rationale for taking two women was that the woman on the team would be under intense media scrutiny. He wanted a back up. He felt that, in exchange for three months of free travel in Nepal, we could put up with some tensions of being still 'on selection'.

We returned to South Africa and went our separate ways. I would only be needed back in Johannesburg at the end of February. There would be six long weeks of waiting. I was trying my best to finish my thesis before I left. However, the topic of 'the selection and presentation of photographs of political violence in South African newspapers' was difficult to get excited about when Everest was looming so large on my horizon.

Sitting in front of my computer in my Grahamstown flat, the whole Everest application experience seemed unreal. It was almost impossible for me to grasp the reality of it all. In a few weeks I would be on my way to the Himalaya, to the slopes of the highest mountain in the world. I was revelling in the anticipation of it all.

However, disturbing rumours were reaching me about the other members of the team. I heard through the grapevine of the climbing community that one of the others, Ed February, was commenting that they, the other members, would 'throw the baggage off the mountain'. Deshun and I were the 'baggage'.

Besides Ian and the two of us, there were four other climbing members. Ian had invited Bruce Herrod, a British mountain photographer. Bruce was a close friend, and would fulfil the photographic commitments to the 31 expedition sponsors. Bruce was a massive man, over six feet high and broadly built. He was highly intelligent, with a doctorate in geophysics, and had spent several seasons working in Antarctica. He loved the Himalaya and had an enormous empathy for the people of the region. Even-tempered, friendly, with a laid-back attitude to life, he was easy to like.

The three other men all originated from Cape Town. Ian had grown up around Cape Town, and his first choice after Bruce was an old acquaintance, Ed February. Ed was in his early forties, an academic and a talented rock-climber. Ed had a big mouth and a lot of attitude. He could be immensely funny. He could also be very nasty.

Ed then suggested his close friend, Andy de Klerk. Andy had been something of a teenage climbing prodigy, and had gone on to become a talented alpinist. He had left South Africa to settle in Seattle. He was quiet, mellow, a bit 'spaced out' in his thinking.

The final climbing member was Andy Hackland, called 'Hack' to prevent a confusion of the Andys. He had been asked mostly because other potential members were not available or not liked by those already on board. He had something of the charm of a puppy. However, although in his late twenties, he had all the self-centredness and ego, and all the insecurities, of a teenage boy. He was in awe of Andy and walked in his shadow.

With the entire organisation being done by Ian, and to some extent by Bruce, these three had been offered a free ride. That turned out to be a mistake. They had watched the television programme that was shown about the Kilimanjaro selection. Before leaving Cape Town to meet up with the rest of the team, they were already antagonistic towards Ian's style, and the women he had chosen. I knew all three of these men vaguely, from my years climbing in the same country. The rumours were unsettling, but nothing could take the edge off my excitement.

Nothing at least, until we all got together for the first time. Then the tension began to rise. We met up in Johannesburg, at the house of Ian's parents. Ian was stretched to the limit with the last-minute organisation and fund-raising. He had little time to be patient with the queries of the rest of us. The three men, perhaps feeling left out of things, took to criticising the organisation. I had seen more of Ian's organisational ability than they had and felt that their criticisms were mostly superficial, and unhelpful in the circumstances. Hack got particularly indignant because stuff sacs for the sleeping bags were not on the equipment list. None of the men took well to Ian's blunt style. Their egos demanded more delicate handling, and Ian had neither the time nor the temperament to give it to them.

They did not take well to the sponsorship requirements. The need to undertake endless photo shoots was complied with ungraciously, to the point that Ian had to apologise to certain of the sponsors. Although the Sunday Times newspaper hyped this expedition as a 'national' event, and although President Nelson Mandela was the expedition patron, it was not national in one important way. There was no government funding or support. All the very large amount of funding needed had been scraped together by Ian from corporate sponsors. For the rest of us, it was as if money and equipment just fell out of the sky. Ian was desperately aware of where each penny was spent, and where it had come from.

Deshun and I lurked in the background, keeping our mouths shut. Only Bruce really made us feel welcome. Even Bruce's life was being made difficult by the presence of his girlfriend, Sue Thompson. She had come out from England to see him off. Bruce had a tendency to avoid confrontation with those he loved. This was to cause us considerable trouble much later in the trip. Sue did not want him to climb Everest. She hated the whole idea but avoided an ultimatum. Bruce knew how she felt, but was determined to go. Rather than talk it through, they avoided the issue. She didn't approve of Bruce's friendship with Ian. I think she feared Ian would lead Bruce into activities, such as mountaineering, which she could not share. She and Bruce had done a lot of trekking together, with him taking photographs and her writing articles. It was a nice partnership for her. Now Bruce was developing interests that shut her out. She did not take it graciously, and sat sulking in the background.

The one positive addition to the team was the base camp manager and technician, Ian's older brother, Philip. Philip was easy-going, friendly, sensible. In Ian's absence he was to become Bruce's confidant in the troubles that followed.

It was not a well-adjusted team that assembled at Johannesburg airport to fly out to Kathmandu, capital of Nepal. However, for the moment, the excitement of leaving and the constant need to display camaraderie for the media smoothed over the problems.

The expedition was on its way. I was off to the Himalaya. Nothing could destroy the excitement of that.

2

Trouble in paradise

Kathmandu was a vibrant city, an intoxicating mix of ancient temples and internet cafes. It held the lure of its past as a forbidden kingdom, but with all the excitement of a modern capital. The excitement of exploring this exotic metropolis held the tensions within the team at bay. However, Ian collapsed with nervous exhaustion almost as soon as he landed. Not all the equipment had arrived in Kathmandu, either.

It was decided that the rest of us, led by Bruce, would begin the walk towards the mountain, taking the long route from Jiri. Ian would catch up with us, with the equipment, by helicopter. Separating Ian from the rest of the team proved unwise. In his absence he became the focus for all complaints and discontent. In addition on the walk-in we had two more people to contend with, and they eventually made life unbearable.

Charlotte Noble was a doctor and a top class marathon runner. She was very energetic, very competitive, on the edge of emaciation. She had been invited as expedition doctor, to be stationed at base camp. She was to prove an immediate liability.

Our first night on trek was spent at Shivalaya. Charlotte collapsed on a bed in the dormitory, shaking with cold. She was huddled in a foetal position, face pressed into the mattress.

Half an hour later she was running around again, full of frenetic energy, pupils as wide as saucers.

Within the first three days of the trek Charlotte had already received verbal warnings from Bruce. These were for holding up the team by consistently being late, for not checking on her patients regularly, for dispensing unnecessarily strong drugs, and for her dress. Padam Magar, our trek sirdar (chief of staff), had approached Bruce to say the staff were uncomfortable with her skimpy running shorts and sleeveless vests. They associated such dress with prostitutes. She was unmoved.

Charlotte was desperate to keep up with Andy and Hack, who often walked way out in front. This drive overcame all common sense. On 10 April we were to cross the Lamjura Pass. This snow-covered pass, reaching 3 500 metres, was the first big challenge of the walk-in. She, not seeing Andy and Hack's rucksacks outside the lodge, assumed they had left without her. She haired off up the trail, alone, without warm clothing or any food, and without knowing where the team would stop for that night. We camped at Tragdobuk but there was no sign of her. We had a suspected sprained ankle in the group, and a porter with blood in his stools. Charlotte, who had become too cold when she had tried to wait for the group, had continued on to Junbesi. There she was found by some trekkers, disorientated, and taken to a lodge.

Bruce consulted with the other team members. He then issued a written warning to Charlotte, with Andy as witness. She had to agree to be present at all meals and in the evenings. Bruce took over control of the medications. On the 14th she again received a verbal warning from Bruce. She had gone for a run alone without telling anyone. In doing so she had missed breakfast, had not checked on her patients, and had held up the porters.

Crossing one of the many bridges on the walk-in. Bruce is in the lead with Ed and Deshun behind.

Four days later she visited the medical centre at Khunde. She asked for drugs in the name of the expedition, claiming we were short of medical supplies. Bruce subsequently returned these drugs. He was by now at the end of his tether with her erratic and self-centred behaviour.

Another disastrous inclusion in the group came courtesy of South Africa's Sunday Times newspaper. The Sunday Times was one of 31 expedition sponsors, but had bought naming rights to the expedition. Control of the newspaper was at the time awkwardly split between Ken Owen and Brian Pottinger. Ken Owen was on leave pending retirement, but still interfered at will with the running of the newspaper. Moody and mercurial, famous for his controversial opinion pieces, he was a hard act to follow. Brian Pottinger was a pleasant man, editor-designate, trying to operate the newspaper around Ken Owen. They sent with us a photographer, Richard Storey, a pleasant, rather colourless individual. And, for reasons beyond comprehension, they sent as journalist Ken Vernon.

Ken was a loud, overweight, middle-aged Australian. It became clear within the first 24 hours of walking that he was hopelessly unfit. It also became clear that he hated walking, hated staying in lodges, hated sharing dormitories, hated squat toilets, hated not being able to shower, hated the wilderness, hated mountains. Why he had accepted the assignment was inexplicable. He seemed to have done no research whatsoever on the Himalaya and to have had no idea what it was going to be like to live at base camp for two months. He had no empathy for the mountains or for the challenge of climbing them. A worse choice could not be imagined.

Unfortunately his ineptitude was accompanied by a huge dose of ego. When still in South Africa Ken wrote to Brian Pottinger to ask why he had not been included on the climbing permit. His goal was to interview the climbers on the summit in person. He asked that if any of the climbers dropped out, he be first choice to replace them. Now he was buckling under the pressure of walking through the lowlands of Nepal. He was not going to admit he was not capable and ask to be replaced. Nevertheless, he was not beyond looking for some other way out of the situation.

Ken enjoyed the sound of his own voice, and his favourite recreational activity was picking a fight. He would home in on someone at the end of a long day and start trying to score points off him or her. He was both chauvinist and racist, and the experience was a trying one. I found the only way I could shut him up was to be deliberately, bluntly rude to him. I hated the whole procedure and avoided him when I could.

To top it all he turned out to be a very poor journalist. Within two weeks of the team leaving South Africa Brian Pottinger had sent a letter to Ken saying that his reporting had been 'disjointed, shallow, dial-a-quote and utterly, utterly unsubstantial'. He also wrote to Ian asking if Ken should be replaced and saying that he had a substitute on stand-by.

With Charlotte and Ken added into the already tense situation among the climbing members, the team was doomed from the outset. The first confrontation came when we reached the market town of Namche Bazar. The town fills a semi-circle of land, in a bizarre indentation into the precipitous mountain slope. It was a long haul up from the riverbed to the town. Namche Bazar was high enough to give us our first encounter with altitude sickness, so we were to pass several days there, beginning our acclimatisation. Ken had baled out at the previous town, Lukla, claiming exhaustion He had chartered a helicopter to fly him up to Namche Bazar, to escape climbing the hill.

We were staying in the Panorama Lodge, situated high up on the east side of the bowl. The dining area was a lovely wood-panelled room, set round a wood stove, with windows on three sides. I was perched on a window seat, reading a book. The others were arriving one by one to settle down for dinner. Charlotte sat down next to Deshun.

'Deshun, you've got my jacket on,' she exclaimed.

'I am sorry, it was a mistake.' The two jackets were identical and Deshun had got them muddled up before.

'It's the Soweto Syndrome,' Ken said sarcastically, in general comment. Deshun turned on him, speechless, taken aback by the casual racism of the remark.

'Oh, Deshun is upset with me,' he announced to all of us. 'I am sorry.' The sarcasm was dripping.

Deshun rose abruptly and left the room. Bruce found her lying in the darkness of her tent, in tears. Bruce then pulled Ken to one side and told him he had had a number of complaints since Ken had rejoined the group that morning. The team found him contemptuous of necessary disciplines, seriously under-informed about mountaineering and felt that he was producing some embarrassingly silly news reports. They found him a divisive influence, critical of people behind their backs and needling people to criticise one another, Ken himself and his newspaper. Bruce said that Ken's reporting was felt to grow out of such material.

This was the third time that Bruce had had to ask Ken to tone down his behaviour because it was upsetting team members. Ken's reply was that if Bruce was going to take any action against him he had 'better have all his ducks in a row'.

The following morning at breakfast Ken stood up and declared that he wanted to discuss the alleged unhappiness of the team. He slapped a recorder down on the table and said he would be taping the session. The atmosphere of intimidation was strong. He offered to leave the expedition if we wanted him to. He then asked each of us, one by one, if we had a problem with him. He chose his order well, starting with Andy, then Hack and then Ed. They all said 'no'. Bruce said 'no comment'. He then asked me.

Walking through the village fields of lower Pangboche, with Ama Dablam in the distance.

By then I was furious. Ken had chosen the question to polarise the issue. He would take a 'no' answer to mean that we didn't object to his attitude in any way. Behind Ken's back the others had been appallingly rude about him. Ed could be bitingly funny in his comments, but in essence they were exceedingly nasty. The 'no' answers were a cop-out, and they served to isolate Bruce, the only one with the courage to stand up to Ken to his face.

I looked Ken in the eye and said I did have a problem with his attitude. And so did the others, whatever they said. Deshun supported me. Ken's solid front seemed then to crumble and he retreated to leave us to discuss the matter. An awkward discussion followed. The grudging agreement that emerged from the men was that Ken would be asked to tone down his behaviour as the 'weaker characters' found him difficult to deal with. Deshun and I were being ever further sidelined.

Neither Deshun nor I found the men easy to get on with, except for Philip and Bruce. Ed, Andy and Hack ignored Deshun completely. I occasionally merited the time of day as the lesser of two evils. I was becoming increasingly depressed at the thought of tackling a mountain as challenging as Everest in such unhappy company.

Bruce received little joy from them either as he battled to take the portfolio of sponsors' photographs. They seemed to feel their mere presence should be enough to satisfy the sponsors, that they did not need to contribute in any way. It drove Bruce crazy. He said to me that he had joined the expedition with the attitude of asking what he could do for the expedition, not what it could do for him.

Meanwhile the myth of Ian as the monster leader was intensifying. The next day Ken was furious, claiming that his copy had not got through to the newspaper and that instead there had been an article extensively quoting Ian criticising the 'headbangers' (Bruce's term for the three men and Charlotte) for going out in front and Ken for staying in Lukla.

'If I haven't hit Ian by the end of this expedition, he'll be lucky,' fumed Andy.

None of us had the article to read. When I finally saw it months later it bore little resemblance to Ken's claims, but by then it was far too late. Increasingly bizarre rumours were doing the rounds. There were suggestions that the equipment Ian was supposedly waiting for did not exist, that he had not bought it. There were implications that he had appropriated the money for himself.

On 22 April we tackled a steep climb up the wooded slope towards the monastery at Tengboche. It was a steep, zigzagging trail, alternating between slippery mud and treacherous ice. We had now been joined by a group of trekkers from South Africa.

Having seen that all the trekkers were safely at the lodge, Bruce looked around for Charlotte. He discovered that she had left, alone, to run back down to Namche Bazar. She was dressed only in her running clothes, carrying no equipment. Snow was now falling steadily. Bruce imagined her slipping on the snowy trail, lying somewhere in the woods, rapidly succumbing to hypothermia.

In the middle of the night I woke up, hearing voices in the lodge. I found Bruce and Philip and a gigantic, mostly empty, bottle of White Horse whiskey. Bruce told me he had dismissed Charlotte at 9 p.m. He had apparently been drinking ever since. He had had enough of her erratic behaviour which endangered not only herself, but also the patients she left behind and the people who might have to rescue her. Ed had supported him, Andy was unhappy, Hack indecisive.

The next morning we woke to a world of white, the mountain slopes, trees, and monastery all being covered with snow. Charlotte, in tears, was slowly packing her things. My sympathy was at a low ebb. I felt that if she wanted to do her own thing, she should be paying her own way. In joining this expedition she had accepted a specific brief which she had failed to live up to. I chatted to Ed, who said he thought that she should go, that he didn't trust her at all. He believed Andy and Hack were simply angry because 'they are losing their plaything'.

'I feel as though a huge black cloud is lifting off me,' said Bruce, as he watched her leave. Andy accompanied her. Rumour had it that Andy had been saying 'if Charlotte leaves, I leave'. His close support of Charlotte came as something of a surprise to those of us outside their magic circle. Earlier in the trip he had been much more clearly critical of her irresponsible behaviour. It was some time yet before we fully appreciated the intimacy of their growing friendship. This intimacy was all the more surprising as Andy was married.

The cloud did not lift for long. Later that afternoon Charlotte reappeared. She and Andy had met Ian on the trail and had pleaded her case. With Ian arrived much of the technical climbing equipment needed for the mountain. North Face, Lowe, Asolo, Rab, some of the best kit in the world in terms of down clothing, Goretex clothing and climbing boots emerged from the barrels. The rumours went up in smoke and the atmosphere that night was calm and friendly. It struck me as a case of 'boys with toys'. The real issues remained to be addressed.

After breakfast we met to discuss Charlotte. She was in tears, admitting she had been irresponsible, promising it would not happen again. Bruce had to prompt her to tell us what she had told him. She had gone to Namche Bazar to phone a potential sponsor. She wanted to be a climber, on the team. She had been discussing the possibility with Andy and Hack for days. When asked by Ian why neither he nor Bruce had been told about any of this, she said they had never quite got around to it. She added that she didn't want to appear to be threatening Deshun and myself.

That struck me as odd. She would only appear to be threatening us if she had set her sights on the vacant sixth place on the permit. Ian was happy to consider her idea. However, she would have to decide immediately whether she wanted to be a doctor or a climber. To get her on the permit both she and he would have to return immediately to Kathmandu to approach the ministry for another place, to organise the transfer of the money, and to attempt to kit her out for high altitude climbing.

Charlotte continued to dither. It was becoming clear that she and her cronies had little concept of what was involved in getting her onto the team. They seemed to think they just had to write her name on some piece of paper, and that more kit would fall out of the sky, the way things had happened for them.

Charlotte vacillated indecisively for the next 24 hours. Eventually she told Ian she would stay on as doctor. He made it clear to her that she would have to consult with him on all medical treatments. A crisis had been averted, but it did not feel as if it had been effectively solved. A sense of doom seemed to hang over the group.

Perhaps the gloom was just me. I was feeling increasingly sick and totally exhausted. By the time I reached the next stop, Pheriche, I realised that I had bronchitis. The next day I remained at Pheriche, with Ken and Bruce, who were also feeling under the weather. When Deshun came to say goodbye to me, before going on with the rest of the group, she was on the edge of tears, so psyched-out was she by the hostile attitude of the men.

In the late afternoon Bruce went to check on one of the Sherpani porters. She had got kerosene burns on her back. He found her with a fellow Sherpani, Nimi, who was lying in the tent semi-comatose. Without immediate aid, Nimi was likely to be dead by morning.

Bruce rushed her to the first aid post, where the doctors put her straight into a Gamow Bag, fearing she was suffering from high altitude cerebral oedema - water on the brain. The Gamow Bag, like an inflated body bag in appearance, could be pumped up to increase the air pressure. As descent is the only cure for altitude sickness, the bag was the only short-term treatment alternative. Once Nimi was in the bag, Bruce began to interrogate her friend. That morning Charlotte had given the girl a course of pills for the burns. Charlotte had left them with the 17-year-old

Breakfast at Pheriche.

mail runner, Khum, telling him to dispense the pills every six hours to the girl. She had told no one else. Ian had then asked Khum to help with the load carrying. He had agreed and handed the pills to the girl. The girl, seeing Nimi getting sick, had passed the pills on to her. No one knew where the pills now were. Bruce and the doctors were faced with the horrible prospect that Nimi's state was the result, not of altitude, but of anything from drug overdose to allergic reaction.

It was finally determined that she had a combination of hypo-glycaemia and cerebral oedema. She was kept in the bag until midnight, checked every half hour until dawn and then loaded onto the back of a porter, and carried back down to Syangboche. Bruce wrote a note to Ian telling him all that had happened, and sent it up the trail by runner.

I left that morning to move back down to Namche Bazar, in the hope of recovering from my bronchitis faster at the lower altitude. Ken came with me. Ian dashed back to Pheriche to check out the situation. As expedition leader, he would be held legally responsible if something happened to his Nepalese staff.

The rest of the team followed him back down. On the morning of 28 April he fired Charlotte. Andy announced that if she went, he went. Ed and Hack followed his lead. They had no intention of attempting Everest if they were not clipped onto the back of Andy's jacket. Ian accepted their resignations. An impasse had been reached.

I was standing outside the lodge when the rest of the team returned to Namche Bazar, one by one. Ed told me briefly what had happened.

'What do you think this means for the chances of those who stay?' I asked Bruce.

'I think it almost certainly improves them,' he replied. 'It gives us as individuals a better chance of going for the summit. And quite frankly, even if none of us get to the top, we are going to have a lot more fun trying this way.'

Both Deshun and I were put under subtle pressure to leave. It was suggested that if we left, Ian and his expedition would be finally destroyed. It was implied that we would put our lives in danger if we chose to stay with the 'maniac' Woodall.

I couldn't see it. Admittedly I was not present at the final confrontation, but I had not seen Ian do anything in the three months I had known him that I considered dangerous or reckless. I felt that if I was in trouble on a mountain, I could trust both Ian and Bruce to help. I did not feel that way about Andy, Hack or Ed. And as for Charlotte, she was orbiting in a different solar system.

'Well?' Ian said. 'I'd like you to stay, if you want to.'

I grinned. 'Oh I'm staying. You can't get rid of me that easily.'

Andy tossed Ian a letter laying out their demands for their continued participation in the team. They claimed they had realised it would be 'life-threatening' to climb under Ian's leadership. Ian was to surrender leadership to Ed, Andy and Hack, jointly. For all the rest of us, these terms were intolerable. We had as little trust in the three of them as they claimed to have in Ian. The parting of the ways was inevitable.

Ian sent the resignations of the three men back to Kathmandu so that they could be removed from the permit. With no way of knowing what the three would go off and do, Ian would not risk being held responsible for their actions. As far as Deshun and I were concerned, Ian and Bruce felt I had the best chance on Everest, so I had the sixth place on the permit. However, he asked if Deshun's name could be substituted for one of the three who had resigned.

The next morning another chopper came in from Kathmandu. It brought with it 15 barrels of equipment. When it left it took Ken and Richard. Neither explained why they were leaving or when, or if, they would be coming back. For the moment Bruce and I took over the task of sending photographs and copy to the newspaper.

We now met Ang Dorje, the climbing Sherpa who would be our sirdar on the expedition. With a wicked twinkle in his eye, a ready fund of humour, and a head of thick, black, wavy hair, he looked more like a candidate for Playboy of the Western World than a high-altitude mountaineer. We began to sort the barrels on the basis of weight - too heavy to be chocolate, too light to be chocolate. At last we found them, four barrels full to the brim with the finest Nestle and Cadbury could produce. We then sorted through piles of ropes, climbing hardware, batteries and yet more food. This equipment was loaded onto zopkioks, the sturdy yak/cow crossbreeds used for transport in a land that has no roads. We eventually had three pack trains in motion on the way up to base camp - 28 zopkioks in all.

Walking back up the trail was a pleasure. An incredible sense of

Zopkioks on the Khumbu glacier.

lightness seemed to have come over the expedition since the three men, the doctor and the journalists had left. There was an ease, an enjoyment among those of us left that we had not felt since the expedition began. At Lobuche a runner came up the trail with a letter. It turned out to be a fax from Brian Pottinger. In his letter, in which he asked for information on what was happening with the team, he included a message from President Nelson Mandela: 'When I met the team I warned them it would not be easy and there would be set-backs. This has now happened. I call upon all members to try and settle the matter. This expedition is very important. It is important for South Africa. Our young sports people are reaching for the stars. I wish the team well.'

That was easily answered. The three men had made it clear in their letter that they would only return if Ian stepped down as leader and they took over. None of the rest of us could accept that. We had each made a strong personal commitment in choosing to stay. Now it was time to fulfil that commitment. We turned our attention towards Everest.

Everest (left) and Lhotse seen from Tengboche.

3

Rivers of ice

Arrival at base camp held enormous significance for all of us. For Ian it meant the end of an endless sea of administration, a chance to become again the climber who had thought up the madcap idea of climbing Everest in a pub one night long before. For Bruce it was a chance to lay aside the responsibilities and stresses of dealing with the rest of the group. For me it was both an achievement and a beginning. I had never imagined I would get even this close to the mountain and to have done so was a triumph in its own right. But it also marked the beginning of the real climbing, climbing that I would now be involved in.

It was strange to me how one could be paddling down the river of life, enjoying calm waters and clear views over each bank and then, suddenly, find oneself hurtling down a gorge, shooting rapids at an insane pace, twisting and winding between sheer cliffs, being taken on a wild ride in totally unexpected directions. Just six months earlier Everest had meant nothing in my life, in my plans. Now it towered over everything. Even when I had applied to join the team, I had had no idea what that was going to mean in terms of experience. The ride was proving tough, but fascinating. All I could do was hang onto my boat and try to ride over the waves, rather than drown under them.

Although Everest base camp is a place marked on a map, it is nothing more than that. It is a stretch of rock-covered ice hummocks on the outside curve of the Khumbu glacier which sweeps down from the jumble of the icefall into the long valley below. Our camp consisted of two large green tents, high enough to stand in, which were used as a mess tent, and a communications and storage tent. We each had our own two-man tent as personal space. Just to pitch these little tents took half a day with a pickaxe to level a site and build a rock platform.

No natural colour existed beyond brown-grey rock, white ice and blue sky. Nothing grew in this barren environment, and nothing lived there, beyond birds which followed the climbers up the valley to scavenge off their kitchen scraps. The ground cracked and groaned as the glacier readjusted to the enormous pressure it was under. The rumble of rock-fall was a common occurrence, while the roar of avalanche was sufficiently rare to bring us all out of the tents, reaching for our cameras.

Yet on this barren wasteland a colourful and cosmopolitan community sprang up. Some 11 expeditions were attempting Everest that season, with climbers from 16 countries present. They were spread out over an area of several hundred square metres.

Mal Duff, leader of a commercial Anglo-Danish expedition, was first to visit. A big, bluff, friendly Scotsman, he had climbed with Ian on the north face of Annapurna some years previously. Mal's Sherpas had the responsibility for fixing and maintaining a safe route through the icefall. Other teams who used the route contributed financially. The icefall was, ever so slowly, flowing downhill, so the anchor points of the ropes and

Everest seen from the Kala Pattar view site. The south-west face dominates, with the south-east ridge as the right skyline. The west ridge of Everest is in the left foreground, with Nuptse on the right.

ladders had to be checked almost every day

Members of Mal's all male team were to become frequent visitors at our camp and we often walked over to them for tea. However, Deshun and I were more interested in the various culinary delights, including French mustard and parmesan cheese, which his table offered.

Temperatures on the glacier varied wildly, a clear, still midday sometimes even bringing out pale arms and legs in shorts and T-shirts. Such experiments were of dubious success, the sight of our leader's pale knees protruding from the type of khaki shorts in which Britain conquered the empire bringing most of base camp to a shocked halt. Light snowfall generally followed in the afternoons. Once the sun sank behind Pumori, temperatures would drop several degrees within minutes and sink steadily from there. At night the mountains stood out as giant, jagged black masses on all sides, with the stars brilliantly clear between. Ignoring the beauty, we would dive for the warmth of our down bags for a serious twelve hours sleeping.

From base camp the summit of Everest was hidden, and only the very tip of Lhotse peaked out between the massive walls of the west ridge of Everest and the west face of Nuptse. The frozen rapid that tumbled down between the two walls dominated the view. In a horizontal distance of about three kilometres, it fell nearly a thousand metres. All day ant-like figures could be seen weaving a way through the maze of snowy blocks, their progress seemingly agonisingly slow from the vantage point of base camp. We watched an injured Sherpa being painstakingly lowered, strapped to a ladder. He had fallen through a snow bridge over a crevasse and broken a leg.

A helicopter then evacuated him from base camp. Base camp was as high as choppers could safely land. Even there the pilots dared not turn the engines off. Once above base camp the only means of rescue would be to be carried out, on foot.

At base camp we finally got to know the Sherpas who would be climbing with us. Ian had deliberately chosen climbers with a high degree of experience who had not, however, reached the summit before. He wanted them to be sufficiently experienced to be able to climb on their own, given the small size of the expedition. But he also wanted them to be hungry for the summit, to want it as badly as we did.

Of the four climbing Sherpas, three had been above 8000 metres on the Nepalese side. Jangbu, 32, had reached the summit of Everest, but from the Tibetan side. He was a lama at a monastery near Khari Khola, and climbed to fund his chosen profession. A reserved man, his face was impassive and his eyes always hidden behind rainbow-coloured reflective sunglasses.

Ang Dorje, the sirdar, we had already met, and we had come to like his friendly manner and ready humour. Pemba Tenging, 28, was shy and retiring, but eager to please, with a wide grin showing off his sparkling gold tooth. His younger brother, Nawang Nurbu, 26, was more of a thug, with a taste for chang, the local rice wine. However, he was friendly and funny.

All the Sherpas were lean and strong, professional mountaineers at home in the harsh environment of the Himalaya. Born on the edges of the mountains, they had less difficulty than we did acclimatising lower down on the mountain. However, they too would eventually use oxygen to reach the summit.

All, except Jangbu, had a wife and several children. This group of Westerners, none of whom had offspring, puzzled them. That Deshun and I could have reached the advanced ages of 26 and 27 and be unmarried fascinated them. We were addressed as 'Didi', a title meaning 'older sister', while the men were called 'Sahib'.

A meeting of all the expedition leaders and sirdars was convened. Ian and Bruce went with Ang Dorje. Following the dramas of the walk-in, our team was fairly notorious. The Americans for the most part ignored us completely. The British were friendly, viewing us with a kind of amused condescension. They wished us well but nobody thought we had a hope in hell

Bruce and Ian descending through the Khumbu icefall.

of actually making the summit.

'I've never seen so many egos packed into so little space,' Ian announced on his return.

The leaders had stood up one by one, and had announced who they were and what they had climbed before.

'They all seem to have been on Everest before,' Ian continued, 'And New Zealand leader Rob Hall stood up and announced that he had reached the summit of Everest four times already, a record for a non-Sherpa climber!'

'I thought Ian was going to burst into tears when he had to confess to never actually having climbed on Everest before,' laughed Bruce.

The teams had agreed on a plan to share the fixing of the safety ropes that would run most of the way from base camp to camp 4. The work would mostly be done by the Sherpas. Our Sherpas would help with the section from camp 3 to camp 4.

Our first jobs were to sort all the equipment. From now on everything moved on people's backs. We began to open the piles of barrels and boxes. The floor of the storage tent became a chaos of stoves, gas canisters, food packs, tents, clothing, and dozens of sundry items. I made up food packs of cheese, biscuits, powdered drinks, chocolate and various sealed, pre-cooked meals. Ian sorted out the tents. Deshun ploughed through the sponsors' promotional material, while Bruce checked medical equipment.

Although we were ready to begin climbing, progress was delayed by the wait for a propitious day on which to hold the puja, the ceremony in which the Sherpas asked the mountain god for safe passage. April 11 was declared an appropriate day. A chorten (stone altar) had been built on top of a small rise near the centre of the camp. Prayer flags were strung from this to all corners of the camp. They ran in a sequence of white, blue, yellow, green and red, representing variously clouds, sky, earth, water and rocks. A fire of juniper at the base of the altar produced sweet-smelling smoke to please the god. Around the chorten were laid offerings: chocolates, tsampa (ground barley), whiskey, milk tea and chang (rice wine). Jangbu led us through a long series of, to us, unintelligible chants. Once the ceremony was over, the party was on and we consumed the offerings, especially the whiskey and chang. The Sherpas believed that the blessing of the goddess was conveyed back to us by our eating the offerings. It was a very practical approach.

The rest of the day was spent doing last minute adjustments to climbing kit, sizing harnesses, pulling gaiters onto boots and gluing them in place, fixing leashes to ice-axes. The next day we would climb on the slopes of Everest for the first time. Deshun, not confirmed on the permit, could not join us yet.

I was consumed with a combination of excitement and nerves. It would be the first time I had ever actually climbed with Bruce and Ian. It would give me a chance to gauge their ability and them a chance to assess mine. I still felt as if I was regarded as one of the 'women', rather than simply as a climber. In a sense it was amazing that this moment had ever come. The chance had seemed so remote when I had first read in the newspaper of this expedition. And then everything that had happened on the walk-in had blunted the excitement. There had been times when I thought the whole expedition would disintegrate. But I had persevered and now, at last, the moment had come.

At 5 a.m. the next morning my only coherent thought was how nice it would be to curl up again in my warm down sleeping bag. Still, twinges of anticipation cut through the fog of sleepiness. Ian was nodding over his cup of tea, like a little old gnome swamped in his huge blue jacket. He looked worse than I felt. I had already realised that early morning starts were not his strong point. Yet he was physically extremely tough. Behind the logic, the discipline, the reserve, I still didn't know who he really was.

Bruce was chatting on, disgustingly cheerful. He had a clear head and an even temper, which was good for the rest of us.

He balanced out both my and Ian's mood swings.

Silence lay over the camp in the dark blue shadow of early morning. It was broken by a brief crack like gunshot. Everyone jumped. A heavy groan followed, and then silence. The ice was imperceptibly on the move.

We replaced our warm down jackets with windproof Goretex ones, pulled on over thermal underwear and fleece salopettes and jackets. Then on went gloves, hats and scarves. On our feet were huge plastic double boots. Finally my rucksack was loaded on. It sat on my back like the weight of sin. We moved slowly across the uneven, rocky terrain. The weight of the boots meant that it was like walking with a cement block on each foot. However, there was no other way up. No roads, no helicopters, nothing except two legs and a lot of will power.

This was risk made real. It was one thing to sit in South Africa pontificating about the risks of high-altitude mountaineering. It was another to be approaching the notorious Khumbu icefall, about to put the theory to the test. The icefall has a nefarious reputation as the most dangerous part of Everest. All the ice blocks are unstable and there is little to be done to minimise the risk. And the icefall is only the beginning.

We left as the first rays of sun were catching the peaks far down the valley. I could see small figures from other teams also moving towards the mountain slopes. We threaded a way over the ice hummocks of the glacier to the foot of the fixed line. The line ran up steep icy slopes, finding complex paths between tottering sculptures of snow and house-sized blocks of ice.

And then the ground vanished. Instead of smooth white snow in front of my feet, there was an ice-lipped chasm, disappearing down into uncharted depths in the bowels of the glacier. It was a crevasse, about four metres wide. The white ice changed colour with depth, passing gradually from pastel blue into

Pemba climbing up through the icefall.

indigo, before disappearing into darkness.

I saw ahead a thin metal ladder spanning the crevasse, as delicate as a bracelet. It was not one ladder but two, tied end to end with a little bit of bright blue rope. There seemed one obvious solution to crossing it. I knelt and gingerly started to crawl across the ladder, staring down in wonder at the inky depths visible between the rungs.

'Give us a smile then, girl. Everest style at its best yet.' Bruce's voice boomed out cheerfully. It seemed there might be another way of doing this. Just when I was trying to look as if I knew what I was doing.

Ian came next. He casually picked up the two ropes that lay slack on each side of the ladder. He twisted them round his wrists and walked across, using the rope tension to keep his balance. I didn't like the look of that at all. But I was damned if I was going to crawl while the men walked. I walked across the next ladder with the handrail ropes wound so tightly round my wrists that I virtually cut off the circulation. But it worked. I could do it.

I climbed on, slowly. Each breath produced a burning sensation, rather than the sweet relief of oxygen-intake. The air pressure at base camp was only half that of sea level. By the time we approached the summit it would be down to a third. Long before reaching base camp we had encountered the first symptoms caused by inadequate amounts of oxygen: shortness of breath, slow movement, mild headaches, nausea. If we

✳ *Ian (left), Bruce and Cathy at camp 1. Bruce's fantasy in red thermals walks past on the left.*

✳✳ *The South African base camp. An avalanche is coming off the Lho La in the background.*

✳✳✳ *Ian enters the chaos of the icefall. Nuptse is in the distance.*

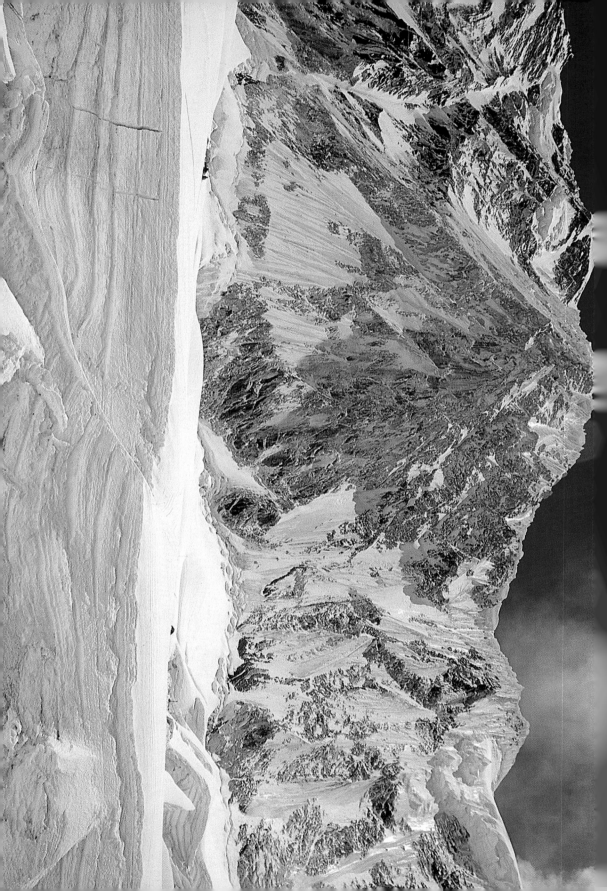

pushed too high, too fast, we risked Acute Mountain Sickness, which could kill in 24 hours. If we were patient our bodies would slowly acclimatise.

The first section of the icefall had been a winding route of ladders and inclines. Now we had to tackle a series of steep snow walls. I was sweating from the exertion, but if I stopped the sweat began to freeze against my skin. As I tackled the next snow wall a cheerful voice came down from above. Ang Dorje grinned down at me, resplendent in his orange climbing salopettes. He seemed unmoved by the fact he had already been to the top of the icefall that morning and was on his way back down.

I watched with envy as the Sherpas moved so swiftly down the slopes I had just toiled up. They were a curious people, with their stoic acceptance of life's hardships and their easy delight in its pleasures. I visited mountains for change, for challenge, for fun, but they lived there. They knew these mountains in a way I never would, and there was so much I wanted to know. But it was not always easy to break through their reserve, or to overcome the language difficulties.

Once the sun emerged from behind the ridge of Nuptse, it beat down brutally through the thin atmosphere. The snow acted as a giant reflector. I concentrated only on moving from anchor to anchor on the safety line, trying not to look beyond

✳✳✳✳ *Ian crossing a crevasse.*

✳✳✳ *Cathy (top) and Ian in the icefall.*

✳✳ *Cathy walking past giant ice masses. The ice becomes an ever darker blue as it is compressed under its own weight. Turmoil as the glacier moves can then bring this blue ice to the surface.*

✳ *The tiny tents of camp 1 are visible below the slopes of Nuptse.*

that, not to search for signs of progress. I had been leading the group and was pleased with my progress. I know I am a slow but steady climber and was glad not to be in the company of 'boy racers'.

We worked our way cautiously under a gigantic overhang. A ceiling of rippled blue ice loomed out into space above us, looking ready to collapse. The adrenalin was pumping. There was a curious fascination about the icefall. It was full of such bizarrely beautiful formations: ice as gnarled as ancient trees, as fragile as giant chandeliers, as intricate as lacework. And the colours were as intense as stained glass. The deep blue ripples of the ice roof were almost mesmerising in their complexity. But the temptation to stand and gawp, like a tourist in a cathedral, was soon repelled by the ever-present awareness of danger.

I emerged from the overhang riding a surge of incredible exhilaration. The awesome realisation swept over me yet again: this was it! This was Everest!

We finally sighted camp 1 at 11 a.m. It was a smattering of tiny tents, dwarfed by the giant silvery wall of Nuptse. We unanimously agreed that enough was enough.

The relief of stopping was so sweet. On the mountains I had climbed in the Andes, this would have been the culmination, a tiny summit with the pyramid of the mountain spreading away below me. This time it was only a small spot low, low down on the slopes of the pyramid that extended upwards for nearly another three kilometres.

That night I crawled into my tent filled with a tired elation. I had no idea if I would make it all the way up this one, but I was not out of the running yet. My greatest fear had been not being able to keep up with my companions. And now I had proved I could do it, proved it both to them (although they had never asked for that) and most importantly to myself. Despite my exhaustion, I couldn't wait for the next day of climbing. I was on my way.

However, we had still not finally escaped from the troubles of the walk-in. A rumour had come up the trail that Ken Vernon and

Richard Storey were on their way back to us. We were all horrified. The thought of facing their lugubrious faces at breakfast each morning was too much. We felt they had chosen their side, leaving with the men who resigned. Neither of them liked the assignment or were well suited to it. Ken strongly disliked Ian, and the chance of any objective reporting emerging from his pen was most unlikely.

The outgoing Sunday Times editor, Ken Owen, was on the trail up to base camp as part of his leave pending retirement. We decided to send a letter to him, asking that the journalists be replaced. Ken Owen's reply was blunt. The reporting team must remain with the expedition, otherwise the newspaper would sue for breach of contract. The rumour went that Ken Vernon had hoped to escape home but that Ken Owen had ordered him back up the trail.

Eventually we decided that we were the ones facing the dangers and the difficulties of the central challenge of the expedition - to summit the world's highest mountain. To have to put up with the sniping criticism, aggression and resentment of Ken as well was too much. Ian and Bruce decided to walk back down the trail to meet Owen. We agreed that if the journalists arrived in the meantime the situation would be explained to them and they would be asked to leave.

The next morning Ian and Bruce left. Deshun and I had been invited to dinner at Mal's camp. After lunch our cook staff were given the rest of the day off. Then I saw Andy walk past the tents and went out to talk to him.

He said that he had come back up to base camp with the hope of joining Scott Fischer's expedition. Scott, an American, was leading a commercial expedition. However, our team's liaison officer had told Andy that his name had been taken off the permit.

'It's not all that surprising,' I said. 'You did resign from the expedition.'

'I don't see it like that,' he replied.

As he did not have the $10 000 needed to try and buy himself a place on a permit, he was going to return to the United States.

He walked off towards Scott's camp. Charlotte passed the camp some time later, without stopping.

I knew now that Richard and Ken were somewhere on the glacier and I sat on a rock waiting. Deshun had retreated into her tent. I was keyed up with anticipation of the confrontation. Richard arrived first, on his own. I explained to him the feelings of the team and said that he was not welcome in our base camp. However, I offered him a place on the floor of the mess tent for the night and said we could find him some food.

Richard made no protest and said he would rather spend the night at Scott's camp.

He walked off and I settled down on a rock to wait for Ken. He arrived in the late afternoon. I told him, as reasonably as I could, what I had already said to Richard, offering him once again the mess tent and what provisions could be found. Ken's eyes lit up as he readied for his favourite occupation of wading into a fight.

He told me that Ian was the spawn of the devil and that I was a puppet under his control. He said that nothing I had told him came from me, I was being used by Ian. My temper was fraying and I replied acidly that he could take it as coming personally from me. He then said sarcastically that he supposed he wasn't even going to be offered a cup of tea. I said that was right. He stalked off to our kitchen tent and demanded tea, which he received. Feeling that the Nepalese staff should not be drawn into the differences between the westerners, I left him there. I knew that if he chose to stay, the staff would look after him. I found Deshun, who had been lying in her tent, oblivious of the disagreements outside, and the two of us went over to Mal's tent for dinner.

The next morning Ken and Richard left, having chosen to spend the night with the Swedish team. They passed Bruce and Ian close to Lobuche.

'You know your boss is expecting you to be back up at base camp,' Bruce said.

Dinner in the base camp mess tent with a visiting trek group. On the right, front to back: Patrick Conroy, Philip Woodall, Henry Todd, Bruce.

Ken simply spat at Ian, and walked on.

The following day our liaison officer, Murari Khatiwada, arrived at base camp. He was a small, rotund Nepalese government official. His job was to ensure that our expedition complied with the climbing regulations and treated our Nepalese staff fairly. He was not only in charge of us, but also in overall charge of all the liaison officers at base camp.

When Ken and Richard had passed him, they had given him a letter of 'official complaint', alleging that they were 'denied all facilities, including food and shelter'. Ken complained that he had been 'exhausted and almost delirious after being lost on the Khumbu moraine'. Mr Khatiwada was furious, not about the peculiarities of the westerners, but about their endangering of their Nepalese porters.

'How could this man have been lost on the glacier?' he demanded. 'Why did he not hire a guide if he did not know the way? And why was he alone, why did he and his companion not walk together? What about the porters he had with him? If no one knew they were coming, who was going to provide food and shelter for their porters?'

In the Sunday Times Ken was to make great play of having been refused a cup of tea as he staggered, lost, across the glacial wastes. Some members of the Mountain Club of South Africa were horrified at this seemingly callous action on my part and tried to have me thrown out of the club. I got something of a reputation as a hard-nosed bitch as a result of all this. Quite frankly, it was all worth it not to have to see Ken ever again.

In the meantime Ian and Bruce had met up with Ken Owen. He admitted that Ken Vernon's reporting was very poor and said that, had it been his choice, Ken Vernon would never have been chosen. However he refused categorically to replace him, stating that no one told him what journalist he should assign. The conversation degenerated into a row. Ken Owen said he did not care if the two journalists were isolated from the team, if we refused them interviews and photographs, but he was adamant that they stay at base camp. The logic of this was incomprehensible. But no one was to tell Ken Owen what to do. The meeting ended on bad terms but with Ian and Bruce agreeing to take Ken Vernon and Richard. They, however, had fled for the safe harbour of Kathmandu and a flight home. Ken Owen was to write an article in his newspaper claiming that in the row with Ian he had looked into 'the heart of darkness'. It all seemed a bit over the top.

There was to be one last fling from Charlotte. While in Kathmandu she had been seen walking along the very edge of the roof of the hotel. The management, fearing that she was suicidal, had called the police. Now she was back at base camp. When Andy left she moved in with the Swedish team. They were there in support of Goran Kropp who was attempting a solo ascent, without oxygen. He had cycled all the way from Sweden to Kathmandu, pulling his climbing kit in a trailer. Charlotte substantially exaggerated her degree of climbing experience, and tried to get onto their team. They made it quite clear that she could not climb without a permit. The penalty for climbing illegally on Everest could be a fine of up to $70 000 or 10 years suspension from Nepal for the expedition leader.

One morning she left alone and climbed through the icefall. She was discovered by Goran, who was horrified. The Swedish liaison officer already knew what had happened, having been told by Sherpas who had passed her in the icefall. Goran could see years of planning, long months of cycling, weeks of dangerous solo climbing on the mountain being ruined by the Nepalese government withdrawing his permit to climb Everest. He ordered her down immediately.

Mr Khatiwada, as chief liaison officer, gave Charlotte two hours notice to leave base camp. He accepted that the Swedish had not known of her plan and allowed them to continue climbing.

Our plan was now to move up to camp 2 for acclimatisation. However, my body was not co-operating. I would jerk awake at night, my throat raw and my chest heaving.

*Cathy at the top of the icefall. Lingtren (left)
and Khumbutse stand out on the skyline.*

Rolling over I would begin long, jerking spasms of coughing. I was worried about of contracting bronchitis again. What I had experienced on the walk-in had not been pleasant.

Yet we had to move up the mountain. The season, which ran through April and May, ended when Everest became engulfed by the summer monsoon storms, sometime during the last week of May. Waiting for me to recover jeopardised everybody's chances. In the end the success of the project had to be more important than that of any of the individuals involved in it. Eventually it was decided that Bruce and Ian would go on without me. I sat by the door of my tent and watch the two figures slowly dwindling in the distance. I had been so buoyed up by my climb through the icefall, and now I was being left behind. I wondered if I would be able to catch up with them again. Was my expedition now grinding to an end? It was a sad moment.

While the men were at camp 2 a young Nepalese runner arrived with three 'registered' letters, one each for Deshun and myself, and one for Ian. We signed a scruffy scrap of paper with a little stub of pencil.

Deshun and I opened ours to find a message from Brian Pottinger. He told us that he had put Ian on 24 hours notice of their intention to withdraw the Sunday Times's name from the expedition unless Ian undertook to meet his contractual obligations. He told us we would no longer be climbing under the banner 'of the country', that he would understand if we wished to withdraw from the team and that our safety was 'of prime concern'.

We were at a loss as to how Brian could stop us climbing as South Africans. Beyond that, we were simply amused. Brian sent the same letter to my father, presumably meant to scare the parents into summoning their little girl home. However, my parents were made of sterner stuff than that.

The era of the runner pounding up the trail ended when Philip Woodall rejoined us. He had returned to Kathmandu to try to get all the satellite communications equipment working.

Once he had got the system up and running, he had had it all carefully packed, first into a helicopter, and then onto the back of zopkioks. Another friendly face was a very welcome addition to base camp.

The yak herders watched in fascination as the satellite aerial was erected. The latest in 20th century technology was provided courtesy of transport that has been used in the Himalaya for thousands of years. On the evening of 23 April we were finally connected to the outside world.

In the meantime Ian and Bruce had returned from camp 2. The return and reunion with Philip was celebrated by Bruce and Philip drinking so much red wine and whiskey that Bruce could not even stand to pee. The resulting headaches apparently had to be experienced to be believed.

Brian Pottinger's letter to Ian claimed he was in breach of agreement for not having a Times Media Limited (the Sunday Times holding company) reporter and photographer with the team and for not keeping TML fully informed of events at all times.

Brian demanded immediate reinstatement of the two reporters and a full report on the status of the expedition. Failure to do so would mean that TML would withdraw their sponsorship. It was clear that Brian had not read the contract that he was quoting from, which, among other things, stated that either party had to be given seven days to rectify any alleged breach of contract. It was clear, too, that in Brian's terms the Sunday Times had already breached the contract through the earlier withdrawal of their reporting team.

Brian phoned within minutes of the satellite phone having been plugged in. He and Ian had a long and reasonably amicable discussion. Ian agreed to fulfil Brian's requirements but was told it was now too late for that.

Brian said that the Sunday Times was now in a position where they had no choice but to pull out, but said that the newspaper would like to continue reporting on the expedition.

Ian explained that that was a little too much like having their cake and eating it. We discovered later that the announcement that they were pulling out had been released before Brian had even spoken to Ian.

Once Ian had put the phone down, it rang again almost immediately. This time it was Cecil Lyons, marketing manager of Radio 702, the Gauteng talk radio station which was one of the expedition's sponsors. Once he was sure the expedition was to continue, he packed a young reporter, Patrick Conroy, onto the next available flight to get our story. Patrick, terrified we might summit before he arrived, rushed up the trail, asking every porter he passed for news of us. He cancelled all the rest days on his schedule, and arrived at base camp half dead. However, he was determined to cover the story.

The withdrawal of the Sunday Times had little direct effect on us. None of the other 31 sponsoring companies withdrew, nor did the patron, President Nelson Mandela, despite Brian Pottinger's urgings that they do so. Radio soon filled the gap in terms of media. The newspaper spewed out negative coverage, aided by the return of Ken Vernon, Ken Owen, Ed and Hack to South Africa. We, of course, did not get to read it and simply heard rumours through the radio presenters and from family. There was little we could do to defend ourselves, so we simply concentrated on climbing the mountain.

However, the Sunday Times could and did hinder Deshun from climbing. We received a fax from Kathmandu saying that the Sunday Times was trying their best to stop the expedition. They had faxed the ministry and the ministry had decided not to help with Deshun's permit. The only alternative was to buy an extra place for $10 000. But the expedition did not have any spare money, nor did anyone Deshun knew have those sort of sums to spare. Then my father offered to pay for her place from his own money. During the two weeks before the expedition left South Africa, Deshun had been staying with me and my parents. They had come to know her well.

We applied once more to the ministry, this time with the backing of our liaison officer, Mr Khatiwada. He had become well acquainted with Deshun in the long days they had spent together at base camp and was as keen that she should get to climb as any of the rest of us.

The drama was not quite over. On 2 May we heard that the ministry had refused to put Deshun on the permit because of negative letters received from the Sunday Times, saying that neither she nor I was qualified to be on the mountain. Then on 6 May we heard that, because of persistent lobbying by friends of the expedition in Kathmandu, she had finally been granted a place on the permit. The last of the saga was over.

The other individuals faded from our lives. Andy and his wife divorced, and he became engaged to Charlotte. Ed cried tears on television about his shattered dreams of Everest but has yet to do anything about realising them himself. Ken Vernon wrote a book about the expedition which criticised everyone, the Sunday Times and his bosses included. Brian Pottinger gave it a scathing review in the Sunday Times. Incredibly, he continues to work for them.

4

The voice of the wind

I stood, alone, in the middle of an immense valley, dwarfed by the giant slopes on either side. The Nuptse ridge rose up in a gargantuan sweep of fluted snow, ice and rock, the sun reflecting off the icy slopes as off burnished silver. The west ridge of Everest was a more sedate affair, bulging snow slopes rising in waves towards the crest. Slowly coming into view in the distance was the south-west face of Lhotse. It hung like a giant white veil of ice, sweeping down from the rocky tiara that crowned the face. Clouds formed and dispersed, as if torn by relentless indecision whether to fill the valley or abandon it.

I was alone on an alien planet, guided only by a line of marker wands, strips of red cloth tied to thin poles. The valley was riven by huge crevasses, mostly hidden by bridges of snow. The wands indicated which bits of the seamless white surface rested on hundreds of metres of solid compacted snow rather than on thin air.

I had decided that if I waited for the men to return from camp 2, I would fall hopelessly behind in acclimatisation. I was not going to give up that easily, so I was climbing up to the 6 500 metre camp on my own. Regaining the initiative was exciting, but the vast scale of the world I was moving through was intimidating. I felt very small and very solitary.

I saw two small figures moving towards me, one substantial, one slight, Bruce and Ian. They were on their way down to base camp. We stopped for a few minutes, passed round a water bottle, caught up on the news of the past few days. Then we went our separate ways.

The featureless snow plain seemed to stretch on to infinity. I appeared to be taking the same step over and over again. The clouds had dissipated and the sun was hammering down on the valley, reflected back by the snow. With no wind the heat built up as in an oven. I pushed up the sleeves of my thermal top and cursed the sweaty warmth of the black fleece salopettes I was wearing. My feet, encased in double boots designed to keep them warm in extreme cold, were now swimming in burning sweat. I draped a scarf across my face and neck and plodded on.

Each time I sat down for a rest, leaning back against my pack rather than bothering to take it off, my backside rapidly became numb with cold, while the rest of me steamed gently. I pulled out more sunblock from my rucksack and smeared it onto my sweaty, dirty skin. There was a long way to go before my next bath. I had to be crazy.

Then I remembered I could have been standing up at 7.45 a.m. to lecture 200 bored first-year journalism students on the history of the South African press. Maybe there were worse things in life than climbing Everest. With the encouraging thought that however bad it got, I was unlikely to be asked to explain, yet again, the structure of the English press, I trudged on.

I stumbled slowly up the final moraine slopes and flopped into my tent like a stranded fish. The French climber who was camped next door sent over a thermos flask of tea. Given that at this altitude water was obtained by melting ice on a gas-powered stove, a time-consuming process, a ready-made flask of tea was a treasure.

I spent an uncomfortable night. Insomnia and nausea made

Cathy (left) and Ian walking up the lower reaches of the western cwm. The wall of Nuptse looms over them.

sure I got little sleep. I lay awake in the darkness listening to music. Once Tchaikovsky had been rescued from sounding like a slow-motion death wail by warming up the walkman batteries against the skin of my stomach, the music provided an escape into another world. Eventually even that began to pall. The tiny green glow of my digital watch was the only thing that proved that time was actually passing, rather than having been forever suspended. When I looked at it yet again I realised several hours had vanished. It dawned on me, to my considerable disgust, that I had been sleeping while dreaming about lying awake being unable to sleep.

The next morning I finally emerged, mole-like, to survey the camp scene: rock, ice, sky, cloud, and a scattering of tiny many-coloured tents huddled together. The various expeditions were camped on one or other of two rock ridges. A street of ice ran between them. The head of the valley was dominated by the huge ice wall sweeping up to the rocky summit ridge of Lhotse. A trail of black dots crawled up an invisible line in the middle of the face, like a train of ants following their own mysterious path up the white tiles of a kitchen wall. I wondered if I would ever make it up that far. However, my solo ascent had boosted my confidence considerably. Up to now camp 2 had been my goal. Based on my previous experience, I had been confident that that was within my grasp. Now I was beginning to set my sights higher. Camp 3 was the next marker. I could see the tiny black dots, clustered in tiers above each other. They were taking shelter in a line of bulging ice pinnacles, seracs, which swept down in hanging waves from the summit of Lhotse. Sometimes I fantasised about being on the summit or about how it would feel to be coming down - never about going up. Mostly I thought about it all in little chunks - each manageable on its own, even if they were a bit much put together. However, all that would have to wait for the next ascent. I spent one more uncomfortable night at 6 500 metres and then headed back to base.

Four days later we were all back at camp 2. This would now

be our base for the rest of the expedition. Deshun, still waiting for news of her permit place, remained unhappily at base camp with Philip, who was acting as base camp manager and technician. Camp 2 was a lot more fun with company. Bruce proved a constant source of amusement. After mountains and photography, his two main interests seemed to be tea and women. The standard procedure with tea was to down six or seven cups at breakfast and then throw it up again about half an hour into the climbing day. He saw this as perfectly logical. Even half way up Everest, he still had an eye for a pretty woman, particularly one of the Americans who tended to cross the western cwm in nothing but full-length red thermal underwear and a harness. Most unusual were his 'lucky under-rods'. They had apparently been to Antarctica three times, and all over the Himalaya. He always wore them on expedition.

After one rest day we set out for a day trip to camp 3, set at 7 400 metres, in order to acclimatise further. The massive bulk of Lhotse dominated the camp at all times, a giant face of glistening ice with a crown of jagged granite rock. It was brilliant white during the day, deep gold fading into rose at sunset, radiant silver at night. And it was big.

I lay alone in the darkness of my tent the night before we left camp 2, questions creeping stealthily into my sleep-deprived mind. What if it was just too far, too steep, too high? I pushed the ever more demoralising thoughts away, and waited for morning.

I followed the others up to the head of the glacier, the Lhotse face hanging in front of me like a giant frosty curtain. As I approached its foot, the deep blue shadow of the valley seemed to deepen, until the cold penetrated my bones. My body seemed only to work in slow motion, as if moving through water. It was the insidious effect of the altitude, the invisible enemy, tangible only in the failure of my body to work properly.

The foot of the face was marked by the bergschrund (a giant crevasse) and a demolition site of avalanche debris. Gravity and cold were constantly at war on the mountain. As soon as the icy grip eased on any of the rocks or ice blocks frozen into the face, they began the rapid tumble down the slippery slope.

We crossed the bergschrund by means of a narrow bridge of snow. The far side was a five metre high ice cliff, breached by a diagonal crack line. I enjoyed the technical challenge of the climb, the careful balancing against the chandelier-like ice formations. Once we were on the Lhotse face, the route moved up in waves, long sections of steep climbing broken by smaller but precipitous ice steps. We climbed on the left-hand edge of the huge stacking of seracs, a nine-millimetre line of rope providing a safety line.

It felt like climbing on a giant treadmill. It became a test of will, of my ability to continue to put one increasingly heavy foot in front of the other, to keep my hand sliding up the rope, to keep moving upwards. However, for the first time I was gaining height rapidly. The cwm slowly assumed its true proportions of a small valley cradled between two huge ridges. The Himalaya west of us became visible, a view of dozens of mountains, presided over by the massive presence of Cho Oyu, sixth highest mountain in the world. I paused to drink it all in: the grandeur of the Himalaya, the brutal blackness of the south-west face of Everest contrasted against the ethereal icy sweep of the slopes of Nuptse. It was all so beautiful. It was hard to believe that it was really me, high up on the slopes of the world's highest mountain. It seemed impossible that all this had come true for me.

'Stop there,' Bruce said. 'It's a brilliant background for a photo.'

'Is it going to make me look way hard, Bruce?' I teased. 'It's all right for you guys, a bit of ice in the beard and you look like rugged explorer types.' I still felt a little apart from these men, with their experience and confidence. However, I felt a rising sense of belief in myself. I expected though, at some point to crash into my limits, to finally find that the challenge had become too difficult for me. But, so far, nothing had approached those boundaries.

Once we had returned to camp 2, the question of what was to happen next was endlessly debated. Ang Dorje said the Sherpas needed three more days to finish moving all the necessary loads up to camp 4, and then a rest day. The weather seemed to be settling. If Everest followed its normal pattern, we should have a good two weeks of stable weather coming. As the Sherpas climbed direct from camp 2 to camp 4, a concept that boggled my mind, we would go again in three days time.

In the next few days the Swedish climber and a Spanish team tried for the summit and were defeated by deep snow. The weather remained erratic, with periodic high winds which sounded like an express train howling past on the horizon. From our camp we could glimpse the south col, the 8 000 metre pass between Everest and Lhotse where camp 4 was situated. Although it would be utterly still at camp 2, spindrift would be whipping off the mountains and off the col like an immense white Buddhist prayer scarf. At times it would drop down across the Lhotse face, whipping up whirlwinds of snow.

Then a message came up from base camp, passed from Rob Hall's team to us via Henry Todd, a British expedition leader with whom we were friendly. The IMAX team, who were making a wide-screen movie of climbing Everest, would be filming up to camp 4 on the 7th, 8th and 9th. Rob Hall would organise to fix ropes on the summit ridge on the 10th, and then Rob Hall and Scott Fischer would move their clients up to the summit over the next two days. Hall and Fischer wanted the mountain clear on the 10th and 11th and were wondering where we would be.

The fairly blunt answer was that where we would be depended on what the weather was doing, although we were likely to be between summit bids. Booking summit slots a week in advance seemed rather cocky. The mountain and its weather dictated the climbing schedules. We had no desire to get involved with the bigger teams. We did not want to use their summit ropes, or to

shadow them up the ridge. We just wanted to be left alone to look after ourselves.

That flurry of excitement over, the hours stretched on. There was no symbiosis between my tape collection and Ian's. His was full of things like Beautiful South and the Cranberries, mine with Tchaikovsky and Verdi. The only books around were the autobiography of the British explorer Ranulph Fiennes and the second volume of Spike Milligan's war memoirs. I read and re-read Fiennes' book until I virtually knew it by heart. The thing that struck me most strongly was his sheer bloody-minded determination to see something through. I was to need some of that myself in the weeks that followed.

However, the most obvious source of entertainment was the IMAX team, camped across the way from us in a small city of yellow tents. Of great value as an object of speculation was expedition leader and film director David Breashears. David, with a multi-million dollar budget at his disposal to make his movie, took his job very seriously. He had descended upon each of the teams at camp 2 to announce that he would be filming higher on the mountain and to request their co-operation. Mal's team had been honoured with a visit, as had Peter Athans's American team. We waited in suspense to see if we too would be treated to a royal command performance. But to date nothing had come of it.

We were reduced to listening to David's frequent radio calls to the United States. Indeed, we could not avoid listening to them, given the volume at which they were carried out. They always followed the same ritual, with David pacing backwards and forwards across the moraine, shouting into his radio in his broad accent about his latest movie deal, or buying and selling stocks on Wall Street.

We sat and waited for the winds to die. We were packed and

Cathy sitting outside her tent at camp 2.

ready to go, but we would never know for sure when we turned in each night whether we would be going climbing the next day or not. I hated the pendulum-like changes of plan, from being all psyched up to move back up the mountain to suddenly being faced with another long day of doing nothing but getting psyched up for the day to follow. I found the waiting tougher than the climbing.

I was feeling more and more grumpy. I really wanted a big hug and to cry on somebody's shoulder. Bruce would probably have taken it too seriously and Ian was out of the question. I found Ian curiously attractive. Perhaps it was simply the enigma of his personality, perhaps the intensity of his drive. He could be very charming when he wished to be, and curiously kind. His rare smiles made his whole face light up.

Then came the news that Deshun was on the permit. The ministry, unable to get hold of our team at base camp, had faxed the news through to South Africa. Ian seemed uninterested.

'I'll believe it when I receive a fax from the ministry,' he said. 'As leader I am the only person who can be officially informed.'

He looked at me with that curious closed look he has, when he has pulled his shutters down. All my tension from the past days swelled up in a giant surge of anger. I was speechless with fury. I wanted to scream at him, to smash those shutters, to force him to acknowledge that the rest of us existed too.

Underneath the pulsing anger, a small, calm voice of reason spoke. We were, hopefully, only days away from the summit. This was no time to have a pitched battle with a fellow team member. In furious silence I withdrew from the tent and stalked off up the glacier. All the things I wished I'd said to Ian hammered through my head. I wandered among the rocks and ice pinnacles that stood at the edge of the moraine, kicking at pebbles. I tried to understand why one stupid comment should have produced such an irrationally angry reaction in me. What was it that was really worrying me?

I felt marginalized, peripheral to the team. I knew that it was partly spatial. Ian and Bruce shared a tent and much of the decision-making happened informally as they lay together, chatting over events. But still I felt left out.

Eventually my patience with my self-pity ran out. I didn't want to go back to my camp, to sit alone in my tent, or to face Ian's complete failure to notice that he had even made me angry. I wandered disconsolately across the ice until a Danish climber invited me over to their mess tent. I spent the afternoon with their team, trading stories of climbing round the world, and speculating about the weather.

The next morning the wind was still blowing, if not as noisily as before. We decided to go up, although with little enthusiasm, and reached camp 3 in the late afternoon. It perched nerve-wrackingly on the edge of the slope, seated on a little platform chipped out of the ice. There was no flat ground around it, only the great sweep of the south-west face of Lhotse behind and the thin air of the western cwm in front. Bruce arrived before I did, and was busy arranging everything.

'Be careful,' he fussed. 'Don't bring in any snow. Dust your boots off.'

'Yes, mum,' I said and collapsed across his carefully organised tent floor.

It was the first time we three had shared a tent, and with three bodies and three sets of equipment, the result was warm but decidedly intimate. We had, by and large, to move one at a time and take care not to dislodge the equipment stacked carefully round the edges of the tent - food, gas bottles, oxygen bottles, personal kit. A subtle manoeuvring was started in order to stay away from the end where the stove was waiting. Somebody was going to end up with the time-consuming process of melting snow and ice to generate the many litres of liquids we each needed to drink. Ian took the bold move of simply lying across the tent and refusing to budge. I ensured I was trapped behind him at the back end of the tent. Bruce found himself sitting right next to the stove.

Cathy (left) and Ian at camp 3. The south col is visible above them.

'Make us a cup of coffee, won't you, while you're there?' I said with a smile.

We were 36 hours from the summit of Everest, 36 hours from the culmination of the expedition. I settled down to sleep keyed up with nerves. I was glad to be sharing a tent. I drew confidence from the company. However, I was worried about the altitude. I repeatedly jerked awake, unable to breathe, with the terrible sensation of imminent suffocation. It was a typical symptom of altitude, but that didn't make it any easier to deal with. Eventually, at Bruce's suggestion, I pulled out one of the orange oxygen cylinders. I put the soft leather mask over my face and tasted the strangely tangy oxygen-enriched air. I slept better that night than I had since first leaving base camp.

The next morning we seemed to be making an unprepossessing start. By 9.30 a.m. we were still mucking about trying to get ready. Our initiative seemed to be leaking away. The Sherpas had already climbed past on their way from camp 2 to camp 4. The pot was back on the boil and I poured us all another cup of tea. It was so much easier to lie back and do nothing than to keep moving towards eight hours of tough climbing.

Slowly the silence was filled by a strange strumming sound. The flanks of the tent began to shiver, the guy-ropes to hum. I peered out. Wind was howling across the fixed ropes. The debate began once more. If it was another windy spell, there was no point in going higher. We would only use up precious energy and supplies. But then again, it might only last an hour or two. We could not afford to delay that long. Maybe we should just climb through it.

As the wind howled, the conversation circled endlessly through the various options, and many cups of tea were consumed. We were sitting in a lazy doze when Bruce suddenly perked up.

'Wind's died. Listen to the silence.'

The wind had died, the sun was out, it was a beautiful day. However, it was too late to make a push for camp 4 and then expect to climb on that night. Staying one more night at camp 3 was the best option. We realised, though, that the Sherpas were going to be unimpressed.

'They'll be wondering what sins they committed in their previous lives to have got stuck with us in this one,' said Ian, as he tried to reach Ang Dorje on the radio.

Camp 2 seemed like a holiday camp in comparison to this tiny tent perched so hazardously on the steep slopes. There was no possibility of even going outside for a short walk. There was nothing to read, nowhere to go, no one new to talk to. Nothing to talk about. I peered out of the tent, seeking at least visual escape from the grey tent interior. The Himalaya stretched out to the west, row after row of icing-coated triangles, like a child's drawing of mountains. As the sun set the triangles slowly turned golden and then were engulfed by the rising cloud layer. It was a beautiful night and felt as if it might be a sadly lost chance for the summit. However, Philip provided an excellent forecast from the Danish satellite weather system. They predicted four days of no wind and clear weather. It looked as though this was indeed to be our window.

I settled down for another night, determined not to use one of our three remaining bottles of oxygen. The pattern of jerking awake to apparent imminent suffocation repeated itself. Time seemed to be slowing down. The thought of a whole night of it filled me with dread. My throat began to tighten with the lump of held-back tears. That made breathing more difficult. I began to panic, the lump grew. I was caught in a downward spiral. My windpipe seemed to be shrinking by the minute. Soon it would be as narrow as a thread. I would never get my breath back.

Ian sat up, pulled in a bottle from the tent's bell and dumped it between us. The metal was icy to the touch but reassuring. He rapidly attached a mask to it and pushed it on to my face. My panic subsided as my lungs filled with air. I wouldn't have minded an arm round my shoulders to tell me it was all going to be okay, but it seemed oxygen was all I would get.

The next morning we were lying in our snug sleeping bags, each waiting for someone else to make the effort of lighting the stoves for tea, when the stillness was broken by shouts from the Taiwanese camp pitched nearby. Bruce stuck his head out to find some Taiwanese Sherpas chattering excitedly and preparing to move back down the ropes.

He pulled his head back in and looked at us with huge eyes.

'One of the Taiwanese team has just fallen down the Lhotse face.'

It seemed that he had gone out of his tent, without putting on crampons or clipping in to the safety ropes and had slipped. Although he was alive when they found him, he died a few hours later.

I was horrified by the suddenness with which someone had simply ceased to be. It was such a careless way to die - as if it made any difference how you died. However, I also felt a curious sense of relief. I knew the statistics, that there was on average one death per season on Everest. Maybe the mountain god would be satisfied. There would be no more deaths this season. What I hadn't thought about was the fact that this season the Nepalese government had allowed far more climbers onto the mountain than in previous years. The statistics needed to be adjusted to take that into account.

Complacency was one of the biggest risks we faced. Humans are almost too adaptable. After so long in a vertical environment we had all become familiar with the steep slopes, the slick hard ice and soft wet snow. With the repetition came confidence. We had to be careful that confidence did not deteriorate into carelessness. In our normal lives we make mistakes all the time. It's just that mostly the consequences are minimal. On Everest there was far less of a margin for error.

Climbers leave camp 3 on 9 May, heading towards the yellow band and camp 4.

Shaken by the sudden death, we left camp 3 later than we had expected and joined the back of the trail of climbers. With the welcome onset of some good weather, four of the thirteen expeditions were on the move - the Taiwanese, Scott Fischer's group, Rob Hall's group and ourselves. We all hoped to leave for the summit that night.

I found myself walking in the footsteps of Scott Fischer, the giant, blond American leader who was climbing at the back of his string of clients. Each in turn crossed the steep icy traverse to the start of the yellow rock band, a wide strip of smooth, angled rock slabs. The rock-faces were scored with hundreds of tiny white scratches, the marks left by the crampons of numerous climbers. I was climbing on oxygen and the difference was noticeable in the growing gap between myself and Bruce and Ian behind me, who were not using it.

At each rest break, I looked out to my left. With each metre of height gained I could see more of the Himalaya, less of camp 2 now so far below me. That ever-increasing view was the reward for all the effort I was putting into the climbing. Whenever I grew despondent at the sheer volume of mountain that still remained above me, I had only to look out and marvel at how far I had already come to regain my confidence.

However, the temperature was starting to drop and I needed to keep moving to stay warm. Scott was stopping his clients to bundle them into down jackets and I slowly passed them, one by one, as I traversed my way across the snow slope towards the

❈ *Ian walks up the western cwm towards the Lhotse face.*

❈❈ *The South African camp 2, looking down the western cwm.*

❈❈❈ *The Lhotse face at sunset.*

❈❈❈❈ *Cathy at 7 000 metres on the Lhotse face.*

rocky outcrop of the Geneva Spur. At the foot of the spur my oxygen ran out. I packed the mask into my rucksack and crouched down for a few moments, hands jammed into my armpits, fingers wriggling determinedly. Little flares of pain ran down my fingers as the numbness retreated. I slowly surmounted the loose rock of the spur and began to traverse round towards the great rock expanse of the south col. The fixed ropes that ran along the traverse became increasingly tatty and finally stopped altogether. The wind was picking up, and spindrift was beginning to swirl. I moved on as quickly as I could to find all the expeditions' tents huddled together in a crescent moon, as if cowering away from the vast col. Our two tents made up the furthest point of the crescent. I scrambled gratefully into a tent, and burrowed my way into down jacket and sleeping bag. Within 10 minutes the wind was howling steadily, snow was blowing horizontally across the col and visibility was down to little more than six metres.

I waited alone in the tent. My sense of time was uncertain, but increasingly I felt sure that Bruce and Ian were not that far behind me. Outside the wind howled, whistling through the guy-lines and hammering against the tent fly. I peered through the flap and received eyes full of stinging spindrift for my trouble.

What to do? How long to wait? Ang Dorje passed over a thermos flask of hot, milky tea.

'I am worried about the men,' I shouted across to him. 'They should be here. Something is wrong.'

✳✳✳ *A tiny Ian on the lower slopes of the Lhotse face.*

✳✳ *Ian coming over the top of the Geneva Spur.*

✳ *Bruce approaches the south col, site of camp 4. The route to the summit climbs up the mixed rock-and-snow slopes on the left.*

*Cathy climbs up the Geneva
Spur on oxygen.*

He gazed at me impassively and retreated into his tent.

I drank the tea, ran increasingly dramatic disaster scenarios through my head and waited. I dozed lightly and lost all sense of time. I jerked out of an uneasy slumber to a hard banging against the tent. I hastily ripped open the door and pulled in Bruce. His black beard was frosted white, his body shaking with cold.

'We got caught in the storm,' he mumbled, through chattering teeth. 'Ian pushed me into the first tent he could find. I don't know where he is now.'

As he and Ian had pulled themselves over the crest of the Geneva Spur it had started to snow heavily. They had reached the end of the fixed ropes and had stared into a curtain of driving snow and cloud, unsure where exactly the camp lay. Staying close together, they had forced their way on through the white void, finally finding a modicum of shelter in the lee of a large boulder. Then, in a fleeting gap in the storm, Ian had seen the outline of a brightly coloured yellow tent. The occupants would only take one member, so he had shoved Bruce inside, and had moved on in search of shelter for himself.

I was squeezed even further into the corner of the small tent as the front entrance was thrown open once again and Ian stumbled in, helped by Ang Dorje and the force of the jet stream winds. He had dived into the tent of Scott Fischer. He told us that Rob Hall was definitely going for the summit that night and Scott would probably go as well. They expected the weather to improve.

Ian was trying to remove his clothing but seemed uncoordinated. His speech began to slur, becoming more and more disjointed. He seemed to be drifting in and out of reality. Suddenly he slumped onto my lap and lay still. Ang Dorje and I manhandled the dead weight into a sleeping bag. As Bruce concentrated on warming himself up, I lay next to Ian, rubbed his icy hands in mine and offered all I had to give, the heat of my body. I peered down into his face, so small as it lay surrounded by great billows of down sleeping bag. I noticed for the first time that his eyelashes, dark near the ends, were red at the roots. The skin around his eyes was so pale by contrast, the skin that had been protected behind his glacier glasses from the harsh glare of the high-altitude sun. He looked so fragile and I felt utterly helpless. Humans weren't really meant to exist in this environment. We might simply trespass for a little while, but always at our peril.

I noticed him shift from unconsciousness to sleep, and he seemed briefly aware of me, as his hands tightened round mine. I continued to lie next to him. He and Bruce were both asleep. I was glad I was not there by myself. In that extreme environment I felt particularly drawn to touch people, to reaffirm my humanity by sharing it.

Ian opened his eyes, looked into my anxious ones. I noticed that his eyes were grey, that he was wearing contact lenses. He reached up to touch my nose and say thank you. I laughed and ruffled his hair. We moved apart. The danger past, we retreated into our personal space. Yet, in some strange way, we had crossed an invisible line.

The danger past, we had to face up to what was to happen next. Ang Dorje and the Sherpas wanted to go for the summit. I felt good and strong, better than I had expected. I, too, wanted to go. I feared that every day spent waiting at this altitude would simply weaken me. Tomorrow the weather might change, the winds might rise again. Our chance would be gone. However, both Bruce and Ian were feeling battered and tired by their passage through the storm, and favoured another 24 hours of rest. None of us knew what to make of the weather.

This was it. The decision. Stay back and miss the summit or press on and risk the weather. I listened to the circling conversation, edgy and impatient. I wanted to go and would climb just with the Sherpas if I had to. However, I was reluctant to go without the other two, after all we had been through together. Was it more important to keep the team together, with the risk that no one would reach the summit, or to split the group to grab a summit chance? I didn't know.

The Sherpas agreed to wait one more day. For better or worse, the decision was made. The wind died in the late evening and the spectacular Himalayan star pattern began to peep through the cloud. At 11.30 p.m. we watched as the other teams left for the summit, one by one. As the tiny, gleaming head-torches slowly made their way off into the darkness in the early hours of 10 May, the unspoken question was whether we had made a terrible mistake. Rob Hall was on the way to his fifth ascent of Everest, a record for any Western climber. Scott Fischer was a experienced and immensely strong mountaineer. Both had decided the time was right.

At least it was our decision. It would be better to have done what we thought was safe and to have made a mistake, than simply to have followed people more experienced than we were, and then to have blamed them if things did not work out.

Nevertheless, the question echoed through the silence of the tent. Had we wasted our only chance because we had been too chicken to push on?

The night was windy and desperately cold, but the next day seemed calm. The south col was a flat plain of angular black rocks, bordered on two sides by the slopes of Lhotse and of Everest. The other two sides fell away down the precipitous slopes of the Lhotse face and the Kangshung face. The various tents were huddled together in one corner of the plain. The sunlit nylon domes in yellow and red seemed bravely cheerful among the black surroundings.

'Many people reach summit, Bara Sahib.'

Ang Dorje was very pleased and eager to go that night. We began to prepare. Bruce's pile of equipment swelled and dwindled as he first added more and more bits he might need, and then, considering the growing weight of his rucksack, began to discard excess equipment. Then he would suddenly spot something that he couldn't live without and the pile would start to grow once again.

I sat among a colourful chaos of sponsors' flags, trying to find a balance between filling all our commitments and carrying so much stuff that we would never get to the top. A knot of excitement and nerves was building up in my stomach. At last, we had the chance to go. Finally we could find out what the summit ridge was really like. However, we might find out that it is just too much, too hard, too far, too high. Anticipation and fear chased each other round my system as the adrenalin began to rise.

Nagging doubts remained. We had not heard the other teams return. The weather was once again deteriorating. At 6 p.m. Bruce picked up the radio to make the usual evening call. Philip asked for Ian. His next words came as an appalling surprise.

'We have just been told that Rob Hall and Doug Hansen are descending from the summit near the Hillary Step and have called for help. Their base camp can't reach their camp 4 so they have asked us for help. They would like you to take them some oxygen as they are both running out.'

Ang Dorje outside the South African camp 4.

5

Anybody out there?

Just take some oxygen up to Rob Hall and Doug Hansen at the Hillary Step, said base camp.

Doug was one of Rob's clients. The Hillary Step was at an altitude of 8 700 metres. The magnitude of this request was horrifying. The bad weather was intensifying, strong winds, extreme cold, snow, low visibility. We were at least eight hours climbing time from Rob, even in good conditions, and, having never been above the col before, would not be able to find the route in a storm.

The obvious question was why ask us? Of all the teams at or above 8 000 metres, we were the furthest away from Rob. The sad answer was that the base camp crews could not contact any of their own members, besides Rob. A second call from Philip, who was now at Rob's base camp, told us that there were another 21 climbers missing.

I found it hard to comprehend the suddenness with which we had been plunged into disaster. What could be going on up the mountain with all those climbers? Experience was supposed to be your biggest asset. I knew the other teams doubted our chances because of our relative inexperience. When Rob had tried to 'book' 10 May for his summit, the official reason was to reduce congestion. I had heard the unofficial reason via the ever-active climbing grapevine - he was saying he didn't want the risk of having to waste time and resources rescuing incompetent climbers from other teams. There was a sickening irony in all this.

Ian made it clear to Philip that, although we could provide the muscle of a rescue, we could not route-find in a raging storm. We needed someone who knew which way the climbers were likely to be descending. It was thought that there might be some Sherpas at Rob's camp 4 and we were asked to look for them.

'Their tents are yellow,' was the unhelpful direction.

A request to go outside that at base camp would have simply meant pulling on a down jacket and grabbing a torch for a few minutes' walk took on a very different dimension at 8 000 metres in a howling storm. Ian battled through the awkward process of dressing, pulling on Goretex salopettes and jacket, hat, gloves, plastic boots. The inner boots were still damp from the previous day's climbing and it was by now a very cold damp.

I was glad it was not me going out. The wind was strumming against the guy-ropes of the tent like fingers over guitar strings. The tent walls shook as if hit by a giant hand. The cold seemed to seep through the fabric. However, inside we were relatively warm, relatively safe. I wondered if I would go out if I had to. I quite frankly thought I would simply become just another victim of the storm's ferocity within ten minutes. I hoped I wouldn't have to make the choice.

I watched as Ian wriggled into the last layers of protective clothing and crawled out into the storm. All those layers that seemed so massive when we first sorted through them in the sunshine way down the trail now seemed so insubstantial in the face of the wind. The figure buried in all the layers of clothing seemed even more insubstantial.

We might be physically closest to the unfolding tragedy but in the face of the elements proximity meant very little. Bruce and I waited for Ian's return, chattering inanely, anything to fill the silence of his absence.

Ian was finding moving through the storm a nightmare. The incredible force of the wind made it like trying to breathe out of the window of a speeding car. His face and eyes were scoured by the flying snow and ice particles. He held both hands up against his face and squinted through tiny gaps between his fingers. The tents had vanished in a pandemonium of noise and ice. The gusting, freezing winds were totally disorientating. Hands jammed under his armpits for warmth, hunched forward against the sting of the gale, he moved crab-like into the eye of the storm. He needed to stop every ten or fifteen steps to get his breath back, yet only moving kept warmth pumping through his body.

He stumbled across the first tent by accident, tripping over a frozen guy-rope. The tent side was vibrating like a drum from the force of the wind. Beating against the fabric made no impact. Shouted words were immediately torn away by the wind. With frozen fingers, Ian could not find the tent zips, let alone try to pull them open. He left the tent and moved on. Finally one tent opened, to reveal the face of Neil Laughton, a British climber on the Henry Todd team whom Ian had last seen over a cup of hot chocolate in base camp. Behind Neil was a pile of cold, tired, frightened Sherpas.

Neil joined Ian to continue the search. Ian recognised a boulder he had previously used as a reference point when moving from tent to tent. It seemed to be bigger somehow, and covered in snow. A figure sat motionless on the rock with his hands neatly folded on his lap and his chin resting on his chest. Neil recognised him as one of his team who had left camp 3 with Neil that afternoon. He had been so slow Neil had thought he had turned back. They dragged him back to Neil's tent.

Ian was once again alone in the storm. Base camp had no more ideas. Rob's Sherpas seemed to have vanished. Philip suggested Ian get himself back to our tents.

Ian returned, deathly pale under his sunburn, with icy cold feet. The risks of going out on any rescue attempt were huge - frostbite, hypothermia, disorientation, losing the tents, losing life. The concept of 'calculated risk' had just been catapulted into a new dimension. When does the time come to forget about other people and concentrate on saving yourself and your friends?

Deshun huddled at our base camp radio base station, linking us to Philip, who was at Rob's base camp. News trickled through, that Rob Hall and Doug Hansen were trapped somewhere below the Hillary Step, that Scott Fischer was out of oxygen and struggling, that the Taiwanese leader, Makalu Gau, and two Sherpas, were in trouble.

I envied the base camp crew, in the warmth and the peace 3 000 metres below us. Yet it couldn't have been easy for them either. Stuck down there, four days' climbing from us with no idea of what conditions were really like, frantic with worry, desperate to help and yet totally helpless. They could do little but radio instructions into a weather chaos that they could not even begin to appreciate. They could issue all the orders they liked. It meant nothing to the people up here.

The next radio call wanted to know how many Sherpas we could contribute to a rescue attempt. Ian made it clear the Sherpas could not be ordered to go to the rescue. It had to be a free choice. At base camp our liaison officer was making it clear to Deshun that he was most unhappy about Sherpas risking their lives in the storm.

About 11 p.m. base camp established comms with someone called Stuart Hutchison at Rob Hall's camp 4. A report had come from him of lights in the storm, but then the comms had gone down. We were asked to confirm it. We peered out but saw little beyond sweeping snowflakes.

There was a strange, dislocating feeling about being warm, well fed and breathing bottled oxygen, when somewhere out around us people were fighting for their lives. The line between

Ian on the radio to base camp during the killler storm at camp 4.

safety and dying was so thin, as thin as the millimetre-thick nylon sheet that made up our tent.

Our tent was a tiny bubble in a world gone mad. It was as if we were plunged into a Dantean hell as the mountain was raked by howling winds, cloaked in swirling snow, frozen to its very core. It was as if we and our mountain had been ripped away from the very earth itself and now swirled distraught through space, caught in a vortex of insanity. We expected moment by moment that the tent fabric would tear, that we would be hurled from our haven into madness in a few seconds. Caught on the line between calm and panic, between safety and death, we could do nothing but wait.

Bruce placed a torch in the tent door, shining out onto the face of Everest, in the hope that it might indicate where the tents were. I lay in my sleeping bag, waiting for the crackle of the radio that would bring further news. Opening my eyes a crack, I could see the light burning in the tent door, like a beacon of hope. However, with my eyes closed the light vanished, while the noise of the wind did not. It howled on, so much more powerful than our pathetic little light. It was a remorseless, unrelenting killer, all the worse in that it could neither know nor care about the suffering it was inflicting on the humans struggling through it.

I dozed on and off. Several times the sound of Ian's voice on the radio woke me, but the news never seemed to bring anything but more confusion. Sometimes I woke in turning over and saw his silhouette against the tent wall, seated propped up on his pack, holding the radio, waiting. He never seemed to sleep.

Around 2 a.m. Ian went out a second time, this time in pursuit of some Sherpas whom base camp thought might be with Stuart. He finally found Stuart, a team-mate and a Sherpa. All three looked completely shattered. Now base camp thought Scott's team might have some spare Sherpas. Ian spent minute after precious minute banging on tents trying to find Scott's camp, but without success. As he stood up slowly from yet another tent he found himself completely disorientated. He began to stumble round in circles. His feet had become wooden blocks jammed inside his boots. He dropped to hands and knees to continue the search. He made it back to our tent and once more collapsed, drifting in and out of consciousness.

Philip spent the night at Rob Hall's camp, huddled in between Americans, Britons and Kiwis, all curled up on the floor in sleeping bags. In our base camp the falling temperatures were taking their toll. The generator had packed up completely and the radio base station was being run off back-up batteries. Patrick Conroy, the Radio 702 reporter, had been nursing his recording equipment inside his jacket throughout the evening. Finally even that froze. He and Deshun spent the night on the floor of the comms tent, huddling together, unable to sleep.

We all woke around 5 a.m. and made a brew of tea. The possibility of being of any help to other teams seemed to have evaporated. The weather continued poor. We had been too high too long. We could be at camp 2 by the afternoon and at base camp the following day.

A 5.30 a.m. call from Philip told us that Rob Hall and a few climbers were still missing, but it seemed that most had managed to make it back to camp 4 during the night. They also had contact with a Sherpa called Lhakpa who was on the south col and prepared to go back up when conditions improved. Would we help? There was nothing to say but yes. Ian asked for one hour's notice so we had time to get dressed. We went back to waiting.

Around 6 a.m. I heard noises that sounded more like voices than the howling of the wind. Unzipping the tent door, I peered into the maelstrom and saw a torch-light in the darkness. Stuart crawled into the tent, bringing with him flurries of spindrift. He brought news that two of his team-mates, Yasuko Namba and Beck Weathers, had been seen lying out on the col near the Kangshung face. Everyone thought they were dead. Although

Ian offered to go out and try to bring the bodies in, Stuart refused on the basis that they were definitely dead.

Once he had left, we continued to talk unhappily about the two 'fatalities'. Although we each knew that the magnitude of the storm made some fatalities likely, these were the first actually to be reported dead. And so close to camp. Surely here we could have helped? We continued to doze, waiting for the call from Lhakpa.

Our Sherpas were adamant that they wanted to go down and they left as soon as it was properly light. The storm was slowly beginning to abate, although the winds were still very high. Neil came over to our camp looking for batteries for his radio and for information, as he couldn't talk to any of his other camps. At the same time Stuart arrived again.

Stuart explained that Doug Hansen had now been confirmed as dead, although Rob Hall was still alive somewhere below the south summit. Andy Harris, one of Rob's guides, was thought to have gone over the edge of the Lhotse face and to have been killed. (This later turned out to be incorrect. Andy disappeared near the south summit.) Stuart reaffirmed that both Beck and Yasuko had been discovered on the edge of the Kangshung face and were presumed dead. Makalu Gau and Scott Fischer were still missing, but all the other clients and Sherpas from all three expeditions were safely back in camp. Everyone was amazed that Rob Hall should have survived the night. Once more, together with Neil this time, we tried to persuade Stuart to accompany us to fetch the bodies of Beck and Yasuko, but he refused, feeling the attempt to be futile and dangerous.

With Stuart's permission, Ian radioed this news down to Philip.

'Philip, I can confirm four people missing, definitely presumed dead. Roger so far?'

Missing, presumed dead. Dead.

This wasn't supposed to happen. This wasn't what we had come here for, what they had come here for. Had they had a presentiment, when they left for the summit 36 hours previously,

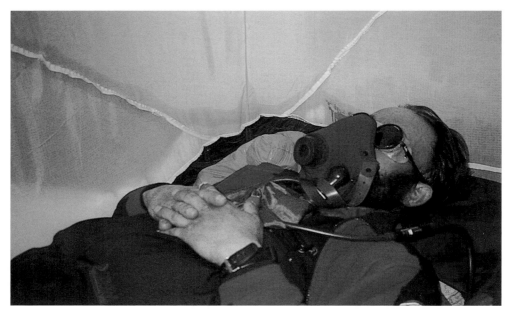

Bruce resting at camp 4, using oxygen.

that they had less than two days to live?

This wasn't an epic survival drama anymore, where everyone escaped at the last minute with various injuries and some great stories to tell round the dinner table in years to come. This was it. Over. For ever.

We were resting, gently breathing from our masks, when suddenly a faint, unidentified American voice broke through on the radio. It asked us to give our radio to some American on the south col, whose name we did not catch. We assumed someone had taken a radio from our camp 2 tent.

The voice came over again, not identifying itself, but insisting we handed our radio over to someone whom we had never heard of on the south col, someone who did not even seem to be part of any co-ordinated rescue effort. Ian refused, and asked who was in charge of the rescue operations at camp 2. He was told that it was the British leaders, Mal Duff and Henry Todd, and so he asked to speak to one of them. Mal took over the radio call and confirmed that we should hold onto our radio as it had provided all the communications thus far.

Henry then came on the radio and requested a detailed inventory of the sick and injured at camp 4, as well as a head count. Bruce volunteered to go out to do the inspection, and was joined by Neil. Bruce was gone for about an hour. Even in daylight with the improved weather conditions, moving from tent to tent was still a tricky and chilling business. He looked in on Stuart and gave the New Zealanders six AA batteries so that they could power up their dead radio. He then visited Scott Fischer's team, who confirmed that they were all accounted for besides Scott himself, but they refused to give any further information. Bruce was cold and tired by the time he rejoined us, and desperately in need of a cup of tea.

Finally five Sherpas left camp 4, two to try and find Rob Hall, the other three to look for Makalu Gau and Scott Fischer. They felt they could move faster without the help of Westerners.

At least it meant we were now free to go down. However, by the time we had packed and secured the tents, spindrift was sweeping across the col and its steep, deadly edges had disappeared into a grey-white haze. We had missed the window to escape.

I felt a curious lack of interest in this news, combined with a remote sense of relief that I didn't have to get up and put in some eight hours of climbing. So much easier just to sit there ... I realised I had to pull myself together. That was how people died, by just sitting around and losing interest, their thinking getting slower and slower. We'd been too high, too long. I started to unpack my rucksack, concentrating hard on each action, reminding myself why I was doing it.

Bruce had spent the last three nights complaining bitterly of being squeezed into the side of the tent. Over six feet tall and broad in shoulders and stomach, he seemed to require more than his fair share of space. Now he chose the colder but roomier option of staying alone in the now vacant Sherpa tent. He came over with some food that he had cooked up. I didn't feel at all hungry, yet opened up a packet of chicken casserole and ate my way through it from top to bottom. It was the first time I had ever finished one of these substantial meals. Having eaten it, I felt neither hungry nor full, just the same as before.

Around 3.30 p.m. Bruce burst back into the tent with startling news.

'Beck Weathers is alive!' he announced.

He had crawled back into camp on his own, badly frost-bitten, but alive nevertheless. We sat in silence, reflecting on the implications of this. The obvious accompanying thought was Yasuko. When had she died? Might she still have been alive in the early hours of the morning when we had considered going after the 'bodies'? Should we have tried harder? The mountain forces hard choices on us, unpalatable questions about how far you go for your fellow man before you just get the hell out to save yourself. They were questions we would probably never have had to face up to, had we stayed in the conventional safety of the suburbs.

An hour later we heard over the radio that Makalu Gau was very badly frost-bitten, but alive. The Sherpas had carried him back to camp. Scott was dead. Rob Hall was still hanging on but the Sherpas could not reach him.

That night Ian and I lay buried deep in our down sleeping bags, holding hands. Through the previous three days we had increasingly reached out to each other for support and comfort. The warmth and strength of one hand holding another could make all the difference. Now I stared into the pitch darkness of the tent and wondered what was happening between us. Was I imagining his changed attitude to me? My feelings were a confused jumble. He began to stroke my face with his fingers. His touch felt fiercely hot in this place of stark cold, almost burning my skin. I listened to the wind wailing round the tent. This had to be the strangest place on earth to be thinking about love. The tent was thick with darkness. If it hadn't been for his touch I would have had no indication that anyone else was there. I rolled over, felt for his face, and kissed him. Once again the warmth of it was intensified by the cold around us. At least I was unlikely ever to forget where we first kissed.

Around 2 a.m. the wind reached a whole new intensity, a whole new rage. I lay awake looking at the thin black nylon above me, stretching and straining under the pressure, the flimsy poles bending and cowering in the face of the tremendous onslaught. I thought of the tiny particles of ice being whipped horizontally across the col, any one of which could potentially slice through the nylon of our tent like a razor, flinging us abruptly into the heart of yet another storm.

Leaving camp 4 on 12 May. Storm damaged tents can be seen on the left.

Climbing down past the yellow band. The summit pyramid of Everest lies behind with the storm clouds still brooding round it.

Ian put on his head-torch and began searching for his boots and jacket. Mine were tucked up by the head of my sleeping bag. He squeezed up next to me, lying watching the tent fabric for any sign of tearing. I closed my eyes and listened to the wind howl.

The descent from camp 4 was a cold and subdued business. We made camp 2 by midday. Bruce and I quickly pulled off our heavy boots to release the feet that had been trapped in them for so long, Ian looked at his own extremities with reluctance. When the boots finally came off the nails of his two big toes were midnight black, with several of the other toes also showing signs of frostbite. We each stared at Ian's feet in silence, wondering what they meant for his chances of another attempt. The last news of the day came from Philip. Rob Hall was no longer answering his radio. The final casualty figure for the storm was five dead.

The next day I plodded slowly down the western cwm, feeling thoroughly depressed. It was a full two weeks since we had walked up this valley. Two weeks in time and an eternity in experience. I plugged into my Walkman and the overture to Verdi's Nabucco came pouring into my head, the glorious music like an audio version of the visual beauty around me. I drank in the views, the icy magnificence of Everest and Nuptse, trying to imprint each angle on my mind. I was desperately afraid that this would be the last time I would see them. I wanted to try again, so much, so very much. I was delighted to have reached 8 000 metres. But how much further could I go if I had the opportunity?

Philip was sitting on a giant rock, at the top of the last slope up to the camp, waiting for our arrival. Patrick, the radio reporter, stood awkwardly behind him. He had spent the last four days filing dramatic reports on our team, but this was the first time he had actually seen us face to face in Nepal.

'Would you like me to carry your pack,' he asked me nervously, trying to be polite.

I stared at the young, slender reporter. I had just spent three nights at 8 000 metres and two days descending Everest.

'I've carried it this far. I think I can manage the last 300 metres,' I replied.

I sat down on the floor of my tent, among the chaotic debris I had abandoned two weeks previously. A pile of mail lay on the floor, blue aerograms, brown parcels. I had expected to be excited to receive news of home, to catch up on events in South Africa, but I felt a strange reluctance to open them. Home seemed so far away and news of it so alien, so irrelevant, to the experiences I had just been through.

I wandered off down the glacier without plan or direction. A lot had changed since I had walked it last, including the facts that I had reached the undreamed of height of 8 000 metres and that six people had died. I battled to find a perspective on these two things, turning helplessly in a deep fog of melancholy. I sat down by a lake and threw rocks at the ice.

That evening Ian knocked on the door of my tent.

'Are you okay?' he asked. I nodded unhappily.

He squeezed my arm. 'If you need anything you know where to find me.'

I watched him walk away and then sat in the darkness of my tent, crying. Finally I couldn't stand the misery of my loneliness any more. Deshun was asleep. Bruce and Philip were celebrating our safe return with a giant greasy fry-up in the kitchen tent.

I walked over to Ian's tent. I had expected a comradely arm round the shoulders, a pep-talk. Instead he pulled me into his arms, under the warmth of his sleeping bag. Once I had cheered up, there didn't seem to either of us to be any good reason for me to return to my tent. We spent the night curled up together. In the morning I could hear Rajan, the kitchen boy, standing outside my tent calling 'Bed tea, Didi. Didi, bed tea.' Not surprisingly, there was no reply. He continued to call with patient insistence. I buried my giggles in Ian's chest and hoped Rajan would give up before the others realised what was going on.

That day we watched laden yaks moving past our camp down the valley. Teams were beginning to move out, heading for the

Cathy (left) and Ian on their return to base camp.

luxuries of home. Intellectually, things like hot showers, real beds, fresh food, were appealing. However, all I wanted to do was go back up. The thought of climbing back up the Lhotse face filled me with horror, but to turn away now was to negate all the effort I had already sunk into this project. Fortunately both Ian and Bruce were as single-minded as I was about trying again. The Sherpas were equally keen. Deshun had been too inexperienced to climb on the mountain on her own. Once we returned to base camp, she had not wanted to push forward her climbing ambitions after the traumas of the storm. She was hugely excited about finally getting a chance.

We did various radio interviews. Death and disaster had, as ever in human history, awoken great interest. The radio staff were mostly horrified at our trying again. I found it all rather ludicrous. No one would expect climbers never to climb on Everest again. So what difference did it make if it was this year or the next? I guess for them the news that people actually died doing this activity came as a shock. Maybe they thought the talk of the danger was just part of the media hype around the event. Now they seemed to find our acceptance of these events incomprehensible.

Part of me was excited to have the opportunity to try again, part of me grimly resigned to the effort and discomfort that the attempt would entail. Best of all was that I finally felt an equal part of the team. The storm, for all its tragedies, did us the world of good in pulling us together as a crew. It had increased my trust, both in Bruce and Ian, and in myself. I realised that my isolation had been to a large extent my fault, founded in my own uncertainty and consequent reticence, my unwillingness to push myself forward in the company of the others. I resolved to be pushier.

We were now low on oxygen but managed to buy seven more bottles from Henry Todd. He counselled us against trying again. He felt the season was over, that there would not be another window of good weather. He had lost several friends in the storm.

His advice to us was to call it quits and try again another year.

Another worrying factor was that Ian was battling a lingering chest infection. Although he looked terrible, he hid the true seriousness of it from us. His chest was on fire, his head throbbing with fever, and he could hardly breathe.

It was an unhappy crew that finally regained camp 2. I had moved off ahead, loving the day. I was fit and acclimatised, the weather was cool. I loved being alone in that extraordinary landscape. I powered up the glacier, cutting my previous time by half. Ian stumbled in much later, exhausted. Bruce followed him, smoking with anger. Deshun could be seen trailing in the distance. She was battling and had taken to whining. Bruce had had a short, sharp fight with her as he had tried to get her to move faster.

'I realised today that my expedition ends here,' Ian said to Bruce as he collapsed in their tent. It was all so unfair. Mentally, he was the toughest of the lot of us, but illness could destroy even the best. After all we had gone through together in the storm, we really were a tight-knit team. To lose any one of us was to lose a whole part of what we were. Bruce had always been easy to get along with, a good friend from the start. Ian was different. I had no idea where he and I were going, but I wanted him to be there on the summit day with me. We kept away from each other now that we were in the company of others. However, Bruce watched us with a knowing smile as I sat with my feet ever so casually under Ian's sleeping bag.

The next day we were enjoying the usual activity of watching IMAX leader David Breashears on the radio. Some things never changed. Suddenly he stopped, listened into his radio intently and then turned to us. He was actually going to talk to us!

'Turn on your radios,' he called. 'Nelson Mandela wants to speak to you.'

We stared at him in stunned silence. Why would the president of the country call up a little mountaineering expedition? Nobody really wanted to radio Philip and find out that it was just a joke.

However, a few minutes later a voice came through, faint but clear.

'This is President Mandela here in South Africa.'

He said he was happy that we were attempting to climb Mount Everest again.

'I am fully behind you. I have a lot of confidence in you and I know you are going to succeed. The whole of South Africa stands behind you because it is a significant expedition and I wish you all the luck.'

When he signed off, Ian handed me the radio and walked away in silence. He was more shaken by that conversation than by anything else that had happened up to then on the expedition. We were all hugely elated. The whole mood of the team had taken an upswing. We were now fully determined to do all we could to get up this mountain.

By the following evening we were back at camp 3. With each step I had taken up the long, steep ice incline of the Lhotse face I had promised myself that it would be the last time I had to do it. It had became a mental mantra, that one done and that one done, never again and never again. However, the Sherpas reported poor weather up at camp 4. The euphoria was evaporating rapidly.

I decided I had absolutely had it with this mountain. With the cold and effort, and above all with the stupid, stupid weather. We should have gone home when we had the chance. I buried my head in my sleeping bag, and tried not to look as if I was crying. With three of us jammed in the tent, there was nowhere to go, no privacy, no space. I could feel the atmosphere cool as the men realised what was happening. Mercifully they said nothing. Bruce continued to melt snow. Ian quietly slipped an arm across my shoulders.

I suddenly felt hungry. I sat up, smiled awkwardly at Ian, and wriggled round to where Bruce was tending the stove.

'Is there any food going? I'm starving.'

He stared at me in bewilderment, unable to keep up with the emotional changes of pace.

I woke the next morning to the howl of the wind, humming against the guy-ropes, slapping wildly against the tent fabric.

Cathy all wrapped up outside at camp 3.

The Sherpas radioed up from camp 2 that they thought the wind too strong and were staying put. Once again it was a round of questions and decisions. Eventually we retreated back down to camp 2.

The next morning brought mixed fortune. Deshun, unable to eat or sleep properly, and plagued by headaches, had set off down to base camp. Philip sent up news of good weather. We decided to head back up the next day. Although I knew weather reports were unreliable, a good one made a huge difference to my attitude. However, Ian was still wracked by coughing. Bruce and I made a half-hearted effort to talk him out of coming with us. He asked only to be allowed to climb up in support of us, to get as far as he could. There was no telling him otherwise.

By the evening the wind had died down and the western cwm was completely clear of cloud. We agreed to leave camp at 5.30 a.m. However, the next morning there was no sign of life from the male contingent. Of all the things we had experienced together, this was what annoyed me most. I could have had an extra hour's sleep, with no difference to our leaving time. All sorts of more important personality clashes passed me by, solved by some kind of mutual compromise. This got me really worked up.

I stalked over to their tent and peered inside. Bruce was fiddling. He had about 11 different pairs of gloves laid out in front of him: fleece ones, wool ones, thick ones, thin ones, red ones, blue ones. He couldn't decide which particular combination to take today. Ian was still asleep, sleeping bag pulled over his head, happily off in the warm and cosy land of Nod which I had dragged myself from a long, cold hour before, at his instruction.

I abandoned them as a lost cause, steaming off up the glacier. Fuelled by righteous anger, I managed a magnificent couple of hundred metres before the altitude, the cold and the weight of my rucksack deflated my energy.

Once on the Lhotse face, rather than battling cold, I was overcome by heat. My body felt immensely hot and heavy with the load and the clothing. It was just too much to feel as if you were about to get heat stroke at 7 000 metres on Everest, surrounded on all sides by ice. However, the heat wasn't the only strange factor. The sky was clear and the mountain absolutely still. Nothing moved. After the weeks of express-train winds that had always sounded in the background, the silence was uncanny.

One last twist of fate stood between us and camp 4. Ian, who was brewing up at camp 3, had placed his lighter on top of the rubbish packet. He then knocked the packet with his sleeve, sending it and the lighter spinning out of the door and down the ice slope.

Bruce's lighter failed to produce a spark. Mine seemed to have been left at camp 2. We looked at each other in consternation.

'And for the want of a nail, the battle was lost,' muttered Bruce as he continued to try to coax a spark from his beleaguered lighter.

No flame meant no heat. No heat meant no liquid. And no liquid, at these altitudes, meant rapid deterioration. Another night and a day and we would be in serious trouble.

'I've got it!' Bruce exclaimed triumphantly as he managed to get a tiny spark to ignite the gas and the stove roared into life.

We reached the south col the following afternoon. All the tents had gone, only our two remained, huddled together in the midst of the vast rocky expanse. Pemba had found some abandoned prayer flags and was busy stringing them up, providing a burst of colour against the black and white of the mountain. To the west, mountain after mountain protruded from a low-lying blanket of cloud. Otherwise the weather was clear and still. It looked to be a perfect night.

Bruce radioed base camp to say we would definitely be going, probably around 11 p.m. I settled down in my sleeping bag, wearing my inner layers of clothing, thermal long-johns and top, with fleece salopettes. The thermal layer had not been taken off since I had left base camp a week before.

The excitement was welling up inside me. It was really, finally, beginning to happen. This time we were on our way to the top. I wished this had come two weeks earlier, when I had felt that much stronger. But I was feeling quite good now. We were so close … and yet still so far. Sleep seemed an impossibility. Butterflies were breeding in my stomach and my mind was racing in circles.

Then Ang Dorje's hand was pounding against the tent door, a thermos flask of tea ready to be passed in to us. The little time there had been for sleep was over. In between cups of tea, working in a sleep-deprived daze in the small pools of light cast by our head-torches, we struggled to dress for the cold night's work ahead. We wore down suits, consisting of salopettes and jackets, over our fleece clothing. It was like wearing a sleeping bag with arms and legs cut into it. It would be the first time we had had to climb in such extreme cold that they would be necessary.

My feet were already encased in warm socks and insulated

inner boots. Now the inner boots had to be forced into the rigid, plastic outer boots, the frozen laces had to be tightened and tied, and last the nylon gaiters had to be pulled up and zipped closed over the bulky down legs. Balaclava, woolly hat, climbing harness, inner gloves, fleece mittens, Goretex mittens, all had to be put on.

Thermos flasks had to be filled with hot juice, oxygen sets checked and attached to bottles in the rucksacks. Sunglasses were stored for easy retrieval at sunrise, a last check for cameras, spare batteries, extra film.

It all seemed to take an age.

'We must leave, we must go,' Ang Dorje urged, fidgeting in an agony of anticipation.

Ang Dorje, playboy, mountaineer and sirdar of the South African team.

6

Stairway to heaven

We pulled ourselves out of the tent, and stood in the clear, crisp night air. It wasn't as cold as I had anticipated, and it was completely still. Bruce was busy sorting out Jangbu's head-torch, which had mysteriously decided not to work. Pemba was still fiddling with his oxygen bottle. Above us the mountain loomed, a huge shadow of a darker shade of black, set against the night sky.

Bruce was speaking to Philip on the radio as I trudged slowly over the uneven surface of the col behind Pemba. I felt disorientated from the lack of sleep, stiff and cold. As I moved awkwardly up the steepening snow slopes, I trawled through my mind for every possible excuse for turning round and crawling back into the warmth of my sleeping bag: illness, altitude sickness, too slow and didn't want to hold up the others. Unable to think of one that would convince Ian or Bruce, or, for that matter, myself, I kept moving. Thinking of excuses became a mental game, to distract me from the slog of the climbing. I dreaded a night like the horrible one I had had reaching the summit of Kilimanjaro, when I had almost talked myself out of the Everest expedition.

We climbed up a snow gully and then over bands of loose rock, sprinkled with snow. We wound a devious route across ledges and up unstable breaks. The insecure surface called for a degree of thought difficult to dredge up in the early hours of the morning. We each moved in a tiny, individual pool of yellow light cast by our head-torches. Strung out below me, the others were reduced to minute stars in the inky blackness of the moonless night. The small circles of light formed fragile bubbles of purpose and direction in an otherwise limitless landscape. The only sounds were the rasp of my breath drawn through the oxygen mask and the crunch of snow underfoot.

The night sky was clear and pitch black. Occasional sheets of lightning on distant horizons turned the sky momentarily electric-blue and the hundreds of peaks of the Himalaya stood silhouetted in jagged black grandeur, before disappearing again into darkness. There was an eerie splendour to it all.

Pemba stopped, fiddling with his oxygen set. I moved up slowly to stand by him.

'No oxygen,' he blurted out, his voice on the edge of panic. 'It doesn't work.'

I tried to focus my attention on his oxygen set, to concentrate through the fog of sleeplessness and altitude. I checked the various indicators slowly and meticulously, assuring myself that the bottle was full and the oxygen flowing. I realised I must be missing something, but what?

The figure below moved up steadily to join us and I saw to my surprise that it was Ian and not Bruce. I waved a gloved hand at Pemba's oxygen cylinder and he leant over to inspect it.

'It's on a one-litre-a-minute flow rate, instead of two or three,' said Ian. With a quick twist of the valve he adjusted the regulator.

We climbed on up the steep slopes of shattered rock and loose snow. Even though Pemba was ahead of me and Ian close behind, I felt intensely alone. No one else could know how I felt, no one could help me find the strength to do this. We were higher than all but a few mountains in the whole world, but still this one loomed above us, disappearing upwards into the inky night. I was frightened. The snow slope seemed so steep, yet not steep enough. It was too precipitous to walk up easily, yet not vertical enough to

129

plunge my ice-axe into properly. Below me it fell away into yawning blackness, the void both concealing and emphasising the drop down to the south col.

I was acutely aware of how much height I had gained in the last three hours. To fall now would be to fall all the way down, to roll and bounce and scream, smashing into rock and ice, before landing on the stony col, still, broken, like a rag doll.

I was aware of Ian's presence a few steps below me. I took comfort in that. I considered telling him that I was scared, but there was no point. There was no way out of this. Even to give up meant returning down the treacherous ground I had come up. For me to freeze with fear only endangered the others.

And besides, I was not that afraid. I had not put in months of effort, weeks of slog, to give up 12 hours from the top. I just wanted to share my feeling. I compromised and imagined telling Ian, while not actually doing so. I feared that he would not understand, that he would read my admission as weakness. I knew it was not. It was acceptance of who I was, knowledge that I could be both frightened and capable simultaneously.

As I was battling my private demons, the snow had been changing from grey to salmon to faint pink. While I moved upwards, the first false light of dawn illuminated the line of the eastern horizon. Slowly the pink smear spread sideways and then reached up into the sky. As the sun rose from the horizon so far below us, the mountain turned vivid pink. The plateau below was striped with pink, orange, blue and purple. The deep valleys on either side of the mountain filled with dark blue shadow. The south col appeared out of the darkness, reduced to a little black postage stamp between Everest and Lhotse, the tents invisible. The yellow orb slipped smoothly into the pale sky, and light and life and confidence returned with it.

Now that the night had passed, I was surprised by how short it had been, and how warm. The sweat was trickling down my back, stewing in the warmth of my massive down jacket and salopettes. In the end it was easier than the Kilimanjaro night. I clambered onto the Balcony, the junction with the ridge that we would turn to follow to the summit. It was marked by a dozen orange oxygen bottles with the names of David Breashears and the IMAX team emblazoned on their sides. I sank down in the snow beside Pemba, resting gratefully against my rucksack, and watched Ian toiling up towards us.

He sat down beside me and pulled off his oxygen mask. I tried to tell him how I had felt through the night. He grinned at me.

'I'm proud of you.'

Pemba, Ian and I looked out over the Himalaya, the black and white mountains now glorious in pink, purple and gold. The sombre pyramid of Makalu dominated the view, a massive mountain of classic proportions, fifth highest in the world. To the left, the deep valley of the Kangshung glacier reluctantly emerged from darkness. On the horizon, the squat form of the giant mountain of Kangchenjunga, third highest, reigned supreme.

I found a deep sense of satisfaction in looking out over so many mountains, and being apparently equal with some of the biggest. The long slog through the dark had yielded its reward, a giant leap in height, concrete evidence that we were making progress and might actually be able to complete this challenge.

Then I turned to look upwards. Above me the long snowy ridge wound up towards the south summit. A tiny line traced its way up it, the footsteps of the Americans and French from two days previously. The main summit was still hidden, the path to it still elusive, the big unknown in my assessment of my ability to reach it.

Pemba, eager as ever, began to move up the ridge. Aware of the cold and stiffness seeping through my body, I started to follow him, with Ian close behind. I found it distinctly depressing to have him following me so closely, given his poor physical condition over the last few days. Then he moved on past me. It was rather like losing a race to a snail, I thought dismally as I watched him plod steadily upwards. We both seemed to be moving incredibly slowly. I assumed it was some time in the mid-morning, but the effort of

locating a watch under the numerous layers of clothing and gloves seemed too great. I marked time by the gradual rise of the sun.

I battled through the soft snow, sinking up to the knee with each step, my axe shaft plunging into the snow as if it were butter. The steps left by others crumbled away under the new weight. The resulting progress up the ever-steeping ridge was slow and painstaking. In a few places tattered remnants of fixed ropes lay in the snow, their anchor points uncertain and their history unknown.

I became aware of a giant pyramid of blue, running across the cloud and the peaks of the Nepalese Himalaya. I stared at it in puzzlement for a moment before realising that it was the shadow of Everest, cast by the rising sun. I stopped to photograph it, thinking, it is so beautiful ... and so big.

'We're above 8 500 metres,' Ian called down to me. 'We've cleared the top of Lhotse.'

We looked towards the giant mountain that had loomed over our trips up the western cwm and our days at camp 2. We had climbed its slopes so diligently and so repeatedly, counting each step done, cursing each step still to take. Now the giant was below us.

I was experiencing a growing feeling of suffocation. My oxygen bottle was empty. I sat down in the snow to change it for a fresh one, to remove my by now unbearably hot down jacket, and to rest. I left the empty bottle to collect on the way down. By the time I was moving again Pemba was out of sight and Ian was disappearing up the twisting ridge. I moved in my own miniature universe, where the only sound was my straining body, and the only sight the few steps directly in front of my feet, the next few steps to be taken.

Achingly slowly, the south summit approached. I blocked it out, watching only the two steps in front of my feet, saving a look

Ian climbing the snow ridge above the Balcony. In the background, the dominant shape of Makalu.

upwards for the occasional treat, to convince myself that I was actually making progress. Still, I wondered how far ahead of me Ian and Pemba were. Was I moving hopelessly slowly? I imagined standing on the south summit and seeing them in the far distance. I imagined Ian yelling to me to turn round, saying that it was too late, too far for me. And I imagined myself telling him to get stuffed.

At last I clambered onto the top of the south summit of Everest - 8 700 metres, higher than any other mountain in the world. I felt an amazing sense of disbelief that it should actually be me who had achieved all this. But could I go further?

I looked across to the ridge that ran towards the true summit. In a few shocked seconds I absorbed several salient facts. It was a classic mountain ridge, knife-edged, corniced, twisting gently up over a series of rises. I instantly recognised the rock step on the ridge as the Hillary Step. It wasn't as fearsome as I had imagined. I noticed the doll-like figures of Pemba and Ian approaching the step. They weren't as far ahead of me as I had feared. I took in the precipitous nature of the ridge and the immense drops on either side of it. That was do-able. The summit was still not in sight but it couldn't be too distant.

From deep within me incredible excitement welled up.

I could do that, I could climb that ridge. I had the energy and the ability. For the first time in the entire expedition, standing on the summit of Everest manifested itself for me as a concrete possibility, rather than just a wishful daydream. All the weeks of uncertainty, of bad weather, of ill health were swept away in the awesome realisation that the goal lay so tantalisingly close.

'Ian,' I yelled, and watched as he turned cautiously towards me. 'Ian, I'm going on.' It was a statement, not a question, but I was still relieved when he waved in agreement.

He asked if there was any sign of Bruce. Looking back down I could see three little black dots, the last just at the Balcony. All were moving upwards. I did not know who was who. We had strung out dramatically along the ridge, more so that we had expected. However, that was how we had climbed all the way up the mountain, often coming into camps several hours apart.

We would descend by the same route, there being nowhere else to go. Anyone who fell by the wayside would be picked up on the descent. I was focused on looking after myself and assumed the others were too.

I moved down the short steep slope to the start of the ridge, past a pile of orange oxygen bottles and a long, blue shape. I realised with shock that it was the body of Rob Hall. I looked away. Crossing of the ridge had to claim all my attention. The trail ran just to the left of the knife-edge of the ridge, staying below the cornices that hung over the Tibetan side, while staying above the unstable dinner plates of rock a few feet down on the Nepalese side. The only flat ground was the footprints left by previous climbers. I moved up the ridge almost as if I had put on mental blinkers, seeing only the two footsteps ahead of me. It was a little like walking along an undulating plank. Not particularly difficult, if you ignored the fact that there was a 2 500 metre drop on the one side, and a 3 000 metre drop on the other.

Despite my concentration, other thoughts and memories wandered through my head. It was ten years and half a world away from orientation week at Wits University in 1987. I had spent the week wandering around the university, looking at all the different clubs on offer. I had watched with disbelief the figures in old khaki shorts and shocking pink lycra scaling the library wall, and listened to the pitch from the Mountain Club chairman. I had not been convinced, and was more interested in joining the Exploration Society. But on the very last day, with the abandon born of spending my father's money, I decided to join the Mountain Club as well. Little did I know then where I would be 10 years later.

My steady progress along the ridge was broken by the wall of the Hillary Step. I stopped short, trying to re-focus mentally from snow to rock. The first section was relatively easy, involving some cautious scrambling. Then a traverse across loose scree brought me

to the foot of an awkward, angled chimney, filled with loose rock and snow. I wriggled my way up it, suddenly conscious of the burden of the bulky clothing, the big oxygen set, the enormous boots and crampons. Jammed awkwardly near the top I contemplated the creeper-like mass of ancient fixed rope that hung down the back of the chimney. Manoeuvring past it without getting it tangled around my rucksack, crampons or ice-axe was as much of a challenge as negotiating the wall itself. Finally I grabbed a huge bundle of it in one hand and pulled, wriggled and flopped my way onto the summit of the block.

Again odd memories floated through my mind. I remembered the first rock-climb I ever did, Donkerhoek Corner in Upper Tonquani, a gorge near Johannesburg. It had been all of grade 12. A classic chimney thrutch, it was an unprepossessing beginning. I quite enjoyed the climbing, was less impressed by the amount of flaming Sambuca being thrown down everyone's throats, and was far from convinced that this was an experience to be repeated. However, I was impressed by a young and handsome blonde called Mike Cartwright. Given that the only place he could be found on the weekends was on a cliff face, I had decided to give this climbing lark another go.

Once above the Hillary Step the ridge widened. I realised with amusement that although the exposure, and the danger, was far greater here than on the slopes lower on the mountain, I felt no fear, only exhilaration. I could see straight down the south-west face of Everest, down to the tiny camp 2 over 2 000 metres below me. We had come a long way since then and a longer way still from home.

I had been moving alone along the ridge for some time. Pemba and Ian were out of sight ahead, the other three climbers somewhere behind. Although I mostly concentrated on the few steps in front of me, blocking out the vast empty spaces that

Ian climbs the Hillary Step while Pemba rests on the ridge above.

surrounded the ridge, occasionally I allowed myself the luxury of looking out across the myriad of snowy peaks below me. With no one else in sight, and no signs of human existence visible below, it was like being the last person alive on earth, having the whole of a magnificent planet to myself.

I felt humbled, aware of how frail and fragile the humans were dotted on the side of this huge edifice of snow and rock. I was also frustrated. The ridge undulated gently. Each crest looked as if it might be the final one, but as I dragged my weary body onto the top I found another one slightly higher, slightly further on. The ridge seemed to run on interminably in front of me. I felt as if I was on a snowy treadmill, a ridge that ran forever with no conclusion. I felt condemned to walk it for eternity.

I tried to suppress all expectations, to deal with the ridge step by step, rather than to face the inevitable disappointment expectation of the summit would bring.

My mind wandered once more, seeking escape from the mental boredom of the slow, plodding ascent. I recalled my first great pronouncement on my climbing career. It was made halfway up a small, loose and aloe-strewn rock face in Wilgepoort. I declared that while I liked climbing, I had no interest in learning to lead rock routes. Within a few months I was leading.

My next great pronouncement came after a friend hauled me up a 300 metre rock-face at Blouberg. The first few hours I enjoyed, but then I was ready to go home. Unfortunately we were only half way up. I announced that I was interested only in walk-ins under half an hour, and climbs of 50 metres or less. Over the next few years I climbed big walls all over Southern Africa, and then moved on to 600 metre rock-walls in the Alps.

My third great pronouncement was that, although big walls were great, you wouldn't catch me dead mountaineering. Too high, too cold, too dangerous ...

I moved slowly up yet another small rise and onto the top of it. And stopped short, aware of two figures and a sudden blaze of colour. Ian and Pemba were seated in the snow with something behind them that to my puzzled gaze looked rather like a ruined tent. After hours in an almost monochrome world of blue sky, white snow and black rock, the medley of red, yellow and green was disconcerting. Then Pemba turned and saw me. A huge grin spread across his face and I noticed his gold tooth glinting in the sunlight. He stood up and began to wave both arms and his ice-axe in the air.

That's it, I thought. That is the summit of Everest.

For the second time that day I was filled with an incredible sense of excitement. At last I knew that not only was I capable of climbing Everest, but that I had actually done it. Only ten more metres. I had never imagined it would get to this.

The last slog up the final slope seemed interminable. I clambered slowly towards the dash of colour, which became a pile of prayer flags covering a metal tripod.

Ian spoke into the radio: 'And then there were three.'

Philip's voice came through in a chatter of excitement.

I sank down onto my knees beside Ian and hugged him, barely able to feel the man beneath the piles of clothing we were both wearing. I turned to hug Pemba, acutely conscious of the pleasure of being able to share the moment with friends. I was glad that I was not there alone.

Ian had reached the summit some twenty minutes earlier, followed shortly thereafter by Pemba. He had announced over the radio: 'We have 9:52 and the Nepalese and South African flags are flying on the summit of Everest.'

The base camp crew had broken out into wild cheering. They had begun to pass round the tins of San Miguel beer that had been chilling on the ice of the glacier. Patrick had answered the phone to find it was the producer of the Radio 702 morning news programme.

'Hold on,' he had said. 'There's a broadcast coming through, they're somewhere on the mountain.' Then he had begun to shout. 'They're on the summit! They're on the summit! Put me on the air! Put me on the air now!'

The news had gone out at six o'clock in the morning in South Africa, to friends and family who had been awake all night, to insomniacs and early birds, to depressed rugby fans who had just watched the All Blacks thrash the Springboks at rugby.

Now Ian thrust the radio at me. Pulling off my mask, I was aware of the immediate drop in oxygen supply. There was only a third as much air here as there was at sea level. I spoke into the little black box in my gloved hand.

'Hello, base camp, can you hear me?'

Everyone offered me their congratulations.

I sat on the pile of snow, trying to order my thoughts, trying to let the enormity of it all sink in. I couldn't believe that I, that we, had actually done it.

Then my mother's voice came through faintly from the black box.

'Hello, Cathy? Good morning, darling. You are the star for us.'

How strange it was to be so far away and yet so intimately connected, to stand on the summit of the world and speak to my mother in her living room in Johannesburg. It was a huge thrill to be able to share with her the very moment that I was on top. My parents had been so supportive through all the difficulty, never hinting to me what worries or fears they might have.

I tried to sort my thoughts coherently, to be able to say something meaningful over the radio. But the emotions that were swelling through me tossed my words into chaos.

Ian handed Pemba the camera and he and I clambered onto the summit itself, holding out Ian's ice-axe with the Nepalese and South African flags hanging from it. After weeks of battling the most ferocious winds, the breeze was now not even strong enough to make the flags flutter.

I looked down at the multi-coloured blaze of the South African flag with a shiver of excitement. I remembered being a teenager in the 'old' South Africa, standing in the hall of my school in Johannesburg, mouthing the words of the national anthem 'Die Stem' and wondering what it would be like to live in a country

Top: Ian (left) and
Cathy on the summit
with the South
African and Nepalese
flags.

Bottom: The view
from the summit.
Makalu is in the
middle distance,
Kangchenjunga on
the horizon.

where one was actually proud to be a citizen, where the anthem and the flag really meant something.

And now I knew.

I never expected to do something under the colours of my country, to make any kind of public contribution to the achievements of the nation. But now as I looked down at what was for a brief moment the highest flag in the world, I was proud to be South African, and proud to have forged a small place in the history of my country.

I looked at what actually marked the summit of the world. The large metal tripod left by the Americans in 1992 as part of a re-surveying of Everest's height was almost covered in vividly coloured Buddhist prayer flags. Beneath them was a collection of tiny photographs in frames. Although I did not know it at the time, Jamling Tenzing Norgay, who was part of the IMAX team, had left them there. He was the son of Tenzing Norgay, the Sherpa who had done the first ascent of Everest with Edmund Hillary 43 years earlier. I removed the South African flag badge that was pinned to my fleece jacket and placed it in the snow.

Part of me wanted to relax, to sit down and soak in the sense of really being on top of the world. But that was overwhelmed by the nagging worry of the long, long way we had to descend. Every one of those steps so laboriously taken on the way up still had to be taken again before we were safe again at camp. The summit was not a finish in any sense, but only a halfway point. I knew the risks of descent, the chances of making a mistake due to tiredness or simply lack of concentration. With the drive for the summit gone, all that remained to keep us moving was the survival instinct.

To spend only 15 minutes on top after months of effort to get there seemed less than logical. But in the end it had been about getting there, not about being there.

Ian and Pemba were packing up to leave and I joined them reluctantly, with one last glance out across the hundreds of mountains below me. Whatever I climbed in the future, I thought, I would never have to climb this high again. I meant that with all my heart. But then my pronouncements about my future never were very trustworthy.

As we moved steadily down towards the Hillary Step, we encountered Jangbu and Ang Dorje moving determinedly upwards.

'Bara Sahib, Didi, *ramro*, very well done,' Ang Dorje said.

'You guys going on to the top?' asked Ian.

'Oh yes.' That decision was theirs to make and neither they nor we ever assumed it would be otherwise. We wished them well and continued on down. They called down to base camp from the summit at 10.55 a.m. Jangbu had been there once before, when he had climbed Everest from the Tibetan side, but for Ang Dorje it was an unexpected culmination to his long career as a climbing sirdar.

Crossing the narrow ridge past the Hillary Step was a trying process. Each time I looked down my glasses misted up from the hot air rising out of my oxygen mask. Yet I dared not take the glasses off, for fear of snow blindness. Ian was climbing a few metres behind me, and, unbeknown to me, he nearly fell off the ridge. He moved his right foot onto the dark outline of a footprint seen through his misted glasses. Only there was no snow, only empty air. As he lost his balance, his heavy rucksack swung slowly but inexorably towards the drop and he began to fall. Even while thinking that these were his last moments, he swung his ice-axe in a wide arc towards the narrow snow ridge. It gripped, leaving him staring straight down the bottomless south-west face, watching his beanie falling on without him. We were, supposedly, climbing together, yet I could have done nothing more than turn and watch him fall.

I stopped at Rob Hall's body for a few minutes, a tiny personal tribute to the life, the achievement and the tragic death of this talented climber. It was strange to me that we should both have been climbing the same mountain and yet have had such radically different experiences.

Encountering bodies on the mountain is not fun. For many people it seems such a horrible concept that they would rather not climb than risk the encounter. These were the first bodies I had ever seen. But he lay there so peacefully. For me what I saw was no more than an empty suitcase. The energy that made up Rob Hall had long

since moved on to the next great adventure.

I crossed over the south summit and onto the steep ridge below. A small figure was visible below me, still moving determinedly upwards. I realised with shock that it was Bruce. I had assumed he had given up. I paused to take a photograph of him as Pemba passed him. As I approached he put out his arms and pulled me into a huge bear hug.

'Pemba gave me the news,' he said. 'Well done, woman. I'm so chuffed you guys have done it.'

We sat down together in the snow and I asked him if he was okay, if he was having problems. He said he was fine, just moving slowly. Then he began to quiz me about the climbing above us, the nature of the difficulties, the length of time I had taken on each section. I realised he had no intention of turning back with us. I was not sure what to say to this and waited for Ian to join us.

Bruce pumped his hand.

'Well done, mate. It's amazing you made it,' he beamed.

Ian asked him to come back down with us. Bruce's ready smile in no way hid the steely determination of his answer.

'No, I've come this far. I'm going on.'

Both Ian and I assumed Bruce would simply go on to the south summit, a major achievement in itself and then turn back from there. Bruce agreed to take a radio and another full bottle of oxygen from Ang Dorje, when he passed him. Ian exhorted him to keep in touch on the radio, with us and with base camp. Bruce confirmed he was happy with the route down, and knew where to turn off the ridge.

We watched him move slowly on upward, before turning round to continue down the mountain. A short while after having left us, Bruce passed Jangbu and Ang Dorje, and took Ang Dorje's radio and another bottle of oxygen. Ang Dorje also suggested that Bruce turn round, but he remained adamant. At 12.20 p.m. he called base camp on the radio.

Ian descends the summit ridge with Ang Dorje and Jangbu catching up behind just above the Hillary Step.

Philip asked him how he was feeling

'At the moment I'm feeling great. Everybody has summitted except me. I'm about 30 minutes below the south summit. What I'm going to do is press on on my own to the south summit, keeping a very close eye on conditions and weather and myself. If everything's all right on the south summit, I'm going to take the radio with me. I'll check in with you, and then I'll press on, just to see if I can top out.'

It was not a situation we had anticipated. I had always thought I might be the one to turn back, or fall behind. That it might be Bruce never crossed my mind. That moment of decision, when Bruce went on and we went down came under heavy criticism after the expedition. Many felt Ian should have 'ordered' him down. However, our expedition did not run that way. And I'm not convinced Bruce would have paid any attention. Ian could hardly have threatened him. At the time, given that Bruce was completely lucid, it did not seem a bad decision. It was midday, the skies were clear and the weather warm. He had nearly seven hours of light left. Other teams from earlier in the season had been at much the same altitude as he at much the same time. In climbing alone along the summit ridge, he would not be doing anything different from what we had already done.

Much was made of so-called 'cut-off times'. But there is no moment when a gong rings out from heaven and announces all climbers must turn round. Each climber must judge when he has run through half his reserves, and then have the discipline to turn back. That point is different from individual to individual, and is not that easily judged. In the end each individual must make a personal decision and then accept responsibility for it.

At base camp the waiting continued. Patrick spoke to President Mandela, who said that, 'the news came to us as a real surprise, and also a cause for jubilation because of the fact that the conditions on top there were not conducive to this achievement, but our children did very well indeed.'

He asked if he could speak to us when we were safely down and began to give Patrick his telephone number. Patrick interrupted frantically. He visualised President Mandela giving out his personal telephone number live on air. He could imagine every citizen in South Africa phoning the President up at home to complain about everything from the state of the nation to the neighbour's barking dog, and he himself, as a result, never working in the media again.

We, meanwhile, had reached the Balcony. I dreaded climbing down the steep snow slope that I had found so frightening on the way up, but daylight and descent made it easier. We moved across the loose rocky ledges relatively quickly, passing Scott Fischer's body all wrapped up in rope. I was surprised by his location, because in the end he was not that far from the south col. I moved on to the fixed ropes, conscious only now of sore knees, deep exhaustion and an overwhelming desire to reach the tents. On my arrival I was too tired to feel anything much, but slowly got on with the chores of pulling on warm, dry clothing, while waiting for Ian.

He arrived at last and stood exhausted by the tent door, huddled over, head down, hands jammed into his armpits. I waited for a few minutes and then seeing that he seemed to be beyond moving, climbed reluctantly out of my sleeping bag. I pulled his oxygen bottle out of his rucksack, fished out his down jacket and bullied him into the tent.

At 4.40 p.m. Ian pulled out the radio and called Philip to report our safe return.

Philip was worried about Bruce. He had not radioed since 12.20 p.m. Ian asked Philip to hold all goodwill messages until the team was fully reunited.

Ian and I crawled into our sleeping bags and I reached across to hug him. I was glad he had made it, and made it first. After all the effort he had put into organising and running the expedition, he had earned that summit a hundredfold.

'No, if anyone deserved it, it was you,' he said to me.

We lay back in tired silence listening to the gentle, reassuring hiss of our oxygen regulators, and keeping an ear open for the crackle of the radio, or the crunch of boots on the rock.

7

A fallen star

Bruce's voice came crackling through the radio. We had been dozing and jerked up in confusion, Ian grabbing the small black box.

'Bruce, mate, where are you?'

'I'm on the summit of the world.'

His voice came through strong and joyful. He sounded immensely proud of himself. Ian and I stared at each other in horror. I glanced at my watch, 5 p.m. My mind was swirling with questions. What was he doing on the summit? And why had it taken him so long?

'I'm just so chuffed that I've finally made it,' Bruce said. 'It's been a long time coming, mate, and I'll be real careful on the way down.'

He said that the weather was benign and he was confident of the descent. We listened as he spoke to base camp, then to his girlfriend, Sue, in London. I wondered if I should get on the radio and congratulate him, but decided to wait. I'd give him an enormous hug when he got back to camp. I desperately wanted him back down. We had all done it and that was great. Now it was time to go home.

Bruce pulled his camera out of his rucksack. He hadn't taken any photographs all day, but this was one scene that he was not going to miss. He pulled off his mitts, now wearing only his red inner gloves, so he could fiddle with the delicate camera controls. He fixed the camera to the top of his ice-axe and positioned it so he could see the summit tripod, the blaze of prayer flags, the pyramid that made up the highest snow in the world, and the curve of the horizon so far beyond and below. Once he was sure it was in place, he moved round to position himself next to the summit tripod. With a big grin, he pushed the button on his remote control. He'd done it!

Meanwhile Ian and I gazed at each other in consternation. He was on the summit. I had assumed he had turned back long since and was on his way down to us. Thoughts of all we had achieved, all we had been through to achieve it, and all that Bruce was still going through, circled round my head. Visions of the steep snow slopes, the broken, rocky ledges, the narrow, curving ridge, the small summit platform. Finally I could stand the silence no longer.

'Do you think he's going to make it back to us?' I said to Ian.

He sought to reassure me. Bruce still had several hours of daylight, a full down suit, plenty of oxygen. He had sounded strong and confident.

'I guess so,' I said. 'It's just having seen the bodies of Rob and Scott lying on the mountain and knowing that Bruce is out there on his own.' I hesitated. 'I guess this sounds silly to you after all your years in the army, but those are the first bodies I've ever seen.'

'Yes, but they're just bodies,' Ian replied quietly.

They were just bodies and we needed now to concentrate on the living, not the dead. We didn't have enough oxygen for the night, let alone to go back up the mountain for Bruce if we had to. I didn't know if we had the strength to go back up the ridge, but I knew that we had no chance at all without oxygen.

I decided to go out in search of unfinished bottles. It was not just the fear that we might need them, but it also provided something to do, an escape from the waiting. Sitting in the tent with Ian was difficult. There was no more we could speculate about Bruce. Yet somehow we could not speak of the excitement of the summit, or of what the future held, with Bruce out in the unknown. We were trapped in limbo.

I moved across the desolate col in the bitter cold of twilight, scrabbling through the piles of bottles left from teams in past decades, searching for the tell-tale orange of the Poisk bottles that fitted our systems. In the confusion of their retreat after the great storm, the other teams hadn't taken down all their oxygen bottles. And once again there were a considerable number left by the IMAX team. Testing each bottle with my regulator, I finally found six with some oxygen left in them.

I sat for a moment in the chilly night air, looking up at the sombre pyramid of Everest, a darker shadow against a dark sky. I wondered where on its great slopes one man was moving. I looked above it to the sky, clear and littered with brilliant stars. So beautiful but so unfeeling. Amid the gloom of worry, a brief flicker of pride shone out. We had done it!

While looking up at the mountain, I radioed Philip to update him on conditions. He logged the call at 6.50 p.m. I could hear the worry in his voice. Unable to see the summit from base camp, he had no idea of what kind of weather Bruce was facing.

'Don't worry, Phil. It's completely clear and still. If there is any night to bivi on Everest, this is the night. And remember, Bruce might take all night, especially if he decides to bivi and climb on down in daylight.'

He agreed with me, and we discussed various possibilities with forced optimism. So we reassured each other, each hiding our own unease behind a brave facade.

I crawled back into the tent with my hoard of orange bottles. I settled down into my sleeping bag and pulled on the oxygen mask, which had transformed itself into a horrible alien object. Damp from the day of climbing and now having been dragged round the col for use testing the bottles, the damp had frozen, leaving a contraption of icy, hard leather, which irritated the skin

Bruce at the door of his base camp tent.

on my face, already chaffed by hours of wearing. However, physical exhaustion overwhelmed the discomfort. I slept like the dead, without waking or dreaming.

I woke abruptly. It was light. I looked at my watch. It was 5 a.m.

No Bruce, no radio call.

He's dead.

No, maybe he isn't. Maybe he's still on his way down. Maybe he bivied and didn't call. Maybe he's nearly here.

But in the depths of my heart, after that long night with no communication, I knew he was dead.

I lay very still, feeling the blood thumping through my pulses. I glanced across at Ian, who was sleeping. I wondered if he had realised.

The radio crackled into life. Ian grabbed it. He was not asleep.

It was only Philip. He could bear the silence no longer.

Soon after that a hand rattled the tent and a thermos flask of tea was trust through the door.

'We go down today. We must leave this morning,' Ang Dorje announced firmly. Then he paused.

'No Mr Bruce?' he asked

'No, no Mr Bruce,' I replied.

He nodded impassively and withdrew.

I watched him go with mixed feelings. I was aware of the prosaic attitude of the Sherpas towards death and had discussed it before with Bruce. He admired their calm stoicism in the face of the inevitability of human morality. However, I was still rather shaken to actually see their apparent disinterest.

I looked out of the tent door and up to the high slopes of Everest. I could see all the way up the slopes that had been so hard won the previous night, and then back up along the skyline ridge to the south summit. The face was dotted with tiny black specks of rock, contrasting sharply with the brightness of the shining snow and ice, but there was no movement. None of the tiny black specks stood up and began to stumble back down towards the South African camp.

Ian suggested Bruce had probably bivied and wouldn't start moving down until the sun caught him and warmed him up a bit. We looked at each other. We both remembered standing on that high ridge in the light of the rising sun 24 hours earlier and we both knew the sun caught that ridge very, very early.

'Listen, Caths,' Ian said quietly, 'we need to think about our options of helping Bruce if he calls.'

'Yes, I know,' I replied.

What were we to do it he called? If he was still moving, we could talk him down over the radio, we could go out and try and meet him on his way down. We would all be pretty slow, but both Jangbu and Pemba were strong climbers. In addition, we had Nawang. He had stayed back at camp 2, feeling ill, but had then climbed up to camp 4 to meet us as we descended. He was fresh. But the Sherpas wanted to go down. And we had little oxygen left.

What if he called and said he could not go any further, as Rob Hall had done? Were we to listen to him die over the radio? Should we try to get to him and probably find him dead when we arrived? Or would we have to sit with him and watch him die, all the time wishing he'd hurry up while we still had some chance of getting ourselves down alive?

Did we have any chance of trying to drag a six foot massive male body back down the mountain? I doubted it.

What if some of us wanted to go and others thought it too dangerous? I wasn't sure I had the strength to climb back up to the summit, and then still be of any practical help when I reached Bruce. So what if Ian wanted to go back up and I didn't? How would we both live with those different choices?

What about the Sherpas? Would they be fearful of not being invited on future expeditions if they declined to go back up the mountain? If he called for help should any of us risk our lives knowing that there was very little chance of saving him?

What would Bruce have wanted us to do?

Eventually Ian turned to me and said he thought that the Sherpas and I should go down. He would stay on as long as he could. What little oxygen we had left would last longer that way. Neither Ang Dorje nor I were very happy with this. The four Sherpas were hell bent on starting back down. Yet for Bruce to finally crawl back into camp and find us all gone would be appalling. I slowly packed up the last of my personal kit. Worry for Bruce was now being subsumed by worry for Ian. Losing one was hard enough. I couldn't bear to lose them both.

We didn't talk. There was nothing to say.

The Sherpas came over to take their leave.

'No go up, Bara Sahib,' pleaded Pemba on the verge of tears.

They walked away. Finally my pack was loaded, my boots were on, there were no more excuses not to go.

Ian reached across and gently brushed me on the nose. I flashed a brief smile in return. Our eyes were fixed together in the moment, passing lifetimes of information and feelings between us.

'Be safe, youth.'

'You too, Ian.'

Without looking back I shouldered my rucksack and strode off towards the top of the fixed ropes.

My last image as I left the tent was of Ian lying on his side, staring unmoving through the tent door at the slope above us. It tore my heart to see him sitting so still, so small. I knew he was waiting for one of the black specks to stand up and begin a slow progress downhill. But they never did. They were only rocks, inanimate and immobile. There was nothing he could do but wait, and the longer he waited, the less chance there was of Bruce returning. It seemed such a waste that everything he had put into the expedition should end like this, that his friend should be out there dead or dying and that we should be totally helpless.

'Damn you!' I shouted suddenly, violently, not sure if I was addressing the mountain or Bruce.

'Damn you for killing him, damn you, Bruce, for not coming back. Don't do this to us. Don't be dead. Come back, for heaven's sake come back.'

The mountain loomed over me in impassive silence, its vast

bulk beyond all understanding of small human miseries.

I walked on, waves of anger and despair rolling over me. My worry for Bruce was overwhelmed now by worry for Ian, waiting alone. I could believe Bruce was safe, enjoying the adventure of whatever comes next in the universe. We were still so vulnerable, ants on the side of this mountain.

By the time I reached the top of the Geneva Spur I was calmer. I turned for what would be the final view of the summit pyramid, the most magnificent tombstone in the world.

I then dropped over the edge and began to move down towards the Lhotse face.

As I climbed alone down the mountain, I was glad of the hours of solitude in which to try and absorb the enormity of what had happened, before returning to the agonised concern of those who waited at the mountain's foot. As I moved, I replayed through my mind all that happened. I analysed our decisions again and again, and I couldn't find it in myself to think that, knowing what we did when we did, we would have decided differently. I discovered that it was difficult to climb downwards with your eyes full of tears, that blurred vision interfered with placing your feet. Already the pragmatism of living was taking over from the seemingly insurmountable trauma of Bruce's death.

I reached camp 3 by 11:30 a.m. and slumped down next to the tiny snow patch that had once held our tent. The Sherpas had taken it with them. My knees were killing me. I pulled out the radio to call Ian. I could hear from the tension in his voice that he had hoped the call might be from someone else.

'Is there ... any sign of anything on the mountain?' I asked tentatively.

'No, love, there's nothing,' he replied.

We had agreed that, if nothing changed, he would make an official announcement at noon. I put the radio on standby and waited for it, staring down the western cwm and out to the distant peaks to the west. A little after noon Ian's voice came over the radio.

'The First South African Everest Expedition regretfully

announces that team member Bruce Herrod has been missing on Mount Everest between the summit and the south col for a period of 19 hours, from 17:00 on 25/05/96 to 12:00 on 26/05/96.'

I turned the radio off and sat alone on the vast expanse of mountain and cried. My feelings swung between a certain acceptance of Bruce's choices, of the risks of mountaineering, and overwhelming pain and sorrow that he wasn't coming back. I ran through it all over again. It was, I realised, a catch-22 situation. I really felt that in Bruce I had found a friend for life. I admired his confidence and determination. Yet I knew it was that determination that had kept him going late in the day, and slowly. To wish him to have turned round was to wish him to have been another person. Yet it was the person he was that I liked so much.

I had no answers.

But now descending safely had to claim all my attention.

I clipped my safety sling to the fixed rope, just below an ice screw anchor point, and eased my weight on to it. The screw wobbled alarmingly. With the ever-rising temperatures, the surface layer of ice was melting and the anchors securing the fixed ropes were coming loose.

Just when I want nothing more than to put my mind in neutral and slide on down to rest and safety, I had to check each point, to remain totally alert, never trusting the ropes fully. The glacier back to camp 2 had stretched out yet again, but at last our two black tents came into sight. I slung my rucksack down outside my tent and sat on it, staring unseeingly at the black rocks in front of my boots.

The radio crackled to life with Ian's voice. He was going to start coming down. It turned out that the bottles I had so painstakingly searched out the previous night might have fitted my regulator, but they didn't fit his. He was out of oxygen. Without supplementary oxygen he could not safely stay on at such high altitudes. It was

Climbing down the yellow band.

157

time to go. He was back at camp 2 by nightfall.

The night before we had slept from sheer exhaustion but now our emotions had had time to brew. I had moved into Ian's tent, in Bruce's place. As we lay next to each other in the dark, we talked softly.

'This probably sounds chauvinistic, although it isn't meant to be,' said Ian. 'But in the end a man had to be allowed to make a man's decision, because if he isn't, then he isn't a man. And Bruce made his decision.'

I smiled. I knew what he meant, even if I wouldn't have phrased it like that.

'Thinking about the summit, my one miscalculation was to assume we would all reach the summit together, or that I'd be the back marker' said Ian.

As the hours wore on sleep still eluded me. We were only 36 hours away from the summit that all six had reached, one by one. And only a day away from the base where we would have to rejoin a world filled with other people. I felt sick and restless, and battled to breathe. Initially Ian tried to comfort me, but I could feel his restlessness and then irritation at my continued movement.

'Get angry,' he told me. 'Channel your pain into anger.'

'No,' I replied, horrified at the thought. I saw anger as destructive.

'Well, for God's sake, don't get all girlie on me,' he said. 'Not yet. We're not off the mountain yet.'

'Sod off, Ian.'

I immediately got angry, with him. Who was he to assume that 'girlie' emotions were weak? That if I didn't suppress them I might not be able to get myself off the mountain safely? Was his bottled-up anger and hurt and fear a better, stronger way of coping?

How could he be both so compassionate and so chauvinistic? As we lay together in the tent I felt so far away from him and his understandings of this mountain, as if we really did originate from different planets. But it worked. In my anger with him, my distress eased and sleep eventually came.

The western cwm had changed dramatically with the rising temperatures and had many more crevasses. This time there was no stopping to gaze at the beautiful scenery. I moved on as quickly as possible. This time it was really over, and it was time to get on home.

The icefall was melting around us, becoming ever more unstable. However, the gigantic overhang of blue ice still stood. We worked our way past it as quickly as exhaustion would allow. Many things had collapsed around it, but this edifice still stood. In the end the mountain was beyond the prediction of the humans that trod upon it.

We walked on together, over the endless glacier. In the distance I saw our camp, with the South African flag hanging at half mast. Philip, who had been sitting on a rock for hours waiting for us, walked towards us. I saw the concern in his eyes as he took in our emaciated figures and exhausted faces.

He hugged me and shook Ian's hand. We walked on together in silence. All the staff had come out to greet us. They stood around awkwardly, not sure whether to offer congratulations or commiserations. Everyone desperately wanted to know all that had transpired in the last 72 hours. How could we explain it all, to people who had never been there? Words became inadequate.

The silence was broken by a cannon-like crack followed by the swelling roar of an avalanche. An enormous piece of serac was crashing down towards the glacier. I grabbed my camera and finally managed to photograph an avalanche in action. I thought with a smile of Bruce, who had tried so often to capture the avalanches around base camp but, because he'd always had to dive into his tent to find his Canon, had never succeeded. Now I had it, and I would never be able to show him.

'Well, I guess that's the mountain declaring that Everest is now officially closed,' I said.

'Yes,' Ian replied. 'The last man is off the mountain and it's time to go home.'

I disappeared into my tent for a total wash, or the best that could be done with a bowl of lukewarm water and a flannel. I peeled off layer after layer of clothing that had not been removed in weeks, to discover the strange phenomenon of a body beneath. My hands were the colour of ochre, my forearms little lighter, while the rest of my body was so white it resembled a grub reluctantly dragged to the surface. Everything was so thin. My skin was stretched as tight as a drum top across my ribs. My forearms were stick bundles of sinew and muscle. I felt as if every bone was filled with lead, every muscle reduced to cotton wool. But at last it was over.

Over but not gone. That night I slid awake to find myself wrapped up in a knot in my sleeping bag, sweating from the unaccustomed heat of base camp. Tangled wisps from some incredibly complicated dream about what had happened on the mountain still hovered in my mind. All I knew was that the dream had it all wrong. That wasn't the way it had happened. Even as I was dreaming I knew it was wrong but found myself powerless to stop the dream, unable to pinpoint the problem, powerless to explain ...

Yet it was still far better to be on the mountain sharing the experience to the full than to be stuck at home, waiting. Our pain was not for the person we had lost, but for ourselves, left to live our lives without him.

The next few days were depressing, as we prepared to leave. It was like being the last people at a party, surrounded by empty

✳ *The South African camp 4 on 24 May, the last camp left on the south col.*

✳✳ *Bruce sitting at the edge of the south col, calling base camp on the radio.*

✳✳✳ *Sunrise seen from the Balcony on 25 May. Makalu is in the foreground, Kangchenjunga on the horizon.*

beer cans and dirty plates. The music and laughter had left with the guests and there was nothing to do but start clearing up the mess.

Base camp had changed dramatically. The glacier surface was melting and the tents now stood on ice pedestals, like strange mushroom houses. Avalanche and rock-fall became ever more common. Giant boulders left teetering on narrow stems of ice crashed down one by one. Even the tents began to become lopsided as the ice beneath them melted. It felt like still living in a house when the demolition squad had already started work.

Life moved on. As each climber got a chance to shrug off his climbing clothing and clean up a little, new people emerged. A wash altered Ang Dorje's matted mass of black hair to a chaos of curls, which, combined with some clean clothing, transformed him from the hard-man sirdar to the urban playboy. His teenage son had walked up to base camp to meet his old man. The son was the mirror image of his handsome father, and clearly soon to be something of a heartbreaker in the villages. Now he was enjoying the reflected glory and fame of his dad, telling everyone he met that his father had just reached the summit of Everest.

Pemba walked round camp sparkling clean and shirtless, enjoying the sun on his skin. The months on the mountain had left him with a lean, muscled torso. Various local women had arrived at the camp to help carry loads down the trail and to bargain for expedition leftovers. They were clearly impressed. Of all the Sherpas, the change in him was the greatest. A shy young man on his arrival at

*** *The ridge leading to the summit, seen from the south summit. Pemba climbs towards the Hillary Step.*

** *Looking back along the ridge. Jangbu and Ang Dorje climb down from the south summit. Lhotse lies to the left.*

* *Ian climbs down the steep snow ridge on the descent from the top.*

Bruce Herrod 1958 - 1996

base camp, cautious in the company of Westerners, his confidence had grown in leaps and bounds as he progressed up the mountain. Returning now with the summit tucked under his belt, he had the air of a seasoned mountaineer.

However, we could not stay within the confines of our little group forever. From the moment of the official announcement all contact with the press had been stopped. We had been able to take some time to come to terms ourselves with all that had happened, without having to display our grief and justify our decisions to the world at large. Nevertheless, the world at large was waiting impatiently. Speculation was rife and South Africa was suddenly full of instant experts, sitting comfortably in their armchairs and air-conditioned offices, each with an opinion to put forward.

Chris Bonnington, who had led five Everest expeditions, and had reached the summit once, said we should not accept any feelings of guilt, that Bruce was determined to climb to the summit. 'It was a risk he took. I mean, he obviously pushed it to the limit. I suspect he pushed a lot, lot further than was wise. And he paid the price.'

Bruce's girlfriend, Sue, described Bruce as, 'an extremely sensible person. Which, I can understand, may make many people wonder why he went for the summit so late in the day. As I say, I have no answer to that apart from the fact that he clearly thought he could do it. And when I spoke to him on the summit he believed he could get down.' The news quoted her as saying that the leadership abilities of Ian were not in question, and that Bruce had been fully behind him.

I was the first of the team to speak to Radio 702. My innate instinct, not discussed with the others, was to defend Bruce and his decision. He was not there to do it for himself, so we, as his friends, did it for him. I did not discuss my and Ian's misgivings about Bruce's choice, and Ian's attempt to get Bruce to turn round. Ian was to do the same. We could have saved ourselves a lot of criticism if we had dumped all responsibility on Bruce's absent shoulders, claiming he had gone on despite our attempts to persuade him otherwise. However, we had stood by each other for too long by now to take any easy escapes.

The presenter asked his final question: 'Cathy, there is no doubt that you've made history by becoming the first woman on Everest from South Africa, and Africa. Will you do it again?'

My answer was categorical: 'No, never! There's no ways. I'm never coming back.'

I told him that I had had some of the best days of my life up on the mountain with Ian and Bruce, but that I wouldn't be coming back to Everest again. I thought then that the Everest saga was reaching the end of its place in my life. I had no inkling that I was barely finishing the first act.

When Ian went onto the radio, the talk was of Bruce once again. As I had, Ian defended Bruce's decision to the hilt.

'The Mountain Club of South Africa, according to the newspapers today, is very, very critical of the decision to let Bruce climb alone,' the presenter said. They were saying it was very unfortunate that Ian had not tried to dissuade Bruce from going for the summit.

Ian's anger was clearly rising, but he managed to contain himself.

'Well, quite frankly, not to put too fine a point on it, the Mountain Club of South Africa could not organise a piss-up in a brewery. They have never been to Everest. Not a single member of their club has been to Everest. They have no idea what they are talking about.'

Once more he defended Bruce's right to make his own decisions and maintained that those who sat 11 000 miles away, with little relevant experience, had no right to tell a mountaineer what he might or might not do.

I, the only one on the team to be a member of the Mountain Club, listened with some amusement. I could imagine the big fish in South Africa's small puddle wedged comfortably into their armchairs pontificating on issues of which they had little knowledge and no personal experience.

The interview over, Ian turned on me, his face dark red with anger, going on about 'your mates in the MCSA.' What do you mean, my mates, I thought. All I was was a member. How could he suddenly lump me in with those guys? Bruce was my friend too.

Tempted though I was to yell back at him I simply walked past him in silence. I followed the uneven path back to my tent, to find that in my absence the Sherpas had taken down Bruce's tent which had stood next to mine. All that remained was a flat rock platform. I stood in the middle of it shaking with anger. Part of me wanted to go back and tell Ian it wasn't fair, but I knew that our mutual stress would end up in an argument. Of all people, he wasn't the one I wished to be fighting with.

About an hour later Ian crouched down at the door of my tent, shoulders slumped, looking deadly tired.

'I'm sorry, Caths. But after months of criticism to be told I am responsible for the death of my best friend is just too much. I didn't mean to take it out on you.'

I could see the misery written in his face. We looked at each other with exhausted eyes, and sat together in silence for a few minutes.

On 30 May we left base camp for the last time, to go down now, rather than up. Once past the end of Khumbu glacier I pulled ahead, finding joyful release in stretching my legs. My muscles moved with such ease, with the fluidity of many days in the mountains. The air was getting thicker with each step, until it was like breathing soup. Fit and acclimatised, I felt like a sports car in fifth gear, just cruising. I felt so light. Physically, to walk without the weight of mountaineering boots and crampons, without the constricting bulk of heavy clothing, without soft snow and heavy rucksack, meant I felt as if I was floating down the trail. And mentally, I had not realised how much of a burden had been lifted from me by the culmination of the expedition. I felt weightless in spirit.

I walked swiftly down the slopes towards Pheriche. A stream ran across the valley floor, the icy clear water meandering between verdant grass tufts. Silky black yaks grazed on the rich foliage. On either side of the green valley great hillsides rose, a thousand shades of brown. Several giant ice peaks dominated the horizon in front of me, immense silver ridges rising up to impossibly small summits. They were partially veiled in mist, mysterious, ethereal beings from another world.

It was all so beautiful and I felt absorbed by all of it. I felt high on being alive.

Buddhist mantras engraved on rocks on the trail down from Everest.

8

The end of the beginning

The days of walking from base camp down to nearest airstrip were a brief time of peace and relaxation, before we tackled the outside world once more. I walked slowly through the woods before Tengboche, savouring the sight of greenery and trees after so many days of rock and ice. The previous night I had lain rereading parts of my diary, including the section where I, sick with bronchitis, had walked back down to Namche Bazar to recover, while the rest of the team moved on up towards Lobuche.

I had written: 'As I walked down I wondered how it would feel when I walked down that path for the last time. Would I bypass it altogether, choppered out ill or injured? Would I be elated with success, depressed by failure or by tragedy with one of the other members, just relieved to finally get out or sorry that it was all over?'

Now I had reached that point that I had once speculated about, walking down for the last time. I felt a funny combination of the elation of my personal success, and of Ian's success, and the tragedy of losing Bruce. On top of it lay the whole emotional cocktail of the expedition experience. I passed, too, the various scenes of the squabbles among the team members. I was glad I had stuck it out. For all that had happened, I would rather have been part of it than be sulking back in South Africa. The knowledge I had gained about mountains, about people, about myself, was beyond price.

The first focus of the walk-out was the little wooden bakery that nestled among the stone houses of Khumjung. The vision of freshly baked bread kept me powering up the steep hill of the Dudh Kosi valley. I managed to dispatch two croissants and three cinnamon buns before Ian and Philip arrived. They manfully took on the challenge of catching up with me, while we waited for Patrick and Deshun. As we sat on the cushioned benches, the smell of fresh bread and roast coffee filling the small room, it was as if we were crossing through a door, from the rigours of expedition living to the comforts of modern conveniences.

The next lure was the helipad at Syangboche and the thought of being whisked away to the luxuries of Kathmandu, starting with the hot showers, followed by clean clothes and restaurants. We arrived to find the landing strip misted in and the IMAX team sitting sulking in the lodge. We waited for the rest of the afternoon, and the following morning. The clouds did not lift an inch. Nor did the faces of the IMAX crew. No amount of US dollars could buy a helicopter when the mountains were submersed in the monsoon clouds.

We abandoned them to their weather watching and hared off down the trail towards the next landing strip, at Lukla. We arrived in pouring rain as darkness fell. Although not quite a Kathmandu restaurant, the lodge did offer a selection of meals on the menu. We swiftly put away double helpings of spaghetti carbonara before collapsing into bed. I only emerged from my room at 2 p.m. the next day. The others were doing little more, lying semi-horizontal on the benches of the lodge dining room.

Only now, when we had at last stopped moving, did I realise how deeply physically and mentally tired I was. We teased Patrick about having to walk the week to Jiri to catch a bus, because no more flights would be possible in the monsoon. But in reality we would have sat out the monsoon waiting for a chopper, rather than take another step. In the end we had only to wait 24 hours.

We arrived in Kathmandu, a lean, sunburnt, weary crew. At the entrance to the hotel was a giant banner: 'Congratulation (sic) to South African Everest Expedition 1996 for successful summited (sic) to Mount Everest. Hotel Harati and family.' The owner and his family were waiting at the door with garlands of flowers. We each received a prayer scarf and the red mark on the forehead.

Once the welcome was over, we all made a wild rush for the showers. Between us, we used up most of the hotel's hot water in the space of a few hours. The hot, clean liquid streamed over my head, through my hair, down my skin. I was washing away weeks of accumulated dirt, sweat, suntan lotion and mental stress.

Although expedition accounts often end at a point such as this, leaving the members to disappear happily into the sunset, life offers no such easy options. The ripples created by this expedition would continue to wash across the shores of my life for many months. Bruce left us an unhappy legacy in his family. His avoidance of confrontation with his loved ones was now to come back to haunt us. His girlfriend, Sue Thompson, spent several unpleasant days with us in Kathmandu. She was understandably devastated by his death. However, she was also eaten up with bitterness. I tried to tell her how much fun he had had in the last two months of his life. I tried to convey to her Bruce's excitement and pride in reaching the summit. I might as well have been telling her he spent those last two months happily entwined in the arms of another woman. Although she considered his decisions on the summit day to have been his responsibility, overall she felt that if he had not been on our expedition, he would still be alive. Therefore, we, and more specifically Ian, had killed him. In our own turmoil over his death, none of us had the patience to deal calmly with her emotional problems. Our parting was not cordial.

Bruce had made the problem worse by not telling his family that he was going to climb Everest. The rest of us had been in regular contact with our relatives via satellite phone. However, Bruce's family was not a close one. Sue only finally told his mother a few

PARLEMENT VAN DIE REPUBLIEK VAN SUID-AFRIKA
PARLIAMENT OF THE REPUBLIC OF SOUTH AFRICA

Telefoon
Telephone   403-2911

Posbus 15
P.O. Box
KAAPSTAD
CAPE TOWN
8000

Verw./Ref.   13/27/3

4 June 1996

Mr Ian Woodall
4 Gary Street
Rivonia
JOHANNESBURG
2001

RESOLUTION

I have the honour to notify you that the National Assembly on 30 May 1996 adopted the following
Resolution:

That the House -

(1)   recognises that there is nothing more terrifying and awe-inspiring than human beings
      pitting themselves against Nature at its harshest extremities, in its loneliest places,
      overcoming blizzards and storms, scaling vertical cliffs in howling, icy winds,
      manifesting in failure, death or triumph, the indomitable human spirit pushing us to
      reach to the outer limits of our knowledge and understanding;

(2)   takes cognisance of the fact that -

      (a)   some of those who attempted to take the South African flag to the very summit of
            the world paid with their lives;

      (b)   Ian Woodall and Cathy O'Dowd overcame great perils to reach the summit; and

      (c)   Cathy O'Dowd joins illustrious women in South Africa who are demonstrating
            that women have come into their own and are contributing to the many glories
            achieved by our nation;

(3)   while lamenting the fact that some of the team of climbers paid with their lives in setting
      steep challenges for themselves, pays due credit to the others who overcame great peril
      to achieve a great triumph in adversity; and

(4)   congratulates Cathy O'Dowd and our country South Africa!

R C DOUGLAS
SECRETARY TO PARLIAMENT
PLP2-NAT10-2/96E
(3rd Session - 1st Parliament)

days before he reached the summit. Having been given no preparation for the concept of tackling Everest, they were completely bewildered by the whole affair. His financial affairs were not in order, either, which led to squabbling over money. It was all a rather sad end to a lovely life.

Back in South Africa, there was something of a media war going on about whether or not Ian should have let Bruce climb on. Unsurprisingly, it was headed by the Sunday Times. There was little attempt made to contact us in Kathmandu to discuss the matter. It was seemingly much more satisfying to speculate wildly in our absence. In these circumstances, the first fax to come through from a newspaper back home was read with some interest.

The Star newspaper of Johannesburg prided itself on providing quality journalism. In the midst of the triumph and tragedy, the success and death, the ongoing controversy, their journalists had one burning question on their minds.

'Is it true that you are romantically involved with Ian Woodall?'

However, there was not going to be any wildly romantic homecoming. Although the attraction between us was still strong, it was buried beneath the pressures of the expedition aftermath. We did want to continue climbing together. I liked Ian's style, the way he climbed, the way he organised, the way he interacted with the Sherpas. I respected his intense drive, and constant barrage of new ideas. Phrases like 'it's never been done like that before' and 'if that idea was going to work someone else would have done it already' simply didn't exist in his universe. He had a confidence I admired, an arrogance I disliked. He drove me crazy at times, but life was more interesting with him around. We were exploring the possibilities of setting up a small company, something through which we could channel any proceeds that came from this expedition, and which we could use in the organisation and funding of future expeditions.

It was a considerable undertaking, a departure in a whole new direction for both of us. To lumber the fledgling partnership with the emotional swings of a love affair was too risky. We backed off from one another.

One television programme did finally get their act together to fly out a crew to interview us in Kathmandu. The best bit of their trip was being flown back to base camp in a helicopter. As the chopper swung up the narrow Himalayan valleys, I began to see, for the first time, how all the valleys I had toiled up fitted together. We flew so low I could see the footpaths I had walked on. We covered a day stage in a matter of four or five minutes, which was both exhilarating and depressing.

Base camp was a truly bleak place. There were no signs left of the teams that had been living there. It was a desert of rock and ice, without colour, without life. The mountain above was wreathed in leaden monsoon cloud. I was sure then that I would never be coming back to Everest.

The worst of the television crew's trip was my growing realisation of how tricky it was going to be to convey to people the reality of Everest. I found it immensely difficult to put into words what it had been like, physically, emotionally, to be so high on the mountain, to be so close to the edge of life.

I was only just beginning to learn what it would mean to have a 'public image'. I had not yet fully appreciated that there were thousands of people out there, whom I had never met, who now had opinions on my character and my choices. In the television programme that was subsequently produced, I was criticised for smiling when I talked about Bruce. Smiling made sense to me. I had liked him, a lot. Apparently, I should have been in tears. That I wasn't proved I was callous.

I learnt a lot in the subsequent months about dealing with the media. Much of it was disillusioning. I had trained as a journalist, and had lectured to trainee journalists. I had never worked in the industry. There is an idealism about student journalists, a conviction that they are entering a profession that has more meaning to it than being an accountant. The reality of the profession was rather more sordid than that. From a small section of the media fraternity came heavily biased reporting, putting paid to any notion of 'objectivity' as a journalistic standard. Dealing with straight lies from journalists who were trying to prove an angle was illuminating. However, most were simply poor at their jobs. They had done no research on the subject, their writing was sloppy, their facts seldom thoroughly checked. Research generally meant copying what fellow journalists had written before them. Thus the same errors were endlessly repeated.

Perhaps most frustrating was the ingrained need of journalists to simplify life into easily understandable stereotypes. At first I was greeted as a kind of Julie Andrews in The Sound of Music, the girl from nowhere who climbed the highest mountain in the world. When it became clear I was not a sweet malleable soul who was going to weep on some reporter's shoulder and give her the inside story on how I climbed Everest despite that devil-incarnate Ian Woodall, things changed. Then I was a callous bitch, stepping over bodies in search of personal glory. There was no room to be just an ordinary person, with good and bad sides, complex, nuanced, human.

The reactions I encountered from the general public on my return to South Africa varied wildly. There was the woman who cornered me at an outdoor show, and told me that there was life out there, beyond our planet, and the mission of the human race was to make contact with them. By my ascent of Everest I had proved I was the one destined to lead this God-ordained mission.

Then there was the internet site that gave a long list of reasons why our summit photograph was faked. It started with the fact that we were wearing fleece jackets and 'everyone' knew the summit of Everest was too cold to survive in just fleece.

Most people were more sensibly somewhere in the middle. Many were proud of the achievement and admired our endeavour, many were bewildered by Bruce's death. With little mountaineering history in South Africa, certainly when compared with a country like Britain, for many people this was their first encounter with mountain climbing as a sport. However, great though the hullabaloo was, it had to be kept in perspective. Ours is a country

The team meets expedition patron President Nelson Mandela.
From left: Cathy, Philip, Madiba, Deshun, Ian.

where the national rugby coach gets death threats if he fires a popular captain. We didn't even merit hate mail.

We weren't the only team, or the only country, to be facing up to the new-found public interest in Everest. The 1996 season embedded Everest firmly in the consciousness of the general public, for better or for worse. Several things happened at once to create that situation. For the first time the Nepalese government had allowed a large number of teams onto the classic south col route. As most teams have some kind of sponsorship, or coverage in their home countries, there was considerable media access to base camp. For the first time teams were running websites about their expeditions, with updates every few days. The public was able to follow an expedition as it unfolded.

And then, in the middle of all this, a journalist walked straight into a sensational story. Commissioned by Outside magazine to write an article critical of commercial expeditions on Everest, Jon Krakauer was a member of Rob Hall's team. The team contained everyone from a postman to a New York socialite. Then the killer storm hit. Jon Krakauer was in the middle of it. Three guides died, two famous ones, Rob Hall and Scott Fischer. Two clients died. He survived, as did others. He wrote a best-selling book, generally blaming everyone involved. Having done little himself to help, he nevertheless criticised Anatoli Boukreev, an immensely experienced Russian guide on Scott's team, who had rescued three people. Anatoli bit back with his own book, and was then killed climbing on Annapurna. The American television talk shows were packed with journalists and with survivors. Discussion forums sprung up on the web, filled with speculation by people who knew very little about it all. It began to rival the assassination of JF Kennedy for conspiracy theories. Everest had become a spectator sport.

As climbers we certainly bear some responsibility for that. We were not the only team to have invited the media in to record the expedition. Not surprisingly, it all gets more interesting to outsiders when things go wrong. It is like watching Grand Prix racing for the crashes. However, given the expense of climbing Everest, an expense largely imposed in the form of permit fees by the controlling governments, sponsorship is inevitable and that means media. Even when climbers have bought places on commercial expeditions, they have normally raised sponsorship to do so. Perhaps all we can ask is for a greater degree of research, and of accuracy of reporting, from the watching media.

The next year was one of change and opportunity. Although it proved difficult to concentrate on something that had suddenly become so much in my past, I did the final corrections on my thesis and was awarded my degree. I moved back to Johannesburg, where Ian and I set up a base for our new company. We called it

Free To Decide, from a song by the Cranberries. The song had become something of a theme song for the expedition, expressing what we felt we had taken away from the whole experience. We wanted, for better or for worse, to carve out our own destinies. In the course of this year Clare Ellis, a tough, talented, above all sensible woman, joined us in the business. She had no pretensions to climbing mountains, and was to become the rock of common sense on which our wilder plans would be founded.

During that year I got to meet many groups of South African society, talking to them about Everest. I received many letters from school children. The worst came from girls in early primary school, saying they were so impressed that a woman could do such a thing. It depressed me that girls so young should already have such fixed ideas about what women could and could not do with their lives. I wanted to shake them and tell them they could strive for anything they wanted. That is not the same as saying they could achieve anything they wanted. Saying that is simply motivational 'rah-rah', uplifting for a few hours and depressing the next morning when you realise life is full of the same old obstacles. However, there is no doubt that we can achieve far more than we allow ourselves to dream of. The barriers we encounter in realising our potential are, more often than not, self imposed. If we start by removing those, we find far fewer real barriers than we had expected.

What I enjoyed more was talking to teenage boys. I liked rattling the cages of their adolescent chauvinism, and challenging them to explain to me why chasing a ball round a rugby field was a completely logical activity while climbing mountains was madness.

I spoke to deprived children from the townships, as well as to captains of industry. Everywhere there was a fascination with the challenge of the mountain, and a general assumption that I was a nice girl, but crazy. I loved telling the story, showing the photographs. I had cut my teeth lecturing the history of the South African media to bored 18-year-olds. Anything was easier than that and my confidence grew rapidly.

I was learning, too, that to strive to please everyone, all the time, was to be a doormat. And people would still complain about the quality of the doormat. The quiet schoolgirl who only wanted to do as she was told was beginning to get a bit of attitude. There was too much potential to life to be wasting time trying to be everything to everybody.

Ian and I began to write a book together about the 1996 expedition. It proved a testing task, merging my creativity with his. However, our egos only clashed occasionally. In many ways it proved a therapeutic activity. In the turmoil of Bruce's death, much of the joy of the earlier days on the expedition had become submerged. In writing about those days, I rediscovered the excitement, the pleasure of the mountain. Plans for future trips began to emerge.

However, there was one thing to be done first. Knowing there would never be a grave, we wanted to build a memorial for Bruce in the shadow of Everest. We returned to Nepal in April of 1997 with a mixed group. Some were members of our families who wanted to finally see this famous mountain that had cast such a deep shadow over their lives for the past 18 months. Also with us was group of boys from a Pretoria school. One had knocked his head in a rugby match the week before we left South Africa. The medics, checking for signs of concussion, asked him what he would be doing the following weekend. On being told he was going to Mount Everest, they promptly shipped him off to hospital. The final member of the group was Jan Horn, the film director who had been with us on Kilimanjaro. He had not been able to film the actual expedition and had jumped at this chance to get into the mountains and see a little of what we had been through.

It was a strange trip. In some ways it was hard. In a sense we were on our way to a funeral. We were also retracing the steps of what had been an emotionally laden experience. In other ways it was great fun. We were simply there to walk, without the pressure of a massive mountain challenge looming at the end of the trek. The boys ranged in age from 12 to 16. Some had never left South Africa before. On the flight out the film *Daylight* was playing. One

The memorial to Bruce.
It stands on top of a hill
near Gorak Shep, facing
the slopes of Everest.

line ran: 'my son went on trek to Nepal and died of fever'. Eight pairs of young eyes turned to stare in trepidation at Ian.

To see Nepal through their eyes was fascinating, the excitement and apprehension of the unknown being very fresh with them. They assumed the hills round Kathmandu were the Himalaya and wanted to know where the snow was. They ran round the hotel dressed up in their thermal underwear and down jackets, demanding to know why it wasn't cold. However as we began to move up into the true mountains, their eyes got larger and the talk got smaller.

We walked up to Namche Bazar and on to Tengboche in cloud. The next morning dawned completely clear, to reveal the Everest massif sitting huge on the horizon, heavy with snow. The cameras went crazy.

I found it strange looking up at the mountain. I had no sense of having 'conquered' it, even of having climbed to its summit. It felt like a dream, or a book I had read a long time ago. It was such an impersonal lump of rock, around which such a broth of human emotions boiled.

No one was camped at our old base camp and the only way we found the site was by placing it against landmarks on the horizon. We walked slowly up the glacier, watching the surrounding mountains, until suddenly the panorama slid into the old, so familiar formation that we had seen each day from our base camp mess tent. The site was no more than a pile of rocky rubble.

In the distance were the tents of other expeditions. Both Mal Duff and Henry Todd were back with expeditions, and there were a few climbers who had not reached the summit in 1996 and were trying again, including Neil Laughton.

Ian's sister and brother-in-law were both eager to see base camp, to experience in reality what they had listened to so closely over the radio. However, we found it impossible to give them that. It was the site but not the 'base camp' that had been ours. It was another year, another group of climbers, another challenge. Our year had been and gone, and all that was left were photographs and memories.

We built a stone memorial on top of a grassy knoll, just beyond Gorak Shep. It stood in the middle of a giant horseshoe of mountains dominated by Nuptse and Everest, and broken only by the Khumbu glacier as it swept down and away from the icefall. For two days two stone masons had sat on that hilltop, with chisels and hammers, cutting the nearby rocks into smooth squares that could be stacked one on top of another. Set into the side that looked out onto Everest were photographs of Bruce and a stone carved in his memory. The stone had been carried for four days up the trail.

A lama came from the Tengboche monastery to perform Buddhist rites. He sat cross-legged on the icy grass, his port-red robes arranged decorously over his grey and red padded mountaineering jacket. From beneath the robes, thick, woolly socks and leather boots protruded.

Spread out in front of him were the implements of his craft, the metal bell, the incense sticks, the bowls of rice and oil. He read from complex papers covered in Sanskrit script, the words running into each other as his voice rose and sank in an endless plainsong chant. Hidden in the words was an understanding of life, death and the Himalaya beyond us mere Westerners. It was an understanding that Bruce had sought to comprehend during his many trips to Nepal.

We sat bundled up in our giant, blue down jackets and black fleecy salopettes, in woolly hats and gloves. Sherpas who had known Bruce, and who had made the pilgrimage to join this memorial, stood silently around us. A bitter wind swept up the valley, swirling round the stone memorial, penetrating every chink of our clothing. A weak sun shone down, illuminating the scene but providing no warmth.

Slowly wispy clouds crept up the valley and the peaks around them gradually vanished behind misty veils. Even the lama began to feel the chill and hurried through the remainder of the ceremony so that he could retreat to the warmth of the smoky lodge in Gorak Shep.

It struck me that the ceremony would have appealed to Bruce's sense of humour, all of us standing around, freezing our butts off, listening to a whole lot of chanting we didn't understand.

The following day the wind had died, the clouds gone. The sun shone down on the small hilltop with a welcome warmth. The great sweeps of Nuptse gleamed as if made of burnished silver, while their knife-like edges glinted gold in the sunlight. Lesser mountains ran round them in a huge circle, sparkling in the crystalline air. The sky swept over the mountains in a monumental blue arc.

We returned to the memorial to perform our own ceremony, spoken in the language we understood. The tension was palpable. Suffering and success seemed so inextricably interlinked in all we have done. When it came to my turn to speak, I began to recite from memory a poem written by another climber for another climber, somewhere else in the world. But the sentiments remained the same.

I would give all the world to have you back,
Remember you not in a photograph,
But in your smiling eyes and wild ideal.
And yet I would not pay a price too high:
I would not dream of asking you to change.

I first saw the poem stuck to the wall of London flat, a flat I was sharing with three other mountaineers. Two years later one of them found the bodies of the other two lying, still, at the foot of a great ice-face in Peru. I had turned to the poem then to give voice to the complexity of my feelings about death in the mountains, just as I did now ...

If you were with me now, I would still help,
Encourage you to reach for the mountain tops,
Would watch you strive for where you should not go.

And you would go again and die again,

And I would cry - cry how much more
If you should ever cease to be yourself.

Ian's voice filled the ensuing silence. For a man so self-contained,
he expressed his pain with a raw honesty that, for the first time that
day, reduced me to tears.

For taking in the rain when I'm feeling so dry,
For giving me the answers when I'm asking you why,
And my-oh-my, for that I thank you.

For taking in the sun when I'm feeling so cold,
For giving me a chance when my body is old,
And don't you know, for that I need you.

Oh! but most of all, for crying out loud, for that I miss you.
Oh! but most of all, for crying out loud, for that I love you.

Back in Kathmandu we heard of a rumour that was running on the
internet. An Indonesian team had become the first climbers to reach
the summit from the south side since we had done it 11 months
previously and they were said to have come upon Bruce's body.
We found it difficult to believe. We had always thought his radio
silence probably indicated a fall. And even if he had died on the
ridge, we couldn't see why the winds of the monsoon, or of winter,
had not dislodged the body. We wondered if they might have
mistaken Rob Hall for Bruce.

As soon as the Indonesians returned to Kathmandu, we
arranged to speak to Apa Sherpa, the Indonesian's sirdar. A highly
experienced mountaineer, he had just reached the summit of
Everest for the eighth time. We walked in tense silence through the
crowded Kathmandu streets towards his hotel. The hubbub of
Nepal's capital city rose all around us, as we dodged rickshaws,
cars, cows and people. The streets were filled with the dense smells
of food, dust and animals. The heat of approaching summer beat

down on the urban chaos. We saw none of it.

We found Apa in the lobby of the team's hotel, surrounded by piles of equipment just ferried back from the mountain. Seated together on the shabby lobby lounge suite, Ian asked him to take us through his summit day, from the south col to where he thought Bruce's body might be. Apa Sherpa described how he had come over the south summit. He had expected to see Rob Hall's body, but it was covered over with snow. He had then started to climb along the ridge towards Hillary Step. It was very narrow, very dangerous. At the foot of the step he saw a man sitting. He wore a blue down suit and a red rucksack.

We had our answer. It had to be Bruce.

Apa said he was clipped on to one of the fixed ropes on the Hillary Step with a jumar and that his face was mostly covered by the oxygen mask. There were no other signs of what had gone wrong.

So we still had no answers, just a whole lot more unanswered questions. Why hadn't he called us on the radio? Why had he stopped there? We were going to have to learn to live with that. At least we now knew where he was. We were not going to have to deal with unconfirmed sightings every few years, as happens with some mountaineers who go missing.

It was a low moment in the assessment of our mountaineering future, particularly for Ian. When Bruce and he had stumbled onto the south col in the middle of that mini-storm on 9 May 1996, he had taken shelter with Scott Fischer and his sirdar, Lobsang Sherpa. Bruce had sheltered with Rob Hall and one of his guides, Andy Harris. A year later, of those six climbers, Ian was the only one left alive. Rob Hall, Andy Harris and Scott Fischer had died in the great storm. Lobsang Sherpa had been killed in an avalanche while climbing above Everest's camp 3 in the autumn season of 1996.

To make matters worse, news had come down from base camp that Mal Duff was dead. He had passed away in his sleep in his base camp tent. Mal had started Ian on his expedition career. In the space of a year Ian had lost his two closest friends. He felt it was time to take stock, to ask if continuing to do this was the right choice.

It was a choice we had to face up to rapidly. We had been spending time in Kathmandu chasing permits for other mountains, for future projects. However, no challenge came without risk.

I tried to work through the muddle of my own feelings on the subject. Presumably we would all in the end reach our own limit, decide we had had enough. I have never been able to come up with a pat answer to the question 'why do you do it?' The famous way of avoiding the subject is to trot out the answer attributed to George Mallory: 'Because it's there'. I think it is more like 'because we're here'. It is part of a drive, in whatever form, to challenge our limits, to try to express the infinite potential we carry within us. That drive is part of what it means to be human and everyone is free to decide what risks are worth it for them.

The last twist in Bruce's tale came a few weeks later. A British team retrieved his camera from his rucksack and gave the film to Sue Thompson. It turned out to contain only a few shots, all the same scene, a self-portrait taken on the summit.

It was a beautiful photograph. Bruce's face grinned out at us, still in his green South African beanie and his blue down jacket. His face was split in a smile, his eyes screwed up as they always were when he was happy. The joy of his spirit shone through as brightly as ever. Next to him were a metal tripod and a blaze of Buddhist prayer flags. Behind and far below him was a curving horizon.

Maybe it was worth it after all. 'So chuffed' was how he had put it on the radio to us. And 'a long time coming'. He looked fit and happy and proud. My only lasting regret was that I hadn't told him over the radio how proud I was of him.

Maybe the answer to why we did these things was simpler than all the in-depth explanations, the esoteric justifications. Maybe we just did it for the love of it.

The love of mountains wasn't the only thing we had rediscovered

I see you still, in my dreams and strangers' faces,
In some expression of my morning mirror;
But cannot reach you in your solitude,
Nor breathe the same thin air that laid you down.
You grow not old, as I am left to grow old;
I age, wane weary, am condemned by years -
Whilst you lie eternal,
Frozen in the beauty of your strength.

I never will again hold back on love;
Love's object may not stay to share tomorrow -
Life, like a welcome guest, too soon departing.
I would give all my world to have you back,
Remember you not in a photograph
But in your smiling eyes and wild ideal.
And yet, I would not pay a price too high:
I would not think of asking you to change.

And though your rope is cut and worlds have fallen,
And though the pain will grip me through the years,
If you were with me now, I would still help
Encourage you to reach for mountain tops:
Would watch you strive for where you should not go;
And you would go again, and die again,
And I would cry - but cry how much more
If you should ever cease to be yourself.

By Mike Thexton

The poem Cathy found stuck to the wall of their London flat in 1992.

in Kathmandu. The attraction between Ian and myself had never died out completely. We were finally safely beyond the stresses of the 1996 expedition, more confident in where we wanted to go with our futures. We gave up trying to ignore the obvious and began to move tentatively down the path of romantic involvement. The media interest in us had not died completely and we kept it all very quiet.

The question was now looming of what we did next. We felt we had now put Everest to bed. It was time to move on. The mountain that shimmered all the while in the far distance was K2, the world's second highest peak, in Pakistan. It is a far harder challenge than Everest, in all respects - technical difficulty, weather, logistics. However, it is an incredibly beautiful mountain, a pyramid of ice in the heart of the Karakorum range. It is an alluring challenge.

If we were to do that at some time in the future, we needed to gain more high-altitude experience. We tossed around all sorts of ideas, mountains in Pakistan, in Nepal, in Tibet. We would decide on one for a while, and then would start considering other plans again. At the heart of the problem was the need to pay for the expedition. Nothing was cheap, and the steady decline of our currency did not help the situation.

Trying to raise money for mountaineering in South Africa is not easy. We have a meagre mountaineering history and it is not a well-known activity among the public. If you mention the likes of Kangchenjunga or Makalu, you might as well be talking about a brand of Japanese car, or the new strain of Asian flu. One day we hoped to be free of the need to use sponsorship money to pay for big mountains, but we weren't there yet.

Of course, Everest was very well known, and the fascination with it continued. But there was no point in going back to Everest. Or was there?

There was one possibility, which became increasingly interesting. Everest is a three-sided pyramid. We had climbed it from the south side, the side that rose out of Nepal. We had ended up on the south-east ridge. This was the route by which the mountain had been first climbed, by Edmund Hillary and Tenzing Norgay Sherpa in 1953. It was considered to be the most straightforward route on the mountain.

However, there was another famous route, rising out of Tibet to find a way up the north side of the pyramid. This was the route, pioneered by the British in the early twenties, on which George Mallory and Andrew Irvine were famously lost in 1924. They were last seen on their way up, a few hundred metres below the summit. The mystery had always been whether they had reached the summit before they were killed. If they had indeed done so, they would have made the first ascent, 29 years before Hillary and Tenzing. The first officially confirmed ascent of the route was by the Chinese in 1960. They followed the north ridge, cut across the north face and finally ended up on the north-east ridge. It is a steep climb, very exposed to wind, with rock difficulties on the final ridge. It is a more challenging route than the south, climbed less often.

It is so different from the south side that it may have well be the slopes of a different mountain altogether. Or that was how the justification began to run as Everest sidled quietly into our field of view.

There was no great decision to return to Everest, no driving ambition to climb it again. I just wanted to go climbing, to gain more high-altitude experience, to get back to the Himalaya. This was the solution that presented itself. Not surprisingly, raising a lot of money for Everest proved easier than raising a smaller amount for a less well-known mountain. However, it is never easy. It took us six months of work, and many, many closed doors, before we finally reached our budget. Big expeditions are in fact made up of two mountains, set back-to-back. You have made the summit of the first mountain when you step on the plane that will take you to the foot of the second one. It is as much of a challenge to climb the first one, and in some ways far more work.

I was busy finishing the book while Clare and Ian knocked on doors, looking for money. More than once I felt ready to pull the plug on the whole plan. However, Ian ploughed on with his characteristic determination. His persistence was finally rewarded. We had the money not just to climb the mountain but to offer two sponsored places on the team and to run a selection expedition to Aconcagua.

We were off to Everest, once again.

The mountains of Nepal.

9

The white wind

We walked up an eroded hillside, slipping on the moist earth. The road below us cut an ugly swathe through the drab brown mountains The village of Puenta del Inca sprawled next to it, a scruffy collection of small buildings. It was a far cry from the magnificence of the Himalaya. Then we reached the mouth of a valley and turned into it. The path curved round a small lake, a turquoise jewel reflecting the cotton-wool clouds. A grass-clad corridor led towards an immense squat mountain, a magnificent presence. It brooded upon the earth like a vast cake, brown-sided and with a cover of icing on the top. This was Aconcagua, highest mountain in the Americas, and the start of our 1998 expedition programme.

We were admittedly looking at the edge of the formidable south face, which was not a challenge we were about to tackle. I had heard it described as the equivalent of several Eiger north faces, piled one above the other. We were going to skirt round the side to reach the west slope of the mountain, a far gentler climb.

This expedition was in some ways the equivalent of the Kilimanjaro trip in 1996. We had with us six South Africans, who were on the short-list for selection for the two open places on our Everest expedition. For Ian and me this was part of our build-up to Everest, as it was for Jan Horn, who was finally going to realise his dream. He had filmed the Kilimanjaro trip and the memorial trek in Nepal. Now he would be in charge of filming on Everest. I was the keen young thing who was going to have to get the high-altitude footage, under his direction.

The initial hours of walking were lovely, up the lush valley floor, by the side of the pebble-filled river. Two dogs of medium size and indeterminate breed, one blonde, one brindled, had joined us. They gambolled up the valley, unconcerned by stiff boots, heavy packs or the growing altitude.

Gradually, though, the grassy fields faded into the distance. Mammoth slopes of brown scree rose above us. Tottering pinnacles towered over that, with rock bands contorted into giant curves by ancient geological forces of unbelievable power. The sun was excluded from the valley. The wind began to rise and snow to fall. The air was icy cold, and getting progressively thinner. The first to succumb was Hennie van Heerden, the gentle giant. He was a massive man, a prison warder, friendly, talkative, sometimes too talkative. He had been radiating excitement ever since he had first heard that he had been selected. Now, battling with the altitude, he collapsed at camp, a fascinating shade of green. We bundled him into a sleeping bag and he lay, shivering and nauseous, unable to understand how his body, so tough in other conditions, could give in so easily here.

The others must have seemed to him depressingly strong and healthy. Gareth Tennant sat next to him, trying to cheer Hennie up with his very different outlook on life. Tall and handsome, he was a life-saver and karate instructor. Steeped in a variety of eastern philosophies, his perspective on life was always unique. Scott Anderson came from the opposite end of the spectrum. He was a police officer, able, disciplined, conventional. However, he had a yearning for adventure that had brought him to us.

The next day was a long, long haul. Aconcagua ably demonstrated how fickle she could be. The morning walk was bathed with sunshine. We moved up a giant beach of white pebbles, a paved road leading into the heart of the massif. A shallow stream

Some of the 1998 Aconcagua team on the walk-in. From left:
Gareth, the blonde dog, Hennie, Scott, Marlie, Andre and Trevor.

meandered across the plain. We stopped for lunch by a field of
boulders, just where the plain ended and the steep walk began. In
a matter of ten minutes the sun vanished. The wind was whipping
round us, carrying the softly falling snowflakes. Cloud cascaded
over the mountain peaks, and came swirling down the valley. Hoods
went up, heads went down, and the walking took on a grim
determination. Even the dogs stopped running around us, instead
joining in the crocodile file to shelter their faces behind our legs.

Of all of us, Jan was the least happy. He had recently freed
himself from 25 years of service at South Africa's national broad-
caster, the SABC. His life had not been focused on this kind of
activity. However, we had enough respect for his intelligence and
balanced temperament to believe he was up to the challenge.
The deal between Jan and me was that I would teach him how to

climb, and he would teach me how to film. I was hooked from the first moment I picked up the video camera. It was taking photographs that moved, that created their own past as you recorded. Now part of the camera crew, I stayed well away from the selection process, leaving that to Ian. However, Jan was faring less well with the mountain challenge. Back problems combined with the lack of oxygen left him battling to walk. Eventually Ian was carrying Jan's pack as well as his own.

I had long since been handed the camera and told to get on with it. No one was in the mood to wait for me, let alone go back and repeat anything. Faces were drawn, hidden behind tightly closed hoods. Shoulders and rucksacks were covered in a lacework of snow. The final hill proved a testing challenge as the path zigzagged up the slope, slippery with melting snow. Base camp was lurking beneath a ceiling of cloud, the mountain hidden above us. All everyone wanted to do was sit down, get their boots off and get their hands round a coffee cup. Elation was deeply buried beneath the sheer relief of arrival.

Our group of six was beginning to get used to my pushing a camera up their nostrils at every vulnerable moment. Asked how he was doing, Trevor Johnston simply stared at me, goggle-eyed, beyond coherent speech. Trevor was a school teacher. He was a laid-back guy, with an appalling sense of humour that he shared with Ian. One of the highlights of Trevor's trip was finding that the dreaded Ian Woodall liked his jokes.

Marlie Malan, a blonde, petite policewoman, looked at my camera and came out with some language that startled the men. She was the only woman in the group. This time Ian had opened selection to anyone interested, and had been overwhelmed by male replies. Marlie was very self-contained, highly competent, always pleasant, but showed very little emotion.

Only Andre le Roux, deeply determined to go on, played down the day's exertion. He was a Methodist minister and embodied a strange package of contradictions. He was thoughtful, introspective, considerate, yet highly ambitious and driven.

Airing equipment and washing bodies at Aconcagua base camp.

The group had some obvious lines of fracture. Gareth the dreamer, Andre the minister and Trevor the teacher stood opposed to the three of military background, trained in discipline, obedience to orders, use of force. Andre had been a conscientious objector during the years of compulsory military service in South Africa. Trevor had fought off the police during student protests in the depths of the apartheid eighties. But the six did not split. The individuals were each too idiosyncratic to be subservient to their career choices. Although a certain caution remained, the overall level of group harmony was higher than with my group on Kilimanjaro.

It was curious for me to be on the other side of the fence. In 1996 I had been on the inside, part of the selection. Now I was on the outside, watching others go through the same ordeal. I had a much better understanding now of what Ian was looking for. It was a kind of indefinable mental quality. Levels of experience, physical fitness and strength, all these mattered. But there was needed something more, a mental toughness, a strange combination of drive and patience, a passion for wild places. It was easier to recognise than to describe.

We started up the rock slope that led to camp 1, at 5 200 metres. It was nothing more than a slog, an endless series of zigzags. A network of paths criss-crossed up the loose slope. Base camp sheltered in the valley head below us. A scattering of snow-capped mountains spread out to the west. Aconcagua is a deceptive mountain. It presents no technical difficulties on the normal route. In good weather, altitude is the only danger. Sometimes it is no more than a long walk up a gigantic scree slope. It has been said you can drive a mule up Aconcagua. As we walked up the slope we passed the skeleton of a mule. The dog that was accompanying us abandoned us for the pleasure of gnawing on the mule's thigh bone. Higher up we were passed by a team bringing down a body. Eight people were killed on Aconcagua in the 1997/98 season. Judging mountains purely on technical difficulty is a dangerous thing to do. Mountaineering requires a far broader range of knowledge than simply rock gymnastics.

One of the most beautiful, most chilling sights on Aconcagua is a crystal disc of cloud moving in towards the summit. It is the notorious 'white wind' - harbinger of filthy weather. Within days of our arrival, the cloud was coming from the west. We were on Aconcagua at the tail-end of a season of particularly unstable weather. The Argentinean guides we were with said they had never seen the windows of good weather so short. We were racing against time, against the gradual onset of a natural force a million times more powerful than we were.

The time on the mountain was beginning to take its toll on our little group. Scott, an avid reader of adventure stories, was beginning to feel that adventure went down better on the pages of a book, when he was comfortably seated in an armchair with a cup of hot coffee. All the endless little discomforts that never get written about, being simply too boring - but which in fact fill up the majority of your hours in the wild - were eating away at him.

Gareth was also not feeling at one with the mountains. He was a son of the beach and the surf. He responded to the call of the sea waves, the powerful, fluid, ever-changing ocean. He found the cold, the starkness, the barrenness of the high mountains too foreign. It was as arid to him spiritually as it was visually.

Hennie was continually frustrated by his body. It simply could not keep up with his level of expectation. The other three were faring better. For Marlie this was just another challenge to be overcome, like any of the courses she had completed in her police training. She had the strength and the determination, but the passion seemed lacking.

Trevor and Andre were loving the experience, despite all the hardships. Trevor was slow to acclimatise and this is always demoralising. Nevertheless, he felt at home in the mountains, fulfilled just in being there, however high or low he might be on the slopes. Andre was coping well, enjoying the environment and thriving on the challenge. Where Trevor expressed his ups and downs, Andre always put a brave face on things.

Chased by oncoming bad weather, we were pushing hard up the mountain. Those acclimatising slowly had to fall by the wayside. When we reached camp 2, at 5 800 metres, the team was down to Ian and myself, the Argentinean guides, Andre and Marlie. It was a beautiful evening, clear blue skies above us but lines of high cloud to the west. We had a magnificent view from camp, across dozens of lines of mountains, like an ocean of umber waves with white caps. Andre and I ignored the bitter cold to stand at the rock edge, watching the sun sink into the cloud, into a fusion of gold and pink and purple. Everyone was keyed up for the next day, an early start and a long climb to reach the summit.

By the early hours of the following morning our tiny tent was rocking like a ship at sea, battered by brutal winds. At 5 a.m. I propped a head torch on Ian's sleeping bag and pointed the camera at him. His voice barely cut through the shrieking wind. This was no weather in which to climb another 1 100 metres.

We had to retreat.

The guides fought to take the tents down while we packed up the kit in a low wooden shelter, rather like a dog kennel, that stood nearby. There was little talk as chilled fingers battled with crampon clips. The winds swept randomly across the slopes, creating mini whirlwinds of snow. Lead grey cloud hovered just above our heads. The white wind was in the process of enveloping the mountain. We escaped below it for a few hours but it followed us down. Base camp was still calm when we reached it in the late afternoon, but that night the snow began to fall. We toasted the end of the expedition with champagne in plastic glasses. The noise of our celebration was deadened by the white silence outside. The snow was falling noiselessly, relentlessly.

Thirty-six hours later it was still falling. We had to make a move for the road-head before we got snowed in. We were the last team of the season and the guides remained behind to sit out the storm and then take down base camp.

We walked out accompanied by a junior guide. He was soon lost and inadvertently brought us down into the steep river valley, rather than staying on the higher slopes. All trails and most landmarks had long since disappeared beneath a blanket of snow. Cloud sulked just above our heads, obscuring the peaks. We were being forced down an ever-narrowing valley. The apprentices were cold, tired and nervous. Scott was particularly tense. Only Andre still managed a lop-sided smile. Of the two dogs that had accompanied us, one had chosen the safety of base camp. The other remained with us and provided a surreal element in the drama.

I was filming as we walked. I needed to be able to move through the group, pass to the front and then drop back. It required a delicate judgement. Ian was focused on trying to work out where we were, and where to go. Everyone else was staring down at their feet, drawn in to themselves. Only the dog seemed happy to frolic

Battling down from camp 2 in the face of high wind and spindrift.

through the snow. Just as a scene I was filming was beginning to give a real survival feel, the dog would trot past, happily unconcerned, popping the bubble. At times I wondered if he would suddenly move to the front and take the lead, bringing us safely through the storm, Lassie style.

In fact we simply had to jump the river and work our way diagonally up the opposite slope to regain the trail. We walked out to the road-head in one long, long day, only emerging from the snow as we entered the last grassy valley.

It was a very grateful group that finally stumbled into the alpine lodge at Puenta del Inca. First on the itinerary were beers and cokes, poured down parched throats. Then came hot showers, and clean, or cleanish, clothes. That was followed by a serious tuck-in at the dinner table, roast chicken, vegetables, bread. We left nothing to be returned to the kitchen.

At last attention refocused on the question of who would go on to Everest. And who still wanted to go on. Marlie, Andre and Trevor had stood out over the others, as much mentally as physically. However, the passion for the project was strongest with the two men. Ian selected Andre and Trevor.

There were congratulations for those two, disappointment among the others. It was difficult for them to just go home, to resume everyday routine, while the rest of us headed off to climb the highest mountain in the world. The apprenticeship scheme was meant to offer a life-changing experience, a chance to try something outrageously different. However, change and challenge could be as disruptive as they could be fulfilling. Nevertheless, as had happened with the women in 1996, several of the group took on their own challenges in subsequent years, or changed the directions of their lives.

The rest of February and early March were filled with expedition preparation. The Tibet base camp of Everest was even more remote than the Nepal one. In Nepal there were a number of villages within a few days walk of base camp and limited replenishment of supplies was possible. In Tibet we would have to be totally self-sufficient. The one advantage, though, was that we could drive trucks in to base camp. Apart from the question of airfreight, weight and size was not an issue. Detailed daily menus had be written out, exact food quantities determined. To avoid what had happened in 1996, all equipment was brought into South Africa first, with the exception of the oxygen bottles.

The team that finally assembled in Kathmandu consisted of Ian, myself, Jan, Trevor and Andre, all fresh from Aconcagua. We were joined by Martin Brasg who was to be our base camp manager. He was a computer geek, more used to air-conditioned offices than mountains, but with a taste for adventure. Short, plump, dark-haired, he had a cheerful attitude to life that left him seldom upset by difficulties. Indeed, at times, he seemed so happily oblivious of difficulties that the rest of us wanted to scream.

Kathmandu was as chaotic, dirty, vibrant, exotic and overwhelming as ever. The dusty streets held an inextricable tangle of cars, rickshaws, bicycles, pedestrians and trucks. Right of way was an alien concept. Through all the chaos walked the sacred cows. Protected from slaughter under the Hindu faith, they wandered the city at will. They were always rake thin and probably thought there were some advantages to being a secular cow being fattened up for the kill instead. Mountaineers, hippies and tourists mingled in with scabby dogs, Sherpas, sari-clad Hindus and Nepalese businessmen. Goods streamed into Kathmandu from all over south-east Asia. It was a shopping paradise for carpets, clothing, jewellery, books, trinkets and outdoor kit. Although it was a city founded on trade, it was steeped in religion. Every street had its little Hindu shrine, meticulously anointed each morning by passers-by, even if the dogs did use them as places to sleep undisturbed. An accidental turning into some shabby back alley would reveal the entrance to a square built around a stupa, the magnificent white circular mounds that stood with the eyes of Buddha peering, ever watchful, from their towers.

The excitement of the shopping and the sightseeing carried the team through the first week. However, once all permits and equipment had been organised, we began to get restless. Unfortunately, the news came through that the pass through the Himalaya, which we would be driving up, was closed by avalanche. A few teams had got through into Tibet before the snow slide, but many, ourselves included, were now stuck, waiting day by day for news of the state of the road. Everyone was getting increasingly edgy with the delay. It was becoming clear that patience was not a strong feature in the makeup of our team members.

At last word came that the road should be cleared within a few days. On the morning of 11 April we left Kathmandu with a massive truck filled with equipment and a bus filled with climbers and Sherpas. We were joined once again by Pemba and Jangbu. Pemba was far more mature than when I had first met him in 1996. He had reached the summit of Everest again in 1997, and was now a highly sought-after climber. Jangbu, too, had moved on in life. He had been climbing on Shishapangma, in Tibet, in 1997, and had met a woman there who lived in Nylam. Now the draw of love was beginning to test his commitment as a lama, lamas being traditionally unmarried. Nawang was with us as well, once more as a support climber. Nawang had developed an unfortunate liking for the bottle, and was being closely watched by older brother Pemba.

Being a big team, we had brought in several more people. Lhakpa Gelu, Jangbu's brother, was a summit climber. He had the same smooth features and calm face as Jangbu, but was very different in character. He spoke excellent English and had climbed Everest four times already, from both north and south. He had considerable confidence and enjoyed interacting with the foreigners.

Keeping it a family affair, we also had the younger brother of Pemba and Nawang, Phuri. Although also a competent climber, he was on our team as advanced base camp (ABC) cook. He had a grin like Pemba's, only more so and collapsed into giggles at regular intervals. Finally we had Padam Magar and Mangal Tamil to man base camp. Both were trek leaders by profession and had worked with Ian before. They were overqualified to be running base camp but the prestige of being part of an Everest expedition made up for that.

Padam and Mangal had never left Nepal. Pemba, Nawang and Phuri had not climbed on the north side of Everest before. Jangbu was going to get to see his loved one as we passed through Nylam. Andre and Trevor were new to the Himalaya. I had never been into Tibet. Everyone was excited as the bus finally approached the border with Tibet.

The road that runs through from the northern border of Nepal up to the plateau of Tibet is a masterpiece of Chinese determination. The pass runs right through the Himalaya, gaining 3 000 metres in altitude in under 25 kilometres of road. However, nothing can protect the road from the catastrophic erosion which the Himalaya undergo from year to year. The Himalaya is the youngest of the world's great ranges, and is still rising as the Indian continental plate grinds relentlessly up against the Asian plate. The mountains are steep-sided and unstable, cut through by immensely deep river gorges. Our road ran up the side of one such gorge. We were rapidly to discover that driving to Everest was not the easy prospect that it sounded.

Things went well for all of 500 metres. We walked across the great concrete span that bridges the river, the Friendship Bridge built by the Chinese. The transition from the shabby mountain huts of the Nepalese border guards to the massive concrete monoliths of the Chinese symbolised our move into a new country. All the expedition goods and people were reloaded into vehicles and we began to make our way up the steep zigzags of no-man's land, towards the official Tibetan border. Soon we found that two bends of the road had disappeared beneath a massive landslide. An entire section of mountainside had gone belly-up. Men with spades were working to clear it. They looked to be some while, a week or three.

Everyone and everything was unloaded. A swarm of locals appeared out of the surrounding forest, offering to porter our goods. An Uzbekistan Everest team was dumped on the road behind us. A chaos of people and goods soon followed. Padam and Mangal guarded our goods meticulously, issuing tickets to porters

The north face of Everest seen from the Pang La.

who began carrying our kit up the steep footpaths that shortcut from one level of the road to the next. Little boys, who stood barely higher than my rucksack, ran around us, desperate to help. Eventually Padam found them small loads commensurate to their size, and they set off up the hill like rabbits. We staggered up after them. Even carrying next to nothing, we could barely keep up.

Once through the second border we checked into a hotel. This was our first encounter with the strange world of pseudo-Chinese Tibet. Tibet has been unhappily under Chinese occupation since the 1950s. A gigantic gold sign proclaimed our hotel to be an official tourist hotel. A vast foyer was floored with marble. The gilded reception desk was backed with clocks giving times in a dozen different countries.

Once we entered the rooms, we were in a different world. They looked as if someone had read a manual about what a hotel was, without understanding what it meant. In the bathroom was the

usual complimentary foambath, in a drab grey box. There just wasn't a bath. In the bedroom a television faced the beds. Loose wires hung out from the back of it. It couldn't be plugged in. The beds were meticulously made but the mattresses were as lumpy as a rock garden. We left with relief the next morning.

The road now ran up the side of the valley, just one truck wide. A sheer drop fell away on one side, a cliff rose on the other. When we reached the site of the avalanche, queues of trucks were waiting on either side. A slot had been dug into the snowy mass. We were rubbing against the icy walls as we inched our way through, walls that towered above us, over 30 feet high.

The final challenge of the day was another landslide, roughly cleared away. The road surface was uneven, tilting at an alarming angle towards the drop. Each section of slide entailed a long wait for our turn to cross. The air was icy cold, and getting thin. We all huddled quietly in the back of the truck, tired, bruised, cold, dusty. The day seemed to have gone on for rather too long.

We spent that night and the next at Nylam, a desolate frontier town on the edge of the Tibetan plateau. We needed to spend time there to acclimatise but there was little to do. We weren't the only expedition that had been held up by the road closure, and there were several expeditions in town. Most notable was a commercial team led by Russell Brice. Russell's reputation preceded him. He had done some intensely difficult climbing on Everest in the 1980s, before going into commercial guiding full-time, specialising in the north side of Everest. He was the most experienced climber on the north side of the mountain. A tall, quiet man, with a laconic New Zealand accent, he was friendly to us, but looked on our motley crew with some scepticism.

'Climbing the south side of Everest is all very well,' he said to me. 'Don't expect that because you could do that, you will manage the north. It's a different challenge altogether.'

After Nylam we transferred to Land Cruisers and the travelling became easier. We had one more bad night, in concrete barracks at Xegar. Some expeditions elected to spend two night there, for acclimatisation. When we came down to breakfast and found a grey goo, masquerading as porridge, accompanied by the previous night's cabbage, reheated, we decided to risk the headaches and press on to base camp.

We had had a glimpse of Everest on the horizon, a deep blue pyramid streaked with white. Now it had disappeared. We turned south and began to drive straight towards the Himalaya. The vehicles wound slowly up a barren hillside. The plains of Tibet receded below us, a vast mass of subtle gradations of brown. At last we crested the hill, to stand on the top of the pass, the Pang La. A blue triangle was visible pasted against a white sky, just like a child's drawing. It was clearly the highest mountain of the range. However, the entire bottom half was still hidden was from us. Its true scale had not yet been revealed. We stood on the pass, shaking from the bitter wind, snapping photographs. The excitement was electric.

As we descended into the undulating lands that lay before Everest, the mood calmed. We still had hours of driving, following riverbeds that wove through the many hills. We passed small settlements of fort-like buildings that looked as if they had risen from the earth itself. In fact they had. They were built with bricks made of local clay, dried in the sun. If left untended for a season or two, the buildings would simply sink back into the ground from which they had come.

At last we turned into a massive valley. It ran directly south, wide and proud, until stopped by a gigantic wall. Everest was back, with a vengeance. The north face stood nearly four kilometres high, a vast bulwark of black rock, covered in part by snow. In the weeks leading up to this point there had been a lot of talk about Everest and how people thought they would manage on it. Now, faced with magnitude of the reality, silence prevailed. We had arrived.

10

Mother goddess of the earth

Pemba was standing, arms crossed, staring down two yak herders. Between them stood a barrel of equipment. The yak herders had red, wrinkled faces and shiny black hair, wound round their heads in plaits, ornamented with yak bone rings and turquoise stones. The two of them picked up the barrel, barely able to lift it between them. They staggered a few steps towards a jet-black yak, and then collapsed. Wild gesturing followed, indicating that she was an ancient and venerable yak and we would cause her death by cruelly foisting such an enormous load on her.

Yaks are the pack animals of Tibet, like cows but with long thick coats and wide horns. Several thousand years of living in a land of bitter cold and little food had done nothing for their tempers. They could spot a white-eye at a 100 paces and took vicarious pleasure in forcing them off the trail. Yaks always had right of way.

Pemba, barely containing his growing annoyance, picked up the barrel in one hand, pointing out that it was well under the allocated weight. The Sherpa people originate from Tibetan refugees who took shelter in the mountains of Nepal. Their language has remained sufficiently similar to Tibetan for them to be able to communicate.

Although the number of yaks hired and weight carried by each was specified in our climbing contract with the Tibetan Mountaineering Association, the reality was a prolonged haggling session. The yak herders knew they held the upper hand. There was no other way to move equipment up the 22 kilometres of glacier to ABC. They insisted we needed to hire more yaks, which they would happily provide, for an exorbitant fee. By late afternoon Ian had told them to get lost and we had reached an impasse. They sulked in their camp, about 500 metres away. They were camped in skin tents, each built round a fire, with a hole in the roof to allow the smoke to escape. We sat ignoring them, looking at our vast pile of equipment.

On the south side the main massif of Everest had lurked coyly behind the west ridge and the mass of Nuptse. The north was very different, with the mountain magnificently dominant all the time. North side base camp was a vast area of gravel plain, lying just beyond the snout of the Rongbuk glacier. The teams were far more spread out that they had been on the south. Our only close neighbour was an Indian team, from Bombay. Their orange tents were only a few metres away from ours. They were the first civilian expedition to come from India to Everest and had funded the expedition mostly through personal loans.

'If we had been going to play the highest cricket match in the world, we would have plenty of money,' sighed Uday Kolwankar, their ABC manager and one of the organisers. 'But in India, no one cares about the mountains.'

Everest is called Chomolungma in Tibet, 'mother goddess of the earth'. The previous day we had done the puja ceremony that asked her for safe passage. The Sherpas had built a chorten on the ridge above our camp and two lamas had come from the nearby monastery to conduct the ceremony. The lamas served as a bridge between the worlds, temporal and spiritual, ancient and modern. Their robes, saffron and wine red, spoke of a tradition older than Christ. Their leather hiking boots and digital watches were firmly part of the late twentieth century. At the end of the ceremony

Snowy yaks wait patiently at base camp.

Jangbu gave each of us a multi-coloured cord, blessed by the lamas. It was to be tied round our necks and remain there for the course of the expedition. We were deep in a land fundamentally alien to us. We were not about to refuse any aid that was offered.

The next morning everything was resolved. The barrels had apparently become lighter overnight and everyone was happy. Those not involved in loading up yaks were trying to trade, anything for anything. Ian was negotiating for an 'eye of Buddha' bead. He and the herder had no common language. Ian was dressed in his vivid red Goretex jacket, the most advanced outdoor fabric available. The herder wore an ancient goat skin coat, which had never been washed, before or after the demise of the goat. However, the language of commerce was universal. From the smelly depths of the goat the herder pulled out an electronic calculator and punched in 100. One hundred rupees were required. The negotiation was happily settled.

The yaks and Sherpas rapidly disappeared into the distance. The rest of us made more gradual progress towards ABC, bedevilled by the altitude which did not affect the Sherpas this low down. I felt dreadful. I could have been at home, warm and comfortable, with lots of oxygen and a car. Instead I was trying to breath air that had less than half the oxygen my body was used to and I was having to walk along miles of glaciers, with all my possessions on my back, to get anywhere. The summit of Everest was nearly three kilometres higher, and I was already shattered. It was altitude, the great leveller. I got no special dispensation for having climbed Everest before. My body had to start from scratch to adjust.

We made use of a transit camp, perched on a hill of shattered rock half-way along the glacier. My resting pulse was up to a 100. Sleep brought little respite, as at night the aches and pains set in. My back hurt, my calves, my feet ... I had become so soft in the city. No amount of pounding the streets of Johannesburg with a rucksack on my back added up to a real mountain. Nearly two years of comfy beds, office chairs and cars had not prepared my body for sleeping on the ground, for climbing with loads day after day, for the mental and physical privations of weeks in remote Tibet. I could only hope my body would remember old habits from other expeditions and settle down.

As we pushed up towards ABC the scenery soon compensated for the effort. The earlier stages were simply rubble-strewn glacier, with all the charm of a vast construction site. However, higher up we were walking on a road of moraine that ran up the middle of the east Rongbuk glacier. Huge fins of ice protruded from the glacial bed. Some were four or five stories high, massive blue pyramids. Between them lay lakes of ice, frozen up against the scree we walked on. On either side white glaciers curved down the brown mountainsides to join this main stream. The east Rongbuk glacier had its source in a bowl-like valley that lay between the north-east and the north ridges of Everest, and the east arm of Changste. ABC was situated on a small rock-shelf below the cliffs of Changste.

It was a beautiful camp. To our west was the snow wall that led up to the north col, site of camp 1. Across the glacier in front of us was the great wall of the north-east ridge, topped by the intricate mass of the pinnacles. To the east the scene opened out, to a jagged line of smaller mountains.

The vast bowl of air above us was filled with the howl of the wind far overhead, the rumble of rock-fall, the creaks and groans of the glacier. The only life was the birds that circled over camp, following the climbers in search of food, and a small, very fat mouse that lived in our storage tent.

All the teams were clustered together, a multi-coloured huddle of tents. Once again there was a wide mix of nationalities on the mountain. The Tibetan side was more affordable for small teams, so we had everything from a large Japanese expedition, with over 40 climbers in all, to some couples, climbing without Sherpas or oxygen. There was some antagonism early on about the use of the safety ropes. The teams were divided between those that had made it into base camp before the avalanche had closed the road, and those who arrived after it. The latecomers, of whom our team was one, were felt to be freeloading. A mass meeting of team leaders and sirdars was held at our ABC camp. In fact ropes had only been fixed up to camp 1. Plenty of work remained to be done and eventually an equitable arrangement was reached, with everyone contributing rope, labour or money, or some combination of the three. Pemba, Lhakpa and Jangbu joined in fixing ropes from camp 2 to camp 3, across the rock slopes of the north face.

ABC proved to be out of radio contact with base camp, our handsets foiled by the mass of Changste. The Sherpas could reach base from camp 1, where they were based as they worked higher on the mountain. Pemba had a particular affinity for radios, and talked on them whenever he got the chance. He would call Padam at base camp each night he was at camp 1. Martin, now out of contact with the rest of the team, would listen to what seemed an eternity of Nepalese chatter. The sheer volume of talk seemed enough to be describing a dozen disasters on the mountain.

'What's happening,' he would demand when Padam finally got off the radio. 'What was all that about?'

'Everybody fine,' Padam would reply.

That was all Martin ever got. What all the other things were that the Sherpas had to say remained a mystery.

Fortunately for him, the Indian team had a radio booster at ABC. I took to using their system to talk to Martin, and gave him a little more information than Padam did. As a result we spent a lot of time with the Indians, at base camp and at ABC.

In 1996 five climbers had died in the great storm. On the same day, 10 May, three Indians had died on the north side, members of an Indo-Tibetan Border Police team. Five Japanese were supposed to have climbed over them as they lay dying, choosing summit glory over aiding fellow mountaineers. This was the subject of much shocked speculation, particularly in Britain. Some quotable name supposedly claimed 'there was no morality above 8000 metres'. Rumours about all of this were running rife on the south side of the mountain in 1996.

It later turned out that six Indians had left the top camp on 10 May. Three turned back while three pressed on despite severe weather conditions. They had radioed at 4 p.m. to say that they were on the summit.[1] However, they did not make it back to camp. Five Japanese and three Sherpas reached the summit the next morning, at 11.45 a.m. They claimed to have passed five climbers, without knowing what teams they were from. None of them had asked the Japanese for help.

I finally had a chance to ask the Indians how they felt about this incident. Their reply was that the whole affair had attracted little attention in India. It was felt the climbers were army members engaged in a dangerous pursuit. It was no surprise that things could go wrong. The Japanese were not considered to blame in any way, and the relationship between the Indians and the Japanese teams in 1998 was one of mutual aid. As was often the case, the truth proved to be far less satisfyingly sensational than the speculation.

1 All times given for events on the north side are Nepalese times, not Chinese. There is a 2.15 hour time difference.

Living at an altitude of 6 500 metres was tough. I had been most worried about Jan, after his poor performance on Aconcagua. He toiled up the glacier to ABC and, having arrived, announced he was never going down again. He battled with the altitude all the time he was there, sleeping poorly and being always short of breath. However, the will of the film-maker overcame all else. In the magnificence of the surroundings and the varied stories of the teams assembled at ABC, he found plentiful material. I enjoyed his company immensely. I found in him a like-minded spirit with whom to share the excitement of the expedition, a mentor in my continued progression into the art of camerawork, a warm and solid shoulder when I was tired or depressed.

The north ridge provided magnificent climbing. There is nothing on the route as weirdly beautiful, or as dangerous, as the tortured ice of the icefall. However, there is a sense of space, and of exposure, that is unrivalled by anything on the south. From ABC we walked up to the head of the glacier, the foot of the wall up to the north col. The junction with the wall was abrupt. Suddenly a great face of white snow reared up, a fragile line of rope running up it into the distance. The route climbed the face in a great arc. It swung out to the right and then traversed back above a massive wall of seracs. Much of it was steady uphill plodding. Sections were depressingly steep, and I was doubled over every four or five steps, battling to get my breath back. The wall blocked out everything beyond it. The goal became the top of it, the chance to look onto the other side. I climbed it for the first time with Andre.

When we turned the last corner of the traverse and pulled our weary bodies over the last rise, we found a huddle of colour in a small depression. The tents were overshadowed by a giant wall of snow that protected the camp from the westerly wind. We had two tents at the tail end of the camp 1 area. We dumped our rucksacks and I persuaded Andre to walk a little further for a glimpse of the

Ian climbing up the ice slopes towards camp 1.

view. We tramped out from the shelter of the snow wall. However, we found we could barely focus on the view for the strength of the wind.

High winds, and resultant low temperatures, are the greatest weather obstacle on the north side of Everest. The four kilometre high north face is the first obstacle the wind encounters in thousands of miles. The human beings on the mountain were inching their way upwards at precisely the juncture where an irresistible force met an immovable object. It was not a pleasant place to be. Andre turned tail immediately for the shelter of camp. I huddled down, putting my side into the wind, and squinted out at the view. Below me lay an ice lake that was the source of the central Rongbuk glacier. The vast mass of ice was buckling under its own pressure, with tortured crevasses clawed across its surface. Beyond it a magnificent scene of snowy peaks spread out to the west, with great towers of cloud rising up between them.

After a short rest, we descended quickly, wrapping the fixed rope around one arm and almost running down the slope with the rope acting as a friction brake. The next day Andre, exhausted, headed back down to base camp. Trevor, who acclimatised slowly, failed to reach camp 1 and then also returned to base. Jan, Ian and I remained at ABC, acclimatising and filming. Andre and Trevor were battling to find the rhythm of a prolonged expedition. Mountain climbing can often be a case of 'hurry up and wait'. On the north the weather was at its most stable in the last 10 days of May. We had over a month yet before we were likely to push for the summit. Proper acclimatisation lower down was our best preparation for those later days.

Although the altitude gain from base camp to 6 500 metres was just the same as on the south side, it was a very different kind of challenge, physically and mentally. It was easier than the ascent of the icefall and the walk up the cwm had been, being simply hiking up glaciers, but was far further as a horizontal distance. It took more days to get up to 6 500 metres on the north, but it did not feel like 'climbing' the mountain. There was none of the spectacular wonder of the icefall, the technical challenge, the danger. There was no feeling of being a proper climber, forging up the mountain slopes. Yet there was just the same need to take it slowly, to acclimatise properly.

Andre and Trevor had tended to spend rather too much time fantasising about the summit and rather too little dealing with the practicalities lower down. They were now demoralised by the difficulty of reaching 7 000 metres. I didn't understand their approach. In 1996 each new camp had been a celebration. Without an enormous pressure of expectation I had managed to keep going, day by day, to heights I had never dreamed of. In 1998 I knew that no woman had ever succeeded in climbing Everest from both its north and south sides. However, I had no idea whether I could climb the north side, so gave no thought to that unclaimed record. I tried to look out as much I looked up, to drink in the beauty of where I was, where I had come from.

One evening I crawled out of the chilly shelter of my ABC tent and made for the warmth of our kitchen tent. Even if dinner was not yet ready, Phuri made a mean bowl of popcorn. Heat and food were the basic desires of our ABC life and the kitchen tent was the primary source of both. Jan heard the crunch of my boots on the rock and grovelled out of his tent to join me.

We entered the kitchen to find a strange woman sitting drinking coffee and chatting to Phuri.

'Hi, I'm Fran,' she said cheerfully, in a broad American accent. 'I've lost my husband. Have you got a radio?'

Her lively attitude did not seem to match with the seriousness of her problem. Jan and I sat down and asked for some more information. She had left base camp that morning ahead of her Russian husband, Serguei Arsentiev, who was a faster walker than she was. He had already climbed Everest once, without supplementary oxygen. However, he had still not arrived at ABC. The two of them were on the permit of a Russian team but seemed to be operating largely independently.

We explained that our radios did not reach base camp but Fran in fact seemed more interested in company than in help. She did not want to sit alone in the one tiny tent she and Serguei had at ABC. She chomped away at the popcorn and chatted happily and incessantly, like a pot bubbling over with words. Typically American, she told us her entire life story. Soon I knew all about her troubles back in Colorado, saving money for her son's college fund. She and Serguei were only on Everest because they had got such a cheap trip. They were climbing without supplementary oxygen or Sherpa assistance and she was rather dismissive of those who used such aids.

'Humping huge loads up the mountain is not my idea of fun,' I commented.

'But it's all part of the challenge,' she replied.

Eventually she returned to her cold and empty tent. Thereafter we greeted the two of them whenever we passed them on the mountain. Neither she nor I had any inkling that there would be one final, disastrous meeting between us that season.

The days at ABC passed with a gentle rhythm. We were now all better acclimatised and so able to fully enjoy our surroundings. Although each team was self-sufficient, there was no shortage of gossip to be shared. Our camp was on the edge of the main route through ABC and climbers often poked their heads into our mess tent to pass on news, or cadge a cup of tea. We were approaching full moon and the entire glacier glistened silver at night, edged by the impenetrable darkness of the shadows of evening. Each tent formed a little bubble of luminescent colour under an inky velvet sky. Once the moon set, the stars came into their own, diamonds filled with a burning fire of inconceivable intensity.

Ian and I would lie in the warmth of our tent, my head on his shoulder, his arm round my back, in silent enjoyment of the peace and stillness of the wilderness night. There was a simplicity to mountain life which I loved, a clarity of purpose which was difficult to achieve elsewhere. There were none of the million different worries that tear you apart in the modern world. We ate, drank, slept, climbed. All progress was focused in a single direction -

Jan filming prayer flags.

upwards, towards the point where you could go no higher.

'I love you,' Ian whispered in my ear. I curled against the heat of his body and smiled into the darkness. Mountains had always been home to my most special moments.

The mood at base camp was very different. As the days passed the base camp group began to brood. The weather was not good, cold and windy with light snow most afternoons, but that was typical of Everest and the north side. No one was climbing high on the mountain. It was barely the first week of May and it might well be another three weeks before we attempted the summit. Nevertheless, at base camp the food was monotonous, the living uncomfortable, the days very long with little to do. And there was no getting away from any of it.

People expect expeditions to fail due to some dramatic event, an avalanche or killer storm. Real life seldom offers anything so sensational. Expeditions crumble because their members crumble. And the members crumble under the constant pressure of the little irritations of life. On a mountain there is no escape, from the place or from the people. For 24 hours a day, week after week, you are trapped together. There is no external stimulus, no newspapers or television, to provide neutral topics of conversation. There is no one outside the group to talk to, with whom to let off steam.

The situation becomes worse when all this is happening around crumbling dreams. In popular mythology Everest is far more than just a mountain. It is a universal symbol of challenge, of achievement. This annoys mountaineers, who know there are challenges far harder that get much less recognition. It also annoys them because mountaineers are a cliquish lot, who want to keep the hills to themselves in the belief they have found a special benediction in the wilderness that the general public doesn't know about.

But the public know about Everest. The British, George Mallory, Edmund Hillary, all made sure of that. At one time only the dedicated mountaineer, or the eccentric adventurer had access to challenges of its ilk. Now the world has changed. The mountain wildernesses have become more accessible. Many more people are interested in gaining personal experience of them. The nineties have seen an explosion in the number of people attempting Everest, and thus in the number that reach the summit. However, despite all the allegations of rich novices getting themselves killed, the percentage of deaths remains the same. In my three years on the mountain, most of those killed were experienced climbers.

People climb Everest for very different reasons, with diverse expectations of it.

Everest as the symbol becomes laden with hopes, expectations, desires. Everest as reality is a large heap of snow-covered rock that happens to stand higher than anything else on earth. There are those who climb Everest because they like climbing, because they like being in the earth's wilderness, and because, after all, it is the highest climb in the world. For them, and I would count myself among them, an ascent of Everest is about the journey. It is about each new day, and what it brings both externally and personally. It is about each new view, each new kind of challenge, each new dawn. What the mountain brings is not always easy, but there is more to be learnt from challenging difficulty than from living in ease. To reach the summit is a great and wonderful bonus, but it is not the point of the exercise.

Then there are those who want to have climbed Everest, to bask in the glory they believe it will bring them. They believe that to have climbed it will prove something about their own self worth. They have a dream of the mountain and its significance that has no place for day after day of bad weather, boring food, altitude sickness, smelly socks, dirty underwear. They love the idea of risk and are prepared to be stopped by spectacular difficulty, but have never thought that they might just grind to a halt because they have come to hate the reality of their dream.

Our crew at base camp was not managing too well with the stresses of the mountain. Safely away from the actuality of the mountain, they began to bark themselves up. They decided that there was not enough oxygen for all the team to go for the summit. We had deliberately misled them, sabotaging their dream of glory. I got a radio call from Trevor asking if there would be oxygen for them above 8000 metres.

I told Ian, who lost his temper completely. He walked down the trail until he could reach them on a handheld radio and pointed out that they had yet to show the ability to get up to an altitude where oxygen was necessary. He told them to get off their backsides at base camp and get back up the mountain if they had such pretensions of climbing it.

Ian, who has a 'put up or shut up' attitude to life, has no space for dealing with other people's uncertainties. He was simmering

The South African base camp, in the midst of packing loads onto yaks. Everest dominates in the distance.

with fury, outraged that people whom he felt had contributed little and put in a poor showing as climbers, should have such criticisms of him and his organisation. The others were insulted by his abrasive attitude, and his undisguised contempt, and headed back up the trail, spoiling for a fight.

It took them two days to get up to ABC. Everyone collapsed into the mess tent. It didn't take much longer than one cup of coffee for the argument to resume. At first tempers simply flared and there was general trading of insults. Once things cooled down grudging apologies were exchanged. Ian went through the number of oxygen bottles, where they were, how they were to be used. We had enough for the entire team to go for the summit together. However, the Sherpas had placed them in the normal places, most at the top camp, contingency bottles at camp 2. The team still had to face up to climbing up to there.

The fight was resolved but the underlying tension was not. The wind continued to howl. Andre climbed back to the north col and spent a frightening night at camp 1 imagining the tent being torn away from around him. He returned to ABC with much of the stuffing knocked out of him and said he had had enough. He was homesick for his two young children, and for the world which he was used to.

Everyone else sulked at ABC, and listened to the wind scream round the upper slopes of the mountain. Ian, angry and hurt by the whole affair, announced to me that he was going to leave the expedition. I was deeply demoralised by everything that had happened and now felt personally betrayed by Ian's decision. We ended up having a bitter fight.

I retreated from him to cry on Jan's shoulder. Jan, who had no personal summit ambitions and therefore less ego at stake in the whole matter, provided a safe harbour for me. He had a head old enough and wise enough to be able to see beyond our immediate troubles. He had known Ian for long enough to know that the storm would pass.

While I was sitting in the kitchen tent, Lhakpa came in and sat down next to me. Although the Sherpas always stayed well clear of team differences, they were no fools. They knew what was going on.

'Is everything okay with the members?' he asked.

'Yes,' I replied, unconvincingly.

'Why do members always fight in the mountains?' he asked eventually. We weren't the only expedition he'd been on where fights had erupted. It was a good question. Perhaps we simply lacked the stoicism of the Sherpas in the face of discomfort. Our city breeding had made us soft in many subtle ways.

Ian calmed down, I cheered up and we made up our differences. We had a deep and long-term commitment to this Everest expedition and to other future projects. It would take more than one fight to destroy that. However, for the moment the mountain seemed in no mood to be climbed. The days spent at the high altitude of ABC were mentally and physically draining to all of us. We decided, as a group, to move back down to base camp. There we would regroup and consider the future.

The strange thing about the mountain is the relativity of its comforts. On arrival from Kathmandu, base camp seemed a bleak place - cold, spartan, uninviting. Coming back down from ABC, it looked like a holiday camp - warm, comfortable, luxurious.

Still, Andre was keen to go home. Martin, having had enough of long and lonely days at base camp, was eager to join him. Ian organised a Land Cruiser to take them back to Kathmandu.

Trevor was suddenly faced with decision time. What meant more to him - to see the expedition through, to perhaps try once more on the mountain, or to return to the luxuries of home? Trevor has a deep love of mountains, and of the world's wild places. He had also grown up in a society where opportunities were not easily come by. He was not about to walk away from this one. He chose to stay.

As I watched the Land Cruiser bump its way across the stones of base camp, I felt a great relief. At last they had left. With all the doubt and the debate now at an end, with the negative energy safely on its way to Kathmandu, we could once again simply revel in being in the mountains.

While still on Aconcagua Andre had told me that he wanted to push his own limits. He spent much of his time counselling people who were at the limits of what they could endure in life. Yet he had no personal experience of what that must be like. He had thought Everest might provide such an experience.

In the end he had found that the challenges he sought were in the heart of his home and his congregation, not on the slopes of Everest. And there lay the achievements that meant most to him. He was disappointed by what had become of his dream but realistic enough to realise that perhaps he had put to much onto the dream.

Those of us who remained all went into the mess tent to tuck into milk coffee, omelettes and tough toast. The summit was there for the climbing and we needed to get back onto the mountain slopes. Jan agreed, with a little reluctance, to stay at base camp as our radio anchor. The following morning, 18 May, we headed back up to ABC. Our base camp was a turmoil of excitement as we left. Our radio base station was more powerful than that of the Indians. One of their climbers had left top camp early that morning in a summit bid. They had been in our mess tent all night, monitoring the radio. On the two previous days Russians had tried for the summit and had failed. Now several teams had members on the move. The tension was high. This might be the first successful summit of the season.

✻ *The avalanche that delayed the drive to base camp.*

✻✻ *The north face of Everest, seen from base camp.*

✻✻✻ *Lamas from the Rongbuk monastery conducting the puja.*

✻✻✻✻ *Ice pinnacles at 6 000 metres on the walk up the east Rongbuk glacier to ABC.*

Now there was no mucking about with a transit camp. We walked up to ABC in one long day. The first news we heard on arrival was that 22 climbers had reached the summit from the north that day, including one of the Indians. Those teams with members in the 22 were jubilant. Everyone else was both encouraged and uncertain. We needed to get up the mountain and make the most of the weather.

'We climb tomorrow?' asked Pemba.

I kept quiet and let the men squash that idea.

'No, we rest tomorrow, go to camp 1 the day after,' Ian replied.

The Sherpas grumbled to themselves. They were anxious to do some real climbing, to get up there with the other teams. They made sure to relate to us in detail all the people and teams who had reached the summit. Ian felt that the weather was likely to improve the closer we got to the end of May, and was tempted to wait a few more days. However, the Sherpas wanted to move. The upward momentum pulled us with it.

Some of the successful summiteers made ABC in the late afternoon of the next day. They made their way through ABC to a ripple of applause from the different camps. For a moment all the teams, whatever their language, whatever their style of climbing, were united in a common joy at the success of some of their fellows. For the Indians that summit made the world of difference. For a short while the citizens of Bombay forgot about cricket and revelled in their Everest triumph. A prominent businessman stepped forward and paid off all the team members' overdrafts. We watched their celebration and hoped that in a week or so we would have something of the same for ourselves. During that day another

✻✻✻ *Ian climbing up to camp 1.*

✻✻ *Tiny figures approach the foot of the face below the north col.*

✻ *A member of the Tibetan team abseils down from camp 1.*

wave of climbers reached the top. We needed to get moving.

Another climber with itchy feet was a Tibetan student, Ci Luo. He had had to finish his exams and so had arrived too late to join the Chinese expedition, which was already packing up to go home. Through the Tibetan Mountaineering Association and Russell, we were asked if he could join up with us. He needed no looking after. He just didn't want to climb alone. Ci Luo spoke no English but he had an engaging smile. We happily accepted his company and began to pack up for a summit bid.

Chorten and prayer flags at base camp.

11

Knocking on heaven's door

I squatted on my haunches, peering at Trevor through the lens of my video camera. By the time his chest stopped heaving and his legs starting moving again, my arms were cramping with the effort of holding the camera steady. It was 20 May and we were on our way to camp 1. I was feeling strong and motivated, ready to grasp this mountain by the horns and show it who was in charge. This is a silly feeling to have on something as big as Everest, but I was buoyed up by the ease with which I was climbing. I was now well acclimatised and my body moved easily, my muscles working in a fluid rhythm. Even with filming on the way, I had constantly been waiting for Ian and Trevor to catch up with me.

Both Ian and Trevor were frustrating to film. So often the legs moving were just a brief aberration. Two or three steps later the man of the moment would be bent over a knee, gasping again. Everything happened in such slow motion that it was agonising to watch. Ian I was not concerned about. He was battling the mandatory chest infection and I had long since learnt that until such time as he was lying comatose at my feet, I could assume he would make the next camp. Trevor worried me more. He simply did not have the pace to cover the distance up to the summit. This was the first day of what should be a five day push, taking us from ABC to the summit and back. I wondered if he would still be with us in a few days time. We only had about 10 days left in the season. We needed to move.

I filmed as Ian and Trevor collapsed wearily into the tent and began the job of squeezing the possessions of three people into a rather small tent. The filming may be part of the expedition plan but there comes a point when it looks suspiciously as though you are waving a camera around to get out of the hard work of pitching tents, sorting kit, chopping ice and cooking meals. And they might just be right. I decided, for the sake of the greater good, to put the camera away for a while.

'I'm buggered,' announced Trevor, and buried his face in a cup of hot coffee made by Ian. The tent was not a pleasant place to be. Six sweat-soaked socks were steaming up the inside of the tent rapidly. The cold might reduce the smell but it could not kill it completely. We were all perched awkwardly on top of sleeping bags and clothing. Each of us was feeling that the other two were taking up an inordinate amount of space. It was the beginning of what was to be an unpleasant night. By 7 p.m. there was no more to eat, no more to say. We settled down into our sleeping bags. On one side I was pressed against the wall of the tent. On the other were various bony bits of Ian, knees, elbows and suchlike. Under and around me were an assortment of clothing and equipment. My inner boots were stuffed into the bottom of my sleeping bag, along with inner layers of clothing, suntan lotion, water bottles, video batteries. Outer boots, crampons, rucksack, Goretex clothing, down clothing, were all fighting for space around me. I seemed to be the overall loser in the affair. None of this helped with the insomnia that came with sleeping at 7 000 metres. Hour after hour I lay awake, staring into the darkness of my eyelids, staring into the darkness of the tent ceiling. Anticipating this turn of events, I had brought my walkman and two tapes. By midnight I knew every hiss, every scratch on the two tapes. Silence was better.

But the silence was filled with Ian's snores, Trevor's groans and gasps. There is nothing more galling than lying wide awake, listening to your tent companions apparently enjoying a solid eight hours. The temptation to shake them awake was very strong, but I figured the risks were too high. I suffered on alone. My digital watch had survived the expedition of 1996 and was with me once again. The lurid green light was once more the only indicator of the passing of time. Ten minutes would pass, maybe fifteen if I was very disciplined about not looking at the watch. Exhaustion, anticipation, nervousness, all made an unpalatable mix. This was the worst of the worst of high-altitude climbing.

By some perverse trick of fate, I fell asleep as it began to get light. By the time the sun was on the tent, I was warm, comfortable, dozing happily. I had spent all night wishing day would come so I could get up. Now day was here and all I wanted to do was stay in my sleeping bag. The three of us formed a grumpy crew as we wriggled out of our warm pits and began to dress and pack.

The sky was crystal clear, the sun blazed down on the snow. It was a winter wonderland. Standing by the side of the tents, it looked like a perfect day for climbing. The only hesitation was the high wail of wind in the distance.

'Well, Trevor?' Ian asked.

He looked uncertain, drained by the previous day's exertions and a night of little sleep. The white ridge that undulated up towards camp 2 looked deceptively straightforward. We had been warned that it was radically foreshortened and was both longer and steeper than it looked.

'I'll climb up for a few hours and see how I go,' he said cautiously.

We nodded agreement, shouldered our rucksacks and set off across the camp site towards the ridge. The idyllic morning ended about 50 metres further on.

As soon as we emerged from behind the snow ridge that sheltered camp 1 from the west wind, we were hit by a gale. I pulled the hood of my Goretex jacket tight round my face, put my head down and soldiered on. The wind howled around me, swirling about my head, creeping down the neck of my jacket, rubbing icy fingers across my face. Before long my cheeks and the

Trevor, tired but proud, at 7 000 metres.

tip of my nose were numb, the rest of my face suffused with a cold burn. I pulled out a neoprene face mask with a fleece neck cover attached. This made all the difference, protecting my face, blocking entrance to my jacket. The mask gradually became damp and gungy from the moisture of my breath, but it was worth it.

I was climbing at right-angles to the path of the wind. My left side climbed in a pool of calm, my right was relentlessly buffeted. The wind gusted, never allowing me to set my balance. One minute I would be leaning into it, supported by its sheer force. Then it would die, just for an instant, and I would be stumbling sideways, out of control. Eventually I turned my back to it and climbed up the mountain slope crab-style, crossing one boot over the other.

It was impossible to communicate with anyone more than a few steps away from you. The wind ripped the words straight out of the depths of your throat. I could see Ian shuffling up the slope below me. His head was bent right down, and he looked like a little red gnome. But he was moving upwards.

Far below him I could see the tiny figure of Trevor - going down. The wind had torn away the last of his determination. He did not have the energy left for the several days and nights that still had to follow. Over the next few days he made his way back down the mountain, to keep Jan company in the lonely base camp vigil.

Far above me the slope stretched on. In the end I found it consisted of four great rises of snow, followed by four easier sections. The rises hide camp 2 from view. The snow stretched endlessly on upwards. Each rise was steeper than the last, and longer. I could not look out to the west because of the wind. The view to the east was hidden by edge of the ridge. The only marker of time became the receding view of camp 1.

What had been a substantial platform of snow, home to a dozen expeditions, slowly dwindled into a tiny ledge, perched precariously on top of great cliffs dropping down to the east and central Rongbuk glaciers. The tents were reduced to little dots of black, sprinkled on the snow like mouse droppings. Tiny black points moved on the snow slopes below the tents. Looked down on like that, it seemed a ludicrous place to camp.

The last of the rises was interminable. I knew I was near the top because I could now see ABC. The east Rongbuk glacier swept up into the valley below us, with the narrow sidewalk of moraine running up the one side. A vague indication of colour was the only visible sign of the tent town that made up ABC.

In the long days at ABC I had watched tiny figures approach camp 2. They had only became visible on the final section just below the tents. They had always seemed to move ludicrously slowly. Now I understood why. I was stopping every 10 steps, puffing into my face mask, trying for once to fill my lungs with air. The air just wasn't there.

The tents slowly came into view. There were six tents, scattered at the topmost point of the snow ridge. Above them the terrain turned to rock. Ours was a very small russet tent, set off to the left.

To pitch the tents a ledge had to be cut into the snow. There was no flat ground. I shuffled up the last slope and collapsed at the tent door. With much huffing and flailing I got myself, and my rucksack, into the bell of the tent. For the first time in six hours I was protected from the force of the wind. At last I could look out to the west, the view that had been hidden from me for so long by the wall of the north col, and all this day by the wind.

That view justified every minute of exertion. Laid out below me was a 200 degree view of the Himalaya. I was high enough to look down on much of it, but not so high that I lost all sense of scale. On the far left lay Pumori and the edges of the valley that held the south-side base camp. Due west was a great highway of glacier, leading towards Cho Oyu, sixth highest mountain in the world. Another giant, Shishapangma, was visible on the far horizon. Below me was the bowl of the central Rongbuk glacier, with the north face of Everest dropping steeply down into it. The north ridge ran down from me, tapering down to a now tiny camp 1, before soaring upwards again towards the summit of Changste. Right of that lay the range of smaller mountains that formed the view east of ABC. Now I was looking down on all of them. The tents of camp 2 provided a brave burst of colour in this world of blue, white and brown.

Once again I was on a mountain high, emotionally and physically. We were at 7 600 metres. We were some 40 hours from reaching our goal, standing once more on the summit of Everest. We were in the most glorious place. I felt as if I was standing in the middle of somebody's expedition book. During my first expedition, to the Ruwenzori in central Africa in 1990, I remember looking at myself reflected in my partner's glasses, standing on a glacier, dressed in all my mountain kit.

'I look just like a real mountaineer', I thought. 'I look just like a picture out of a book'. This camp, with its views of the great glaciers, of the dozens of snow-peaked mountains, was straight out of a mountain story.

Through the last of the afternoon I sat by the tent entrance, melting ice and brewing drinks. To Ian's annoyance I kept opening the outer door to peer out at the setting sun. Each opening brought a flurry of spindrift and a wave of cold air, but it was worth it. A rising tide of cloud had washed in among the massive peaks. The sun was sinking slowly into it, a ball of deep orange turning the surrounding cloud hazy gold. As the sun slipped down into the cloud sea, it changed colour to brilliant pink, set over shadowed purple, shot through with the last golden rays. Slowly darkness began to take over. Now the clouds were turning to sombre blue, glimpses of soft pink still visible in the far distance. It became too cold even to peer out of the tent door. The last colour was left to fade away without an audience.

With the high-altitude team now down to two members we had oxygen to spare. I spent a night in solid and happy slumber, aided by a gentle trickle of oxygen-enriched air. The excitement was mounting.

But then again the mountain has no interest in the plans laid by the fleas that scuttle up her skirts. She measures time in geological ages, not in years. The change from one day to another means nothing on such a scale. Yet to us it meant everything. We woke before dawn to howling wind. The guy ropes were strumming, the tent skin pushed taut. We were a tiny boat in a sea of moving air, our prow pointed straight into the wind. I peered out of the tent door and got eyes full of spindrift for my trouble. The wind was considerably stronger than the previous day. The climbing ahead of us would be higher, harder, longer, more exposed than the previous day. It was an unhappy combination.

At 6 a.m. Ian called down to the Sherpas, who were sleeping at camp 1. Sheltered from the wind themselves, they were keen to climb. We were unsure. Ian said he would call them again at 8 a.m. We lay in our sleeping bags and watched the yellow fabric ceiling surging under the pressure of the wind. A full day of climbing might well be feasible, but what would conditions be like up on the summit ridge? We didn't want to be stuck waiting at 8 300 metres, our top camp.

Two Uzbek climbers were camped a few metres below us. Shortly after dawn I had watched them set off round the corner and up onto the rock ridge. Shortly before our second radio call they came stumbling back down and dived back into their tent. That decided the issue.

'We will wait here,' Ian said to Pemba.

There was an unconvinced mumble over the radio. The Sherpas were beginning to wonder how seriously we were actually taking this.

'No Pemba, don't worry. We are not coming down. We stay here until the wind dies and then we go on up'

With that out of the way, we settled in to wait out the next 24 hours. We were trapped in a tent smaller than a double bed. There was little room to manoeuvre, nothing to do. We dozed, made cups of tea, talked about nothing in particular. By mid morning the wind seemed to have lessened. I began to wonder if we had made the wrong decision.

Ian huddled in a corner as I dressed in my full down-cum-Goretex suit, and pulled on my boots and harness. Taking the cameras, I ventured outside. The wind was persistent, steady, but not unbearable. The Uzbeks had gone to ground and there was no other sign of life. I moved gingerly round on the snow. With the exception of about a square metre of ground in front of our tent, there was no flat surface in any direction. I explored a tatty white tunnel tent pitched on the slope above us. Inside was a mess of empty food packets. The fabric had been torn by the force of the wind, and hung forlornly from the metal hoops. The owners were in for a nasty surprise when they came back.

I then ventured across the snow slope towards the start of the rock ridge. The main north face was hidden from our camp. As I moved cautiously round the snow bulge I found out why. I had fortunately clipped into the safety rope, because I rounded the corner into a brutal wind that brought me down onto my knees. I could hardly lift the camera to my face, let alone hold it steady. The tents were situated to protect them from the full fury of the

Cathy mixing juice in a thermos flask at camp 2.

wind raking across the north face. Any doubts I had had about the wisdom of waiting a day were literally blown away. I edged back round the corner and stuffed my hands into my armpits, trying to regain some warmth. All the while the sky was brilliant blue and the sun was shining down benevolently.

The afternoon was occupied by the venerable activity of weather speculation. I sat by the bell of the tent, melting ice, and looking out periodically for any sign of action. At last a tiny figure appeared over the horizon of the ridge below us. It moved at a steady pace, so looked like a Sherpa. However, the colour of the clothing suggested to me that it might be Russell.

'Does he have Sumio with him?' Ian asked. 'I doubt he would move her up the mountain if he wasn't confident of the weather.'

Russell's team was down to one client, Sumio Tsuzuki, a Japanese woman. All his considerable expertise was now focused

From left: Jangbu, Lhakpa and Pemba at camp 2, waiting for Nawang to catch up with them. Camp 1 is visible on the right.

on getting her to the top. It was her third attempt. She had failed on the south in 1996 and the north in 1997. Russell had the most sophisticated weather forecast information of any of the teams on the north side. We reckoned that if Sumio was on her way up, he must think the weather would stabilise. We began a 'Sumio' watch, looking out for her brightly coloured down suit. It was a long wait but at last she was in sight. Our mood improved no end. Only a direct notification from God would have been a better indicator of good weather.

As the afternoon progressed, camp 2 began to fill up. A British climber, Mark Jennings, arrived, with a Sherpa. Then two Americans turned up. Both were big men and they proceeded to crawl into the smallest tent I have ever seen. I doubted that they could both lie down at once in it. It was a funky design, with transparent panels and orange and purple colouring, but it wouldn't have made a decent dog kennel, let alone a tent.

Not surprisingly, the Americans were first up the next morning. The rest of us were just stirring in our respective tents while they were busy dressing - outside their tent. One told me that they had a hanging stove in the tent. The buffets of wind had been washing the water out of the pot and all over them. They had had little sleep and even less to drink. They were keen to move on.

We packed up in a much more relaxed manner. Our little tent seemed positively luxurious by comparison with theirs. We were just getting under way when Lhakpa, Pemba and Jangbu arrived. Nawang, who was not in the same class as a climber, was toiling some way behind. They were all carrying enormous loads. Pemba had been a little over-optimistic when he told Ian that camp 3 was fully supplied. Perhaps they had not wanted to hump too much stuff up to top camp until they were convinced that we were serious. There can be little more depressing for a Sherpa than to have all your team give up half-way up the mountain, and to be left to go and retrieve all the equipment you carried up to top camp.

However, the result was that everyone was moving slowly. For the first, and probably last, time in my life, I was keeping pace with our Sherpa team. The ridge became steeper and narrower, a hazardous jumble of loose rock slabs interspersed with snow patches. It was classic mixed ground with the crampons on our boots alternately a help and a hazard. Tents were scattered up the ridge. Unlike other camps, with so little flat ground on the ridge, there was not a common camping site. Most people who put in camp 2 as low as ours put in two more camps, not one. The Americans, the British, Russell and the Uzbeks all eventually stopped, camping again around 7 900 metres. Only Ci Luo and ourselves kept on moving.

Climbing the rock ridge required concentration, and patience. The ridge just kept on coming at you, level after level of scattered scree. I was climbing steadily and felt good. I finally stopped at the Americans' camp, and looked around to see who was where. Ci Luo, Pemba and Lhakpa were just ahead of me. Jangbu, Ian and Nawang were below me. The ridge we had climbed was still clear, but scoops of mist were wandering across the north face. Above me I could see the tell-tale snow plumes that indicated strong winds higher up. Light sprinkles of snow began to fall as I waited. I decided it was time to pull out the oxygen. Oxygen not only enables you to climb faster, but it stops you getting so cold. The temperature was falling as the weather worsened. This was no time for heroics. I dug around in my rucksack to find the bottle I was carrying. The cold leather mask went onto my face, under my jacket hood. I opened the bottle valve and set the regulator to 2.5 litres per minute. Then I turned my attention to the great north face.

At about 7 900 metres the route turns off the north ridge and begins a diagonal traverse up and across the north face. A ramp of snow ran below a line of black cliffs. Once we had rounded the cliffs, we began to climb steeply up a huge snow bowl. Below us the face dropped away over a rock rim. Nothing more was visible until I saw the Rongbuk glacier, riddled with crevasses, lying a little under three kilometres below me. The exposure was immense. We were clinging to this vast wall, with an infinity of air spread out beneath us. The size of the face was breathtaking.

Pemba load-carrying to camp 3.

It seemed ridiculous to imagine that I would ever surmount it, would ever be standing on the summit ridge I could glimpse in the distance.

Mist swirled around us. At times it would clear completely, revealing ever more mountains spreading into the distance. Then it would return, drawing a veil over the view, settling like a damp cloak over me, dropping tiny pellets of snow onto my arms and hands. I was bitterly tired, with little idea of how much further it was to the last camp. My mind roamed aimlessly, seeking any distraction from the grind of the climbing. Sometimes I thought about what the summit day might bring, but mostly that was too depressing. I barely felt as if I could reach camp, let alone climb 600 metres higher. Sometimes I thought about home, about warmth and greenery and life. I imagined the freedom of being on a sun-baked rock-face, dressed in little more than a few scraps of lycra, feeling the rough warmth of the rock under my bare hands.

Then for a while I redecorated the living room of my house. I happily spent thousands on a complete makeover of the room, changing colours and patterns and furniture.

Eventually all the distractions began to pall. I started to count footsteps, sometimes in patterns of four, sometimes in eights. Then I set my focus on the next anchor point on the rock and counted down until I reached it, trying not to stop on the way. I seldom managed.

The snow bowl was finally below me. Once more we were on mixed rock and snow. I fixed my eyes on each rock ridge we approached, hoping that when we surmounted it I would see little coloured blobs of tents. So far I had been disappointed. What I could see, though, was the summit ridge. It was clear of mist and I could now appreciate the full length of it. I ran my eye back down from the summit. There was the final rock and snow ridge. Then came the steep slope, a pyramid of snow. Below the snow ran a ridge of rock, marked by three distinct features. The Third Step was a round hump of rock, looking like a high-altitude paper-weight. The Second Step was like the blade of a cleaver, a square, thin-edged cliff. I could see what looked like tiny figures moving along the skyline. I took them to be climbers descending from the summit. A narrow line of rock then led to the First Step, an elongated dome with a patch of white snow at its foot.

I noticed movement on the white patch. Watching intently, I could see two black dots. One was still. The other circled round and round. This all happened very slowly. Each time I stopped to get my breath back, I would look up and watch the dots. They had to be climbers but I couldn't think why they should be spending so much time in one place. The bottom of the First Step seemed an odd place to stop.

The puzzle of the dots was driven out of my mind by the appearance of coloured blobs much closer to me - tents. Our camp 3 lay at 8 300 metres, higher than all but five mountains on the planet. It is the highest regularly used camp in the world. It is not, however, any great shakes as a site. It was on steeply sloping ground, mixed rock and snow. Piles of snow had been scraped together to form platforms. I collapsed next to the tent Pemba and Lhakpa were pitching. It was late afternoon and the other three were still on the slopes below us. It was not the best planned run-up to a summit night. Mist continued to swirl around us. It was difficult to tell what evening would bring.

Ian arrived, looking exhausted, and none of the Sherpas seemed too fresh either. We sat in the tent, drinking luke-warm tea out of a thermos. Ian called Jan at the 6 p.m. radio check and said we would call back at 8 p.m. to tell him what we had decided to do. Then we looked at each other.

'Now what?' he asked.

'I've felt better,' I said.

We did not know how hard the summit ridge was going to be, only that it would be harder than that which we had climbed on the south side. The day had been too long, the rucksacks too heavy. We had made camp too late, and were ill-prepared for the night ahead. There was too little time to rest, to recuperate. The weather was too uncertain.

It was not difficult to talk ourselves out of it. Ian called Jan, and told him and Trevor to shut off the radios until a 9 a.m. call the next morning. We then crawled into our bags and settled in for solid sleep undisturbed by expectations of the summit.

'Tea, Didi. Didi, tea ready.'

The voice filtered through into my dreams. Tea. How nice. Tea in the tent before getting up for breakfast.

I opened bleary eyes and fumbled for the tent zip. Pemba handed me a thermos, his face a faint blur behind the glare of his head-torch.

'We must get up now, Didi. We go for the summit.'

I stared at him in sleepy confusion. I thought we'd decided to give up. Obviously the Sherpas had not reached the same conclusion. I gazed out of the tent door. The night sky was pitch black, jewelled with stars. The cloud had gone, the wind had died. I nudged Ian.

'Wake up. Apparently we're going climbing.'

At that point it seemed easier just to go with the flow. In some ways it had been an advantage. I had slept solidly, without being keyed up with the knowledge of leaving for the summit in a few hours.

However, we had not prepared ourselves to go, so dressing and packing took some time. I was feeling neither strong, nor particularly co-ordinated. But then I always felt like that on night-time starts. I took the half-used oxygen bottle off my mask and begun battling to fit another one. The valve was screwed too tight. Ian had to find a penknife, and, battling to focus through the glare of his torch, numbed with cold and too little sleep, made the fiddly adjustment. He was swearing under his breath. Base camp was solidly asleep, in the knowledge we were not going anywhere. So there was no one to tell. It did not seem the most auspicious of starts.

We finally stumbled out of the tent at 2.30 a.m., picked up our rucksacks, adjusted our oxygen sets, and moved off into the coal-black night. With no moon, the Himalaya spread out below us were the faintest outlines of deep grey against the black sky. We each moved in a tiny yellow bubble, the fragile world of light and warmth cast by the head torches. Six tiny bubbles moved up the steep slope of snow, like six fallen stars trying to crawl their way back up to the heavens. Lhakpa led, followed by Ci Luo. I followed with Pemba on my heels. Ian and then Jangbu came behind.

The snow ended and a line of dark cliffs ran off in both directions. Jangbu and Ci Luo were busy climbing diagonally up and to the right. The narrow beam of torch-light made climbing tricky as we tried to work out where variously to place hands and feet. We were not dressed for rock scrambling. Massive Goretex mitts impeded sensation and made it difficult to use rock edges. Worse than that was trying to rock-climb with crampons on my boots. The metal spikes meant my foot did not end where common sense told me it did. The spikes tended to slip on the rock. In the torch-light I could see dozens of tiny yellow lines scored into the brown rock - crampon scratch marks. Remnants of old ropes lay across the rock. Although these sometimes provided a welcome handhold, something I could curl my glove right round, mostly they provided a potential hazard in which my crampons would tangle.

Climbing the rock cliffs took concentration and focus. It provided a distraction from the heavy tiredness of moving at 3 a.m. It also took a lot of breath. I stopped on each ledge, panting and huffing into my oxygen mask. The damp leather sat cool against my skin. There never seemed to be quite enough of the sea-fresh air emanating from it. After five or six heavy breaths, I would start moving again.

Between the rock steps were sneaky ramps of snow, taking us diagonally upwards. The night was cold but still. The resulting temperature proved reasonable, when mitigated by all the clothing. With my eyes adjusted to the torch-light, the surrounding darkness was as impenetrable as a coal face. I had no idea how far we were up the north face, how much further it was to the summit ridge. Below me was over 3 000 metres of inky space, but it could have been three metres or three million metres for all I could see of it.

Looking back down, to judge how those behind me were faring, I was confused to see six crawling stars, instead of three. My brain ticked over slowly, as deadened by lack of sleep as by lack of oxygen. Eventually I realised they must be other climbers, also on their way to the summit. I turned back to the task at hand. All that mattered to me was to keep a reasonable distance ahead of Ian and Jangbu, so that I wasn't slowing the team. Beyond that it was just about taking one step, and another, and another. As long each step went roughly upwards, I was doing the right thing.

I climbed through yet another band of rock, and up mixed rock and snow slopes, to find Lhakpa and Ci Luo standing, waiting. Looking up revealed sky, rather than more mountain. We had reached the ridge. I looked to my right, where the snow wound off into black distance. To my left, however, behind a wall of spiky rock formations, was air. And in the farthest distance was a thread-

Cathy dressed to keep out the wind.

thin line of pink, the merest suggestion that light would be returning to the world in the near future.

A figure stumbled up behind me, and moved off into a hollow to the right, where he huddled down. He wore a purple down suit and I realised he must be one of the Uzbek team. As we waited for the rest of our team, the pink glow was slowly spreading. The pitch black rocks turned deep purple. The bed of cloud that lay below us to the east was tinged with salmon pink. I fumbled in the pocket of my down jacket for a camera. I was not about to try and muck around with the controls of my SLR. One Goretex mitten came off, shoved into the other armpit. The tiny compact camera was lifted, the button pressed, shoved back, and my hand was back in the mitten within the minute. Even so, I could feel the fingertips of my right hand tingling with cold.

As soon as the other three had joined us, we moved on. There was no conversation, only the sound of our boots crunching on the snow, the rustle of our jackets. We left the Uzbek waiting for his team-mates. A little further along, the snow wall that guarded our left side was breached for a few metres. I looked out, and stopped in amazement.

The north face of Everest makes for a climb of half a world. To the west you have the most spectacular views, 180 degrees of Himalaya and of Tibet. To the east you have nothing but the giant wall you are perched on. It blocks out the rest of the world as surely as if it did not exist at all. Now, suddenly, I was afforded a glimpse into that hidden world. The face fell away vertically just beyond my feet. Far below, out of sight in the murky distance, was the Kangshung Glacier. Most impressive, though, was the great falling sweep of the Kangshung Face, tinged rose colour. It was topped by the snowy line of the south-east ridge, set against an indigo sky. There lay the ridge we had climbed one year and 364 days previously. Behind it lurked the rocky crest of Lhotse. The sombre blue pyramid of Makalu stood clear and proud to the east. Once more the camera came out, very briefly, and popped its tiny flash across the blue void at the 4 000 metre high snow wall.

However, the new world to the east brought mixed blessings. With the magnificent views came a less welcome element - wind. It was a nasty, sneaky sort of wind, winding its way deviously round my body, before stealing down the collar of my jacket to attack the very heart of my body heat.

Slowly the copper-orange orb of the sun slid up out of the grey mantle of cloud, but its warmth did not reach me. The snow along the ridge turned golden before my feet, but it was the coldest gold I had ever seen. Before, the light of dawn had always brought both hope and warmth, signalling that the worst of the challenge was over. This dawn was different. The temperature dropped steadily as the wind rose.

My toes were still warm in the massive protection of my boots, but everywhere else my heat was retreating towards my core. My fingers were feeling numb, and so slow to move. My face had a strange, mask-like sensation, as if it no longer really belonged to me. Fumbling in the massive mittens, I pulled the down jacket hood close round my face. Determinedly wriggling my fingers, I walked on along the ridge.

Two strongly opposed forces were at work. My only weapon against the icy wind was my own body heat. As long as I kept moving, I felt tolerably comfortable. However, we were approaching

8 600 metres above sea level. Even with supplementary oxygen, the air was bitterly thin. I was wanting to stop every 10 or 15 paces to get my breath back. Each time of resting became a race between too little air and too little heat.

I was not enjoying the experience. However, I felt I could just tolerate it as long as nothing further went awry. The ultimate goal was worth the current discomfort. I retracted my vision, my expectations, to concentrate on nothing more than the next few steps.

The ridge was a steady, but relatively straightforward upward rise. Snow and rock were mixed. The path was bordered by a corniced snow wall on the left, hiding the drop. On the right it veered off steeply down broken rock slopes. Looking back, I could see the first line of sun catching the snow curve between Everest and Changste. Climbers at camp 1 would be waking up as their tents began to warm in the sun's heat. The glaciers of the central and east Rongbuk were still shrouded in dusky blue shadow.

We had spread out as we moved up the gentle incline. Each climber had his own rhythm, took his own time to stop to catch a breath. Ahead of me the ridge rose abruptly. A great heaped mass of rock squatted in our path. This was the First Step. With all the time that had been spent debating the Second Step, I was taken aback by the sheer height of the First. Although in a less precarious position than the Hillary Step on the south-east ridge, it looked like a tougher climb. Steeply angled rock slopes were sprinkled with snow. Jangbu was already several metres up it, with Pemba on his heels. Ci Luo followed closely behind. I would be next to tackle it.

Something off to the right caught my eye, blotches of colour. I looked across and saw, slightly down the rocky slope, a boulder. Just below it lay a body with a purple jacket and red boots. That surprised me. I had not realised that there would be bodies on the trail. But bodies I had seen before on this mountain. I looked back towards the Step.

Then the body moved.

12

Don't leave me

I stared at the body, blinking in disbelief. The area was in the shadow of the First Step, so the light was dull. The body lay about 10 metres from where I stood and was angled away from me, difficult to see in its entirety. It jerked again, a horrible movement, like a puppet being pulled savagely by its strings.

You think you are travelling in one direction in life, and then without reason and warning your path suddenly switches. You think you have one set of options and suddenly you have a whole new set to deal with, to deal with now. Everything you planned for, everything you anticipated has been summarily thrown away, without your participation or consent. A whole new reality is presented and you have to start making decisions about it immediately. We had been on a well-organised and so far successful trail towards the summit, worrying only about ourselves. Now a stranger lay across our path, demanding a totally different perspective on what would happen next.

The body moaned. That screwed the tension up to yet a higher level of urgency, of reality. Disbelief and horror circled through my head. Who on earth could it be? We had heard nothing of anyone in trouble. And what was I to do now? Lhakpa shouted down to me. I looked up at him and he waved at me to move on, to follow him up onto the Step. I looked back at the raggedly jerking figure.

Each team, or solo climber, did, or should, arrive at the foot of the mountain self-sufficient. That was self evident. Any one who turned up assuming they could borrow food or clothing or tentage off others would receive short shrift. Similarly, you could not climb yourself to a standstill and then expect other teams to risk their lives to save you.

Saving someone was not a straightforward exercise either. There was no one else to offer aid. There was no 911 to call, no Mountain Rescue to whom the problem could be handed over. We would not be able to walk away, feeling we had done our civic duty and that 'the experts'· were now in charge.

Anyone who becomes immobile on a mountain as large and as remote as Everest is probably going to die. That was self-evident, and had been reinforced by the experience of 1996. Then Makalu Gau, and Beck Weathers, both severely frost-bitten, deeply traumatised by their experience, had still to climb back down the mountain to 6 000 metres. Only from there could they be evacuated by helicopter, and that evacuation had been highly risky to the helicopter pilot. Scott Fischer, Yasuko Namba and Rob Hall had all collapsed, and had all died. On this side of the mountain, we would have to get the victim all the way back to base camp, before we could contemplate trying to find a helicopter. If he had to be carried, that would require the co-operation of a number of teams, dozens of people in manpower, at least three days of climbing.

Whoever it was on the rocks in front of me was so badly incapacitated that he had spent the night out on the mountain, rather than crawl down. Life lay in keeping moving, as it generated body heat, and with every metre of descent, moved you into thicker air. I suspected we had virtually no chance of saving the life of this man.

Should we then even try?

We stood to throw away an entire expedition, the money, the time, the thousands of vertical feet of physical and mental effort. We had sponsors who expected us to go for the summit. We had personal ambitions that pointed in the same direction. We were only 240 vertical metres from the summit, only four or five hours in climbing time. We were so close to fulfilling everything we had set out to do.

Should we throw it all away for some rescue attempt that was doomed before it even started? The body was lying in a ghastly inverted V. It looked as if the climber's spine might be broken. If he couldn't walk he was probably condemned. Why waste time, stand around getting cold and demoralised when the attempt was destined to be futile? Why not just turn away and climb on?

It is one thing to have these kind of debates in the comfort of the base camp mess tent, when the whole issue is theoretical. Or to analyse some famous incident that had happened to strangers and to wonder what you would have done in that situation. Nothing can prepare you for the real thing, for standing at 8 600 metres on the north-east ridge of Everest, at 5 a.m., in freezing cold, as you try to make moral choices.

This all ran through my head in the space of a few seconds. Time seemed to have slowed down, the way it sometimes does if you are in a car accident, or fall off a rock-climb. The ground seems to approach in slow motion. You have plenty of time to think about the fact that you are going to hit it, very hard, very soon.

But all the debates, the issues, the logical analysis was useless. I simply could not do it. I could not put the summit of a mountain ahead of a human life. I would not want to live with myself if I could. However hopeless this man's situation might be, I had to try.

I walked back to Ian, who was standing with Jangbu, watching Lhakpa climbing the First Step.

'That body's alive. I'm going to have a look.'

It took him a moment to understand what I was talking about.

'We can't just leave him,' I insisted.

He nodded and I stepped down from the trail and walked gingerly across the loose shale towards the body. He lay with his head towards me, long brown hair lying over his face. I thought perhaps he might be one of the Russian team. As I approached I saw he was lying with his harness clipped to a line of fixed rope. His stomach was uppermost, his head and legs dangling down on either side. I wondered if he might have fallen and broken his back.

The unstable rocky slope fell away steeply below him and I knelt down cautiously next to him. I brushed the hair away from his face.

'Don't leave me,' she said.

Her face had the waxy perfection of fairytale drawings of Sleeping Beauty. The skin was milky white, and totally smooth. It was a sign of severe frostbite but made her look like a porcelain doll. Her eyes stared up at me, unfocusing, pupils huge dark voids.

'Don't leave me,' she murmured again.

I felt physically sick. With her long, dark hair, she looked a bit like me. For a shocked second I felt as if I was glimpsing a possible future for myself. The fact that she was conscious both encouraged and appalled me. It might be possible to save her. Or we might yet have to leave her.

'I need to fetch the rest of my team,' I said to her. 'We have several people here. We will try and help you. I will come back, I promise.'

'Why are you doing this to me?' she asked. I looked at her in shock, and then realised that the question was not directed at me specifically, but seemed to be asked of life in general. Why, indeed? It was unanswerable.

Ian and Jangbu came back with me. Lhakpa, Pemba and Ci Luo, seeing the turn events had taken, began to descend towards us. Ian took over and I was happy to let him do so. The woman had no visible trauma injuries and her bizarre position turned out to be the result of complete muscular limpness. She was as helpless as a rag doll. It looked as if someone had clipped her harness to the end of a fixed rope, presumably so she would not slip down the slope, and had then left her to go for help. Next to her was an orange bottle of oxygen, of Russian make, and a mask. The bottle was empty.

While Ian and Jangbu pulled her straight, I collected her down gloves, which had been thrown to one side. Her jacket was over her shoulders but her arms were not in the sleeves. Our bodies can be bizarre in their reaction to trauma. A fairly common occurrence with severe hypothermia is a sensation of extreme warmth. The victim may start tearing off his clothing, and it looked as if she might have done this.

The men tried to replace her clothing. Her hands were swollen masses, her arms completely limp. She had no motor control. As Ian tried to get her arms into her jacket sleeves, she gave no resistance, no assistance. Jangbu was trying to give her some of the hot juice from his thermos.

They then each grabbed her under one arm and tried to pull her into a sitting position against the boulder. She was a complete dead-weight, unable to help in any way. The two strong men took several heaves to get her sitting, and then both were doubled over, gasping for breath. It put perspective on what it would take to try and actually carry her anywhere, let alone carry her or drag her for days down the mountain.

We had no capacity for giving her oxygen. Her mask would not fit our brand of oxygen bottles. We carried spare bottles but no spare masks. For the oxygen to have any effect on her condition, she would have to be put on it, at a high flow-rate, and stay on it for hours. A few whiffs would have no effect. It would mean one of us had to go off oxygen permanently, to give her a mask, and that we would run through all our spare supplies very quickly. Until we established that we had a real chance of saving her, the risk this involved was too great.

We had no means of communication with the outside world. Pemba tried calling base camp, but their set was not switched on. They were happily asleep in warm sleeping bags, with no idea we

Fran and Serguei Arsentiev walking towards Ian as they make their way back down to ABC.

were so high on the mountain. Last they had heard, we were to stay at camp 3, and would call them at 9 a.m. That was still four hours away.

I found one crampon lying near her, black crampons. Scratched on the inside of one of them was 'Frankie'. Frankie? I had not known who she was. I had wondered if she might be one of the French climbers on the mountain. There were some women among their team. Ian was attempting to talk to her. So far she said only the two sentences she had said already to me: 'don't leave me' and 'why are you doing this to me?' Now, she added one more.

'I am an American. I am an American.'

American? But the American team was below us. Their first wave of climbers had camped at 7 900 metres the day we moved up to camp 3. They were a full day behind us. My mind wandered back to the sight I had seen the day before, two tiny figures at the foot of the First Step, one still, one moving around.

Could she be Fran? Could she possibly be the bubbly American woman who had sat in our ABC kitchen tent that one night, passing the hours while she waited for her husband, the Russian climber, Serguei. It might make sense. She and Serguei were climbing as a twosome. They had no Sherpas, no oxygen. They would not be in radio contact with other people on the mountain. That did not explain how she came to have an oxygen bottle lying next to her. Nor did it explain where he had gone. I stared over Ian's shoulder at her face. She looked far younger that I remembered Fran as being, but that was probably the effect of the frostbite. I couldn't be sure.

Three Uzbek climbers were approaching us.

'Will you help us?' I asked. 'This woman is dying. We might be able to carry her down. Would you help?'

The leader of the three looked down at me reluctantly. His voice was muffled behind his oxygen mask.

'We tried to help yesterday. We left her with oxygen. She is too far gone to help.'

His words made little sense to me. He began to speak into his radio, presumably talking to his base camp. However, they did stay, watching Ian and Jangbu to see what decision they would reach.

Ian had her by both shoulders and was speaking directly at her, his face only inches from hers.

'You have to help us. If you can help us, we can try and move you back down the mountain. If you don't, you are going to die.'

He was staring intently into her face, looking for some reaction, any reaction, to his words. There was nothing.

'You are an American. Americans fight. If you're going to live you must fight.'

It was becoming clear that although she was aware that we were there, she was not mentally coherent. She did not understand what was said to her, and she herself could only say her three phrases. It was difficult to know what was left in her head.

As Ian continued to try and get some reaction from her, I noticed her other crampon lying a few feet below us. I took a tentative step down the slope to try and retrieve it, and immediately thought better of the plan. The slope was covered in loose rock shards, like a million smashed dinner plates. They were slipping away under my feet, rolling down the slope towards the Rongbuk glacier, which lay 4 300 metres below us. It was like trying to move across ball bearings. I could see how a climber, having once lost his balance, would not be able to stop the downward momentum. Was that what had happened to Serguei?

Ian and Jangbu had been trying to pull her into an upright position. Ian's thought was that if she could take some of her weight on her feet, even if she could not actually walk, it might be possible to move her down the mountain with a climber at each shoulder. However, her legs simply crumpled under her weight, as useless as strands of spaghetti.

We were all in the shadow of the First Step. The Step, however, did not block the wind, which still wound itself round us. We had been with Fran for nearly an hour, standing still in temperatures of around -30°C. Perched perilously on the steep, unstable slope,

I could not even stamp my feet for warmth. I was beginning to feel deeply, profoundly cold. My fingers were almost totally numb. Orders from my brain for them to wriggle met with a lacklustre response, a minuscule, slow-motion movement. I had full body shivers and my teeth were chattering behind my oxygen mask.

The strangest sensation, though, came from my chest cavity. There were 'things' floating inside it, things that were cold. In normal life I had never made conscious contact with the organs that lived in my chest, whose smooth functioning kept my body alive. Now they felt like grey lumps, discrete entities, and cold ones. The cold was attacking the very heart of my body core. It was time to start moving.

The decision to leave her came upon us without much discussion. The Uzbek climbers and Lhakpa had long been of that opinion. What hope I had had, had faded in the face of her incoherence, her physical incapacity. Now Ian and Jangbu straightened up and turned away from her. She had stopped talking, and seemed to have sunk into unconsciousness.

'What do you want to do?' Ian said to me.

'I want to go down. Will you come with me?' I said.

The thought of going on was intolerable. I had lost the will to summit. Besides the physical drain of the cold, which made thoughts of trying to climb the First Step unpleasant, I was emotionally

❋ *Camp 1 sheltering from the west wind behind the snow cliff. The Changste ridge is visible beyond it.*

❋❋ *Looking past the South African camp 1 to the snowy north ridge that leads to camp 2. The north face stretches out to the right.*

❋❋❋ *Ian on the north ridge, climbing up from camp 1. The tiny dots of the tents are visible below him.*

❋❋❋❋ *Camp 2, looking west towards Cho Oyu.*

shattered. I had never encountered anything like this. I had passed bodies, I had had friends not come back, but I had never watched anyone die. Nor had I had to decide to leave them.

It was all that much harder for me because she was female. It is not that I thought women immune to the risk, but it was such a male dominated environment. Everywhere you turned, everyone you talked to was male.

I climb because I enjoy it. I climb for the pleasure of the activity, of the surroundings. There was no pleasure left. I wanted to be down, to be off the mountain, to have both feet on flat ground. I could not push Fran to one side, mentally, and find again my drive for the summit.

'Yes, I'll come down,' said Ian. I had assumed he felt the same way I did, and that if he didn't, he would say so. Asking for company was a reflex action, out of my mouth before I knew what I was saying. Had he said he wanted to go on, I would have readily accepted that. I did not expect him, or the Sherpas, to be as traumatised by the situation as I felt. They had all seen more of such things. I did not realise then that he in fact wanted to go on, but put that aside to accompany me back down.

Ian then asked the Sherpas what they wanted to do, encouraging them to go on if they wished. They had a brief discussion. Pemba

❄❄❄❄ Ci Luo climbing up the rock section of the north ridge. The site of ABC is visible below him.

❄❄❄ Jangbu moving diagonally up the north face. The summit pyramid of Everest looms in the distance.

❄❄ Ian climbs up the last snow slopes before camp 3. The central Rongbuk glacier lies three kilometres below him.

❄ Pemba looks out from a camp 3 tent, with the plains of Tibet lit by the setting sun.

decided to go down. It was the decision of a leader. Although they were all superb climbers, Pemba was first among equals. It was a brave choice. He had the least summits of the three, and was the only one who had not climbed the mountain from the north. A summit from the north would have made a difference professionally. But he felt his responsibilities lay elsewhere.

That left Lhakpa and Jangbu. The two brothers looked at each other. Lhakpa had climbed Everest four times already. Jangbu had climbed it twice. Both had climbed it from the north before. To reach the summit this time would make little difference to their professional reputations, no difference to their expedition wages.

'We go to the summit' said Lhakpa.

I had always wondered why the Sherpas climbed. The effort was enormous, the risks obvious. Yes, it was a highly paid job by Nepalese standards, but I had always wondered if they enjoyed the experience, if they felt the lure of the challenge. Now it seemed the mountain still called to them, despite multiple previous ascents.

Lhakpa and Jangbu moved towards the Step. Ci Luo and three Uzbek climbers followed them. I turned away, retracing my footsteps back along the ridge. Ian and Pemba followed. Fran sat, half-slumped against the boulder. She seemed thankfully oblivious of our leaving.

The descent was a haze of cold, disappointment, and emotional exhaustion. We moved slowly and made camp 3 around 9.30 a.m. I dumped my rucksack by the tent door and crawled into it. Nawang, who had stayed at camp 3, brewed up hot juice. Ian pulled out the radio and called base camp. They were oblivious of all the drama and he filled them in. He said we thought the woman to be the American, Fran, but were not sure, and asked Jan to try and find out where other teams thought Fran and Serguei to be. Jan had one question for me. The television director's mind was already at work. Had I shot any video footage?

'No bloody way!'

Practically I had been too cold to try and operate any of my cameras, but it affected me more deeply than that. I had a purely

258

instinctive revulsion to recording her misery for our gain. If she was the person we thought she was, she wasn't just a sensational death high on a mountain. She was the bouncy woman who had drunk coffee in our kitchen tent at ABC. She was the mother to a son, still at school. His last memory of her was presumably an affectionate good-bye at the airport. Did I really want to be responsible for replacing that with a picture of her as helpless, incoherent, dying slowly and horribly on the mountain slopes? Within our team we had agreed to record whatever happened, and then sort out afterwards what we would use in any documentaries that were made. But she was not part of that agreement. She had no say as to how our material would be used. I had found watching her to be deeply traumatic. I didn't want that turned into a twisted thrill for armchair viewers.

Shortly after Ian had signed off from Jan, an excited voice came spurting over the radio, chattering at a million miles an hour. It was Lhakpa. I was surprised by the intense excitement. They had done it before, after all.

'Summit, summit! South Africa on top,' he shouted happily.

Lhakpa, Jangbu and Ci Luo had reached the summit at 10 a.m. They were a few minutes behind the Uzbek climbers. With Ci Luo taking the photographs, they had even remembered to fly our sponsors' logos, and the Nepalese and South African flags.

The greatest pleasure of the moment for me, apart from their achievement, was their confidence of being members of the team. It didn't matter to them what passports they carried. They were part of the South African team and the expedition had reached the top. It was a sweet ending to the trauma of the morning. I felt that something good had emerged from all that had happened.

Three days later we were back at base camp. Already the razor-edge of the trauma was fading, and I was beginning to wonder if I should not have pushed on for the summit after we had decided to leave Fran. All I needed to do, though, was to re-live the feelings of that hour with her at 8 600 metres to know exactly why I had turned back.

The brothers Jangbu (left)
and Lhakpa on the
summit, 24 May.
Ci Luo took the
photograph.

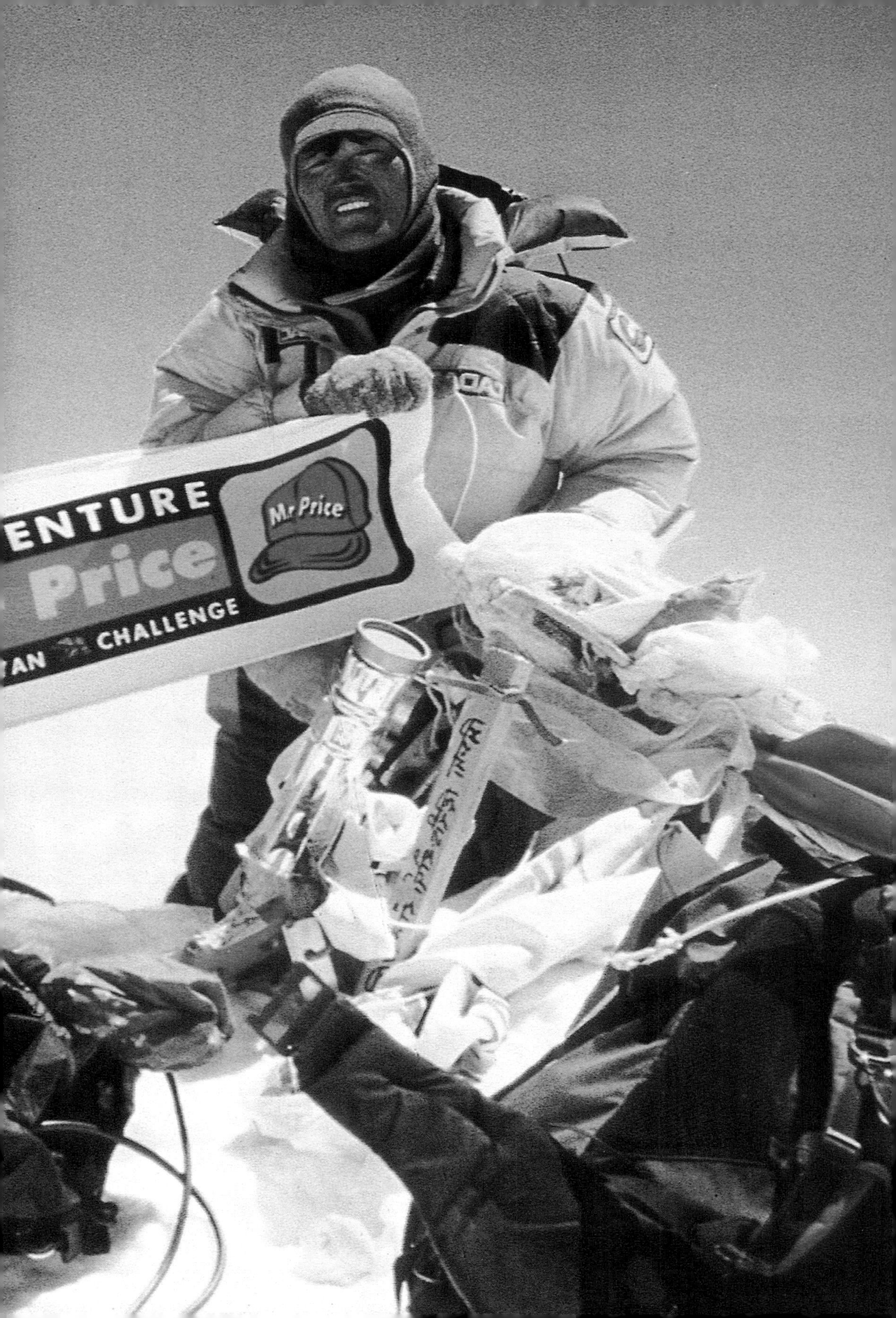
ENTURE
Price
Mr Price
CHALLENGE

Word had spread fast across the mountain. As I descended from camp 3 I passed first the Americans, then Russell, then Mark Jennings. Everyone knew what had happened and offered their commiserations. They all seemed confident the woman was Fran, and so she turned out to be. She was alive when Lhakpa and Jangbu had passed her on their way down, but unconscious. She was dead when the other teams came upon her the following morning. They all went on to summit.

Fate feeds us a fickle line. If we had gone for the summit one day later, she would have been dead and we would have climbed on. If we had left camp 3 just two hours earlier, we would have passed her in the dark, not seeing her until we were descending. If we had left a day earlier, we would have found her in a better state and might have been able to save her. All we could do was live with the hand that fate had dealt us.

Slowly we pieced together some of the story of what had happened to her and Serguei. Members of the Russian expedition had, after two unsuccessful attempts, reached the summit on the 18th and 21st. The Arsentievs were the only members to go for the summit on the 22nd, and the rest of team had retreated back down the mountain. The couple had already spent one night at 8 300 metres, without oxygen. They had no radios with them. They had left top camp about 10.45 p.m. A Japanese climber, a Sherpa and an Uzbek also climbed to the summit that day. The Uzbek had passed the couple climbing up when he descended. He had advised them to turn back as it was too late in the day. They had replied that they were prepared to bivouac and had climbed on. They were seen on the summit from base camp through binoculars around 4 p.m. They had been climbing for over 17 hours. The next day five Uzbek climbers reached the summit. Around 7 a.m., on their way up, they had passed Serguei on his way down to top camp. He had not asked them for help. A little later they had found Fran at the First Step in bad shape, standing motionless and unable to speak. Two of them had given her oxygen and had made her sit down. After an hour, having got no response from her, they had climbed on. Although they had radios, they had not notified any-one else.

Serguei reached top camp around 8 a.m. He left again, on his own, to climb back to her in the afternoon, carrying oxygen, medicine and drink. He was never seen again and his body has yet to be found.

When we found Fran she had been at an altitude of over 8 000 metres without oxygen for more than four days. It was 37 hours since she had reached the summit and she had spent two nights out above 8 600 metres. That she was still alive was a miracle.

We obtained information in bits and pieces, in discussion with various Uzbek and Russian climbers. The information raised as many questions as it answered. Who exactly I had seen below the First Step I will never know. Why Serguei did not make more effort to get other climbers involved we will never know. On his own he had no chance of getting her down to safety. Could the Uzbeks perhaps have done more? All I know is that it is incredibly easy to point fingers with hindsight, but far harder to deal with a situation as it occurs.

The end of the expedition was something of an emotional roller-coaster. The last few days of the season were calm and clear. From the comfort of base camp the mountain looked serene, benign. However, it continued to take its toll on human life. As I had descended from camp 3 I had passed Mark Jennings on his way up to the top camp. I had found him taking a rest, lying back beneath a rock cliff, admiring the view. He was on oxygen, and seemed strong enough. The next day he was one of 10 people to reach the summit. Among them were Russell, Sumio and one of the Americans. Mark returned to sleep at top camp. The following day he left his Sherpa packing up his tent and began to go down, still on oxygen. His Sherpa found him a little later, sitting on a snow slope some hundred metres below the camp, dead.

On the same day a New Zealand climber, Roger Buick, was discovered on his way up from camp 1 to camp 2, at about 7 400 metres, also sitting hunched over the fixed rope, also dead. There

Cathy on the descent from the top camp.

were no explanations for either death. Their bodies had simply given up on them.

Why these two men should have had their bodies pack up on them so easily, when Fran was able to hold on for so long, with so little air and warmth, is a puzzle. The bodies we inhabit are wonderful creations, but they are also strange to us. Sometimes we are capable of such tenacity in the face of intense suffering, yet sometimes we snuff out as easily as a candle.

The disappointment of neither Ian nor I reaching the summit sat heavily over our group. In 1996 we had fought hard, had fought on, and had succeeded. This time we learnt that the best laid plans could come to nothing in the mountains. We issued a press release to South Africa, explaining what had happened and why we had turned back. However, we did not release Fran's name, as we could not ascertain whether or not her next of kin in the USA had been informed. The Star newspaper quickly found an ill-wisher to quote, saying the so-called female victim did not exist, and that she was simply an excuse we had created to justify our failure to summit.

To have the heart-rending end to Fran's life reduced to a fabricated excuse for my 'failure' floored me. To be capable of assuming that someone would lie about such horrible events, events that I now felt to be burnt into my brain, took a peculiarly twisted mind. Once all the facts had emerged, several days later, and Fran and Serguei's deaths had been reported internationally, it was old news in South Africa. Something newly shocking was having its 15 minutes of fame. Depressed and disillusioned, I tried to find sense in this expedition.

In seeking an explanation for what had happened to Fran and Serguei, people were, as ever, casting around for somebody to blame. Nothing can happen without someone being held accountable for it. There are no right answers to questions of risk and responsibility. There is no set line, dividing the acceptable from the suicidal. We each create a line for ourselves.

To some people climbing Everest using oxygen is unsporting, an indication you are not good enough for the challenge. To others to climb it without is simply stupid, a ridiculous risk. We are always searching for ways to quantify risk, searching for 'experts' and 'arbiters' who will create rules, who will decide what is or is not acceptable. In taking on a challenge like Everest, I assess the danger and do what I can to minimise it. I set limits that I do not go beyond. Climbing well above 8000 metres without supplementary oxygen is one risk I choose not to take. Fran and Serguei took it. For them their personal balance of risk and reward was different. And I do not believe that, because I would not do it myself, I am in any position to condemn their choice, whether or not it proved to be the right one.

If they had lived, their ascent would have been a superb achievement. Fran would have been only the second (arguably the third) woman to have climbed the world's highest peak without oxygen. But they died. What becomes of the achievement then? And who is to blame for it all? Perhaps blame is not a relevant issue. They made their choices and those choices didn't work out as planned.

Mark climbed with oxygen. He was just another one of the 117 people who reached the summit that season. No particular hero back home, except in his personal circle. His choice didn't work out either. His wife and children had to pay the price for that. But what does it mean to the rest of us, except to serve as a warning that this is a serious business? There are no 'yak routes' on the world's great mountains.

As human beings we have a complex relationship with death. We love to discuss it, circling around its perimeter, but we are not good at facing up to its realities. That each of us, and everyone we know, will die, is the only complete certainty of our existence. We make choices throughout our lives, balancing out quality and quantity of existence. Why do we venture into the mountains, Ian, myself, Serguei, Fran? Presumably we find there something life-affirming, something that gives us far more than we risk in the venture.

Within a group of climbers who have chosen to tackle a challenge on the level of Everest, no one can be held accountable for the others. Each step higher is a personal choice and a personal responsibility. We need to be very clear about that before we venture out. If I walk on the narrow edges of life, I do it because I choose to. If that edge breaks under me, I accept that as a consequence of my choice. I cannot blame others for what happens. Nor do I expect that those who accompany me on that edge, if they do, should carry blame for my decisions.

'Why are you doing this to me?' Fran had asked of an indifferent universe. I have no idea why she should have had to suffer on such a level before she died. Yet, when I hear of an acquaintance of my age, 30, dying of cancer, I'd take Fran's choice, to die in the places I love, doing what I find most fulfilling. Life does not go easy on us just because we choose to play it safe.

Ian and I did interviews with Jan about what had happened, but we did them separately. Later I sat in the comms tent, watching his interview on the monitor. I had not realised how badly he had wanted to go on to the summit, and felt rather guilty about having got in the way of that. Still, it had been his choice. What was more important to me was what he said next.

'What keeps you focused as a climbing team is the trust between the two partners. When that trust is broken down, that team will almost certainly disintegrate. The mountain will always be here, but it's not easy to find climbing partners. The loyalty and trust is more important. I'd rather have a climbing partner and a long list of future projects.'

Everything we had experienced on Everest had drawn us together. The trust we were building had been tested harshly by the fires of experience and it had come through unscathed. We might walk away from the mountain, but at least we walked away together.

The voyage of Everest 1998 had taken some unexpected directions, but nevertheless was overall hugely enjoyable. Up until the moment I saw Fran at the foot of the First Step, it had been a great expedition. The north side was far more attractive to me than the south. Perhaps it was the sheer magnificence of the north face or the incredible exposure of the climbing, the breathtaking situations of the camps, the technical challenge of the rock-climbing. Already I was wondering whether I might, someday, get the chance to return to the north side, to try and finish the climb.

Ian felt the same attraction to the route. Quite how we were going to find the time, and the money, to do a third Everest expedition, we had no idea.

But the seed had been planted.

13

One step at a time

The Tibetans believe that mountains rest lightly on the earth and that, if they are not pegged down, by chortens or prayer poles, they are liable to fly off. It seems a fantastic theory for something as heavily grounded as the pyramid of Everest, with its many thousands of square tons of rock. But the Tibetans do not get bogged down by the narrow-minded geophysics of the situation. One has only to see a mountain peak floating above a sun-lit cloud to realise they are indeed creatures of myth, and of wonder. The spirit of the mountains surpasses all their physical realities.

Right now it seemed as if Everest had indeed taken wings and vanished. We had been driving across the Tibetan plateau for hours and not a glimpse. Even crossing the great Pang La pass, from where, a year ago, we had first seen Everest's majestic pyramid bisecting the horizon, there was nothing. A dusty haze hung in the air, the result of a winter and a spring with very little snowfall. Of mountains there was no sign. As we drove through the convoluted maze of foothills, I had a bizarre vision of the inhabitants of some remote tropical island looking up to see a massive rock pyramid flying towards them, in search of a spot for its summer holiday.

We finally turned the steep corner into the Rongbuk valley. The valley ended abruptly - a four kilometre high wall of rock and ice.

Everest was back.

Everest was back, and so were we. Once more we were going to be crawling up her skirts, hoping to teeter briefly on her crown without disturbing her - Chomolungma, mother goddess of the world. Despite all the media hype, no one 'conquers' a mountain like Everest. We just hoped to trespass on her mighty slopes long enough to nip up to the summit and back before she shook us off like unwanted fleas.

When passing through Kathmandu I had filled Elizabeth Hawley in on the details of our expedition. She is a Nepalese institution, and has kept records of Himalayan expeditions since time immemorial. She had finally given up on mountains such as Shishapangma and Cho Oyu, which dozens of expeditions now attempt each year, but she was hanging on grimly with Everest, looking besieged by the sheer volume of information she had to process. She interviewed each expedition on its way in to the mountain, and again on its return.

As she meticulously wrote down our expedition details, she had commented that maybe the following year I would finally come to do something different, 'get over the Everest obsession'. We were back to finish off the north ridge of Everest. This expedition was small, and totally focused. Ian and I were joined by Pemba and Jangbu, with Phuri in support. That was it. The sole aim was to get ourselves to the summit. Was it obsession? I wondered about that but decided it was not. It was the final bow to a magnificent mountain.

We had spent the rest of the year of 1998 in South Africa working on other things. We had made no firm decision about a return to finish the north ridge of Everest. Only early in 1999, when we had to make a final commitment to getting a permit, if we wanted one, did we seriously face up to the issue. There was a certain 'oh, what the hell, why not?' feeling to our decision to try one last time. I was certain that if we did not succeed this time, I would not be coming back.

However, in 1998 I had simply had no idea if I was capable of climbing Everest's north side. Now, though, I thought I could, if weather, health and conditions allowed. Those were some big ifs but it seemed worth a try. We still needed to pay for all this. We cut the expedition budget right down and started looking for money. Some was personal money, some was raised from companies, some came from a group of trekkers we organised to come and visit us at base camp. It was a close run thing, and there was more than one time when I thought that it simply wouldn't happen. As it was we ended up coming out to Tibet nearly a month later than all the major Everest expeditions.

This time, though, I was intimately involved in the chasing of finance. I called company after company, made polite noises when they said no, and then phoned some more. I went on radio looking for trekking clients, talked prospective candidates through all the details, gave slide shows, and waited to see if they would finally sign a cheque. By the time we had finally accumulated enough to go, I felt this was my expedition in a way neither of the previous two had been.

We set up our base camp in the same spot that we had had the year before. This time Padam would be running base camp, with Mangal back to help with the trek group. Our chorten was still standing on the great boulder above our camp. Once our tents were in place and the prayer flags strung out from the chorten, it was almost as if we had never left.

The mountain dominated everything, as ever. This year, though, it was particularly stark. There had been very little snowfall, right through winter and spring. The north face was a massive rock wall.

On our east side was Russell Brice, back with a new group of clients. On our west were other friends of 1998, Wilfred Studer and his wife Sylvia. Wilfred was an Austrian mountain guide. The first thing one noticed about him was that this big man had tiny feet. He had lost all his toes to frostbite. Now, for his holidays, he and Sylvia were attempting Everest without oxygen.

'An Austrian, Peter Habler, was one the first two men to climb Everest without oxygen,' he explained. 'In Austria, to have climbed

Jangbu (right) sneaks a peek at Pemba's hand during a base camp card game.

Everest with oxygen is not to have climbed it at all.'

It was their third attempt. In 1998 Wilfred had turned back at the top of the Second Step, deciding that it was too cold for him to risk continuing. I had enormous respect for a man who could be that close to his goal and have the strength of will to turn away from it. Wilfred had no pretensions about his considerable abilities. He had a ready smile and a humorous outlook on life and climbing. He proved good company.

The first few days, and the first explorations up the glacier towards ABC, were uncomfortable, as ever. My body took time to get used to sleeping on the ground, to walking hour after hour, to carrying loads. But the old ways soon reasserted themselves. Lying in our tent at night, totally encased in a cocoon of down, falling asleep snuggled up against Ian, I could imagine no better place to be.

On 8 May we were resting at base camp, watching the summit ridge through Wilfred's telescope. Three tiny figures were crawling up the final snow slope to the summit. The weather was perfect, clear and warm. They were from the Ukrainian team and would be the first climbers of the season to summit. Every team on the mountain would have swopped places with them just then.

But the mountain is fickle, and the weather seems to be less stable in the earlier weeks of the season. During the afternoon the group of trekkers arrived to spend some days with us at base camp and above. The wind was howling, snow was falling. They huddled into our mess tent, bitterly cold, depleted by the new altitude, watching the tent fabric flap and shudder. They looked out across the barren, stony wastes towards a mountain that had long since disappeared in cloud. I could see from the horror in their eyes that they would hardly agree with me on the beauties of base camp.

They were agog for the latest news from us. While in Lhasa they had found a report on the internet that on 1 May an American team had found the body of George Mallory, the British mountaineer last seen making his way towards the summit in 1924. Now 75 years later, his body was apparently almost perfectly preserved. There was no sign of his camera and so no concrete proof of whether he had reached the summit before his death, or not. Speculation was raging.

We had no idea all of this had happened. Communication was limited. When everyone was crowded together in a camp like ABC news passed round quite quickly. But once climbers moved away they could disappear for days without other teams knowing what was happening. Each team assumed themselves and others to be self-sufficient. We were one of the few teams still at base camp, so those who were watching the internet knew far more of what was happening on the mountain than we did.

However, the next morning news was travelling faster. We heard that the three Ukrainians had reached the summit around 2 p.m. However, they had battled on the descent, climbing in poor weather, struggling to find the right route. Vladislav Terzyal was safely back at top camp by 9 p.m. Vasili Kopytko disappeared, and was presumed to have fallen. Vladimir Gorbach was stranded above top camp, badly frost-bitten, and out of radio contact. Only their doctor was at ABC, their leader was at base camp. Russell went down to see the doctor, taking a spare battery to power their radios, and began co-ordination of a rescue.

The drama played itself out over the next few days as I took a group of our trekkers up the east Rongbuk glacier. We had several couples in the group. Although it was the men who all talked big back in South Africa, in most cases they were now languishing at base camp, felled by altitude, while the women had quietly and successfully made their way to the higher camp.

The Ukrainians had two more waves of climbers, at 7 800 metres and at 7 000 metres, waiting to move towards the summit. They climbed up the mountain, and met Vladislav struggling down with Vladimir. All his toes were frost-bitten, as were all the fingers of his left hand and his nose. The Sherpas of another expedition dumped the loads they were carrying and helped to carry Vladimir down to camp 1. The rescue took all day, reaching camp 1 around 7 p.m. Luckily, he was a little man, only 65 kilograms, and they simply took turns to piggy-back him down.

In the meantime, climbers from the American team, a few others and about fifteen Sherpas had climbed up to camp 1 with a stretcher. Pemba and Jangbu were among the Sherpa group. The victim was then lowered down the steep ice slopes through the night, reaching ABC around 2 a.m. There Russell had turned his camp into a field hospital and rescue kitchen. Vladimir was unconscious on arrival and was put on a drip. They worked on him for five hours, until dawn. He remained at ABC for the remainder of that day, while a group of yak herders came up from base camp for the next carry, down 22 kilometres of glacier back to base camp.

The following day I was up at 6 000 metres, with the hardiest of the trek group. We walked along the tongue of moraine, which ran between two seas of ice pinnacles. The pinnacles rose 20 or 30 feet above us, an angry sea frozen mid-storm. Their surfaces were pure white, dusted by snow as powdery as icing sugar. In the cracks that led into their icy hearts, the white turned to pale blue and, where the ice was most compressed, deep lapis lazuli.

The trekkers were running all over, passing round cameras and posing by the most extravagant ice pinnacles they could find. Their vision broadened mine. I became too caught up in the climb, focused always on the next horizon. They, without that single-minded concentration, looked laterally, discovering scenes to which I was blinkered.

A little black snake moved towards us in the distance. It slowly resolved itself into a line of 12 people, walking slowly. It was the Ukrainian rescue party. Vladimir was now being carried by the yak herders, piggy-back in a makeshift chair. They disappeared from view and then reappeared virtually on top of us, stopping next to us to give the injured man a drink. His nose was pitch-black, his hands were wrapped up in down gloves, his eyes were glazed and exhausted. But he would survive.

Memorials to climbers killed on Everest.

Despite being part of a strong and well-organised team himself, it had taken the efforts of dozens of people from his own and other expeditions to get him down to the safety of base camp. He still had to spend a night at base camp before he could be driven out over the rough dirt roads and across the plains of Tibet to a medical facility. He had to live through four days of whatever medical treatment his and other expeditions could provide before his ordeal was over. Rescue is possible from high on Everest, but it requires a victim who will survive the days it takes to get him or her down, and it requires the efforts of many people, generally from other teams. Other teams, in helping, are often using up their supplies, particularly of oxygen. They are also using up their physical strength. Helping may well mean the end of their own summit hopes.

Despite all this, most climbers and most teams do all they can to assist. Accusations are thrown around about climbers not helping, mostly by people thousands of miles from the event itself. People fail to realise that in a world this remote, climbers may well be beyond what it takes to save them. If they have hours left, rather than days, all the well-meant intention in the world is not going to make a difference.

Then we received much better news. Lhakpa had elected to climb with a big commercial expedition on the south. He was the team sirdar, a very prestigious post. On May 12 Pemba and Jangbu were sitting on the north col as Lhakpa reached the summit of Everest, for his sixth time. They were able talk to him on radio, and patched him through to us at base camp. The moment was particularly poignant for the brothers Lhakpa and Jangbu because with Lhakpa on the summit was their younger brother. It was his first big expedition and he had reached the top of the world. The excitement of this summit fired up both the Sherpas and ourselves. As soon as the trek group had left, we readied ourselves to move up the mountain.

I walked back and forwards in front of our kitchen tent, restless, anxious, and increasingly angry. We were due to walk from base camp to ABC, a long, stiff hike. We had too much kit to carry. I was not fully acclimatised to ABC yet. Ian had developed yet another chest infection and I was worried about what that meant for the expedition. I wasn't sure I would make it to ABC in one day.

It was 8.30 a.m. We were supposed to have left at 8 a.m. Ian had barely begun to pack. I began to fume. We rubbed through on most things, but the time-keeping still drove me crazy. I walked over to ask when he thought he would be ready. What was meant to be an innocent question triggered a short, nasty row. I called him lazy and he called me selfish. After trading insults for a few minutes we stopped talking to each other altogether.

An unpleasant start stretched into an unpleasant day. I was passing transit camp around midday, feeling tired, over-loaded and sorry for myself. It began to snow heavily and I decided enough was enough, and dived for shelter in Russell's transit tent. Ian made a similar decision about half an hour later. We ignored each other.

The storm passed, although snow continued to fall lightly, and the long afternoon hours were crawling by. I picked up my camera and headed outside to look around. In the middle of the worst of times, the mountain once again created a moment of magic.

A few hours previously it had been a world of rock, but now a lace blanket of snow covered the ground. The big rocks still resisted, melting the snow as it landed and glistening black and wet in the white world. Clouds filled up the valley, with high peaks making the occasional eerie appearance, floating above the mist.

The next day I moved into new territory, for this expedition at least, over 6 000 metres. Tired, and miserable from the ongoing stand-off with Ian, I turned to music to disguise the effort of the climb. When I heard heavy panting coming from somewhere when the tape ended, it took a moment to realise it was my own breathing. I was passed by various French climbers going down. They had arrived, heavy with attitude, to climb Everest without oxygen. They were 'real' mountaineers. Having reached 7 900 metres, they had thought better of the whole thing and were headed home.

Then I met up with Mangal, who was coming down from ABC with a flask of hot coffee. He poured me a cup, and then continued on down to meet Ian, who was, to my malicious relief, well behind me. The hot, sweet coffee felt like a blessing as it poured down my parched throat. However, my altitude-troubled stomach was less convinced. I had not eaten all day and my stomach was in no mood to have to deal with the sugary liquid. An unhappy bubbling feeling was rising.

Through my headphones came the dulcet sounds of Vivaldi's Four Seasons. They discreetly masked the retching as I threw the coffee up all over the icy rocks. It was not a good day.

It was not a good day high on the mountain either. The previous day two Americans from the Mallory search team had topped out. Now, in the afternoon, five members from two expeditions, Belgian and Polish, were reaching the summit. Sporadically cheers would go up from their camps. But at dinner I gathered three climbers were not yet back at top camp.

That night I lay in the darkness of the tent, unable to sleep from altitude. Bored with my selection of music, I stared into the blackness of the night. There were no lights to be turned on, nothing to do, no-one to talk to. Inside the tent it was -10°C, so it was not even an option to get out of my sleeping bag .

Sometimes I wondered why I did this to myself. I could be living comfortably back in my house in Johannesburg, curled up under the duvet with my cat. Why put up with the discomfort and the risk? I had already climbed Everest. And climbing any mountain was not the most logical activity in the world, when you really thought about it. You just ended up back where you started - at the bottom.

My watch inched past 2 a.m. I could tell that Ian was also unable to sleep. We were together physically, separated by a million miles emotionally. I was simply miserable. I dislike fights, my temper tending to cool off almost as quickly as it flares up. Ian takes longer to get angry and longer again to get over it.

An arm reached across the darkness, bumping into my face.

I took that as an invitation to reconcile, and curled myself round it. The cold of the night was replaced by warmth and happiness. The dawn brought a rose-pink hue to the slopes of Everest, while golden clouds rose over the north col. The deep blue shadow of the valley floor was slowly dispelled by the sun's light. I watched from the door of our tent and I remembered why I did this.

That night we had dinner with Russell's team in his camp. Russell's expeditions were superbly organised, and most luxurious. I was particularly taken with the special sachets of chocolate powder for sprinkling on top of the cappuccino. His dining tent had a proper table, with chairs. We found it laid with tablecloth and cutlery. One of Russell's clients, Helge Hengge, had cooked up a cheese fondue, with freshly baked bread. Helge, a slim blonde German, was friendly and uninhibited. She had already turned the heads of all of Russell's Sherpa team.

The discussion obviously opened with events on the mountain. We already knew that Joao Garcia, a Portuguese member on the Belgian team, was frost-bitten but on his way down. The Polish leader, Ryszard Pawlowski, had survived a night out on the ridge and was also on his way down, with slight frostbite. Tadeusz Kudelski, a member of the Polish team, had disappeared. The Belgian leader, Pascal Debrouwer, was also missing. Now Russell had the latest news. In the mid-afternoon, members of the Italian team had seen a climber fall from the ridge. It was thought to be Pascal. We had also heard that Michael Matthews, a member of the OTT expedition that Lhakpa was on had disappeared on the descent from the summit on the south side.

Russell was gloomy. Deaths on commercial expeditions always raised more stink than those on private ones, and rebounded on other commercial operators. The image of rich novices buying their way up Everest had lodged firmly in the mind of the public after the events of 1996. None of the facts stuck: that most deaths were experienced climbers, that the percentage of deaths had not risen in all the years climbers had attempted Everest, that there was no guarantee that climbers on private expeditions were more experienced or those on commercial ones less so. Commercial clients were as often sponsored as private expeditions were. Everyone had to find the money somewhere.

Guiding was a tradition as old as mountaineering itself and making use of people expert in local conditions makes a lot of sense. Russell and his Sherpa group had the best organisation and the greatest experience of any team on the mountain. The result was that he inevitably ended up organising rescues for other expeditions.

Perhaps what had taken many people by surprise was the way, in the 1990s, the number of people attempting Everest had expanded, and therefore the number who reached the top had increased. Previous summit climbers seemed to get huffy about it mostly because it made their personal ascents look rather less awesome. The way the two most popular routes on Everest are climbed has changed. The sheer number of people climbing makes it easier for all concerned, as work can be shared. However, as we saw with Fran in 1998, it does bring other problems. Modern equipment helps, as does the volume of knowledge now available about the mountain. What has not changed is the cold, the weather, the altitude, the climbing. For those for whom that is not enough, there are a dozen other routes up Everest, each difficult, even more remote, mostly ignored. For any that hanker after an old-fashioned challenge, it is there for the trying.

On 19 May Ian and I set out for an acclimatisation climb to camp 1. The 1999 route came as something of a shock. The previous year, and for some years before that, it had followed a pleasant curve, sweeping up to the right, before traversing back above a large ice cliff to the camp site. This year the safety line ran straight up from the bottom, disappearing into the distance above us, like an Indian rope trick. It was a route with a mission. This was partly the fault of the Ukrainians, who had up put the route. They had a summit to reach and had no intention of going in any direction other than up. It was also due to the enormous crevasse that had opened up across the previous route.

I was barely a third of the way up the climb and I was already doubled over, gasping for breath. Sweat was pouring down the inside of my thermal top, and I felt dizzy. This time it was not the altitude but the heat. Just 12 hours earlier it had been -9°C, and that was inside my tent. Now my thermometer was telling me 41°C, a 50 degree fluctuation in just 12 hours. Days like this were not that common, but were dreadful when they occurred. There was not a breath of wind, not a wisp of cloud to cast any shade. We were climbing a section of the mountain where there was no rock, every inch was snow-covered, every inch was reflecting the sunlight back. The atmosphere was much thinner than we were used to, the sunlight was less diffused. My face and hands were slathered in total sunblock but the sweat was washing it away. The rays reflected off the snow were reaching all the sneaky bits I had forgotten, the underneath of my ears and nose, under the chin. It was not the best of conditions in which to try to climb 400 metres of steep snow and ice.

I battled on up a nasty 60 degree slope. Through the whole of April there had been no snowfall on Everest, but we had had several storms recently. The result was soft powder snow that wouldn't hold the weight of a footstep. Under it was glass-hard ice that was barely scratched by the metal points of my crampons. Tired and frustrated, I reached a ledge at the foot of an ice cliff. A short section of vertical ice was followed by a long slope of 80 degree ice and snow. A safety rope ran all the way up it, so it was not dangerous. But it was going to be exhausting.

A tinkling sound was followed by a shower of ice particles onto my head. Climbers were coming down from above. Suddenly, like lemmings over a cliff, the entire Tibetan expedition, 12 members in all, came cascading down the ice slope one after another. I knew that they had been camped at camp 1, in preparation for moving higher up the mountain, and was surprised to see them descending.

Ian following an American climber on the way up to camp 1.

Their English was not good (although better than my Tibetan) but the import of their news was clear: 'too windy, too cold, go down!' It was hard to believe in this 40° furnace but the face I was climbing blocked the wind. The mountain was not yet ready for climbing.

More worrying than weather was illness. The harsh environment was taking its toll on our bodies. Ian's chest infection still lingered, resulting in body-wracking fits of coughing. I was paying the price of climbing in the heat, with mild heat-stroke and a badly burnt lower lip.

Health is such a fragile commodity. Months of planning, thousands of dollars, all of it can be rendered worthless by some minor illness. At these altitudes the body does not recover. Even a small cut on a finger, one that would heal in days at home, can stay open week after week at high altitude. Any more serious illness meant going down to base camp or even lower to recover.

Jangbu and Pemba had been supposed to do the final lifts of equipment to our top camp over the next few days. Once that was in place, the team would be ready to make a bid for the summit. However, Jangbu radioed down from camp 2 to say he felt sick, hit again by a stomach bug we thought we had cured at base camp. They both decided to come back down to ABC. The delay was going to push our schedule back again, and we were running out of time.

We sat in the kitchen tent as Ian and Pemba debated logistical alternatives. Jangbu was asleep in his tent. Phuri was melting ice, and listening intently. There was simply too much equipment still to be moved. We were risking running into June. Although we had the time to do that, at some point the mountain would be affected by the monsoon storms. Every day we delayed increased that risk.

Phuri started talking to Pemba in Nepalese. Phuri was an exceedingly strong man and an able mountaineer. His main problem in life was being Pemba's younger brother, by eight years. Phuri regularly led clients up the trekking peaks of Nepal, and in 1998 had done day trips up to camp 1, carrying loads. However,

Pemba was reluctant to concede that Phuri might be able to go higher. Phuri saw his chance in Jangbu's illness. With his help, all the equipment could be lifted from camp 1 to camp 3 in just two days. At last Pemba reluctantly consented to the plan, and proceeded to lecture Phuri on all the risks involved. Phuri listened with great seriousness, but nothing could disguise his bubbling excitement.

Phuri went on to sleep at camp 1, his first night ever at 7 000 metres, and then carried loads from 7 000 to 8 300 metres two days in a row. It was an astounding performance. When the three Sherpas returned to ABC, neither Pemba and Jangbu were carrying anything, while Phuri carried equipment for all three of them. He had clearly been cast in the role of the apprentice, but once again nothing could suppress the huge grin. He was delighted with himself.

On the night of 24 May we were ready to leave for the push to the summit. The excitement was mounting. I felt weather would be the only obstacle. We were once again fit and now ready and well prepared. The weather seemed to be stabilising, preparing for a spell of several days of good weather. A lot of teams were on the move. We were deliberately holding back, hoping to be able to be the only team on our summit day. We wished no one any harm, but did want to be able to do our own climb, our own way, without getting messed up in other team's dramas.

We were sitting over cups of coffee after dinner, trying to work out where the other teams were, when Russell walked through the tent door. He was supposed to be at Camp 2, on his way to the summit, with the rest of his team. He was one of the strongest climbers on the mountain, and probably the most experienced. He said he had been throwing up everything, even water, for three days. Dehydrated, and with no fuel for the body, he had had to turn back. Even the strongest of humans were so vulnerable in this extreme environment. We were living on the edge of what the human body was designed to do.

Climbing up to camp 1 was a pleasure. As Ian tackled the

Resting on the north face on the way to camp 3. From left: Cathy, Phuri, Jangbu, Pemba.

vertical ice wall, he was climbing straight into the sun. I waited below, taking pictures. The ice glistened, the snow sparkled. Ian stood profiled against the skyline, yellow gaiters, yellow mat rolled on his rucksack, red shirt, blue harness. He contrasted beautifully with the white-silver snow and deep blue sky. I photographed upwards, getting bursts of sun flares exploding from the hot white star of the sun. In the next three hours of climbing I ran through three films - all of Ian climbing above me. I didn't even notice the exhaustion of the steep walls, the visual opportunities were just too exciting. I just hoped that what I was capturing on film was living up to the compositions my eyes were marking out.

The following day spent acclimatising at camp 1 was not a pleasure. I had passed a bad night. Every time I reached a pleasant drowsy state and began to drift off to sleep, I'd suddenly jerk back to wakefulness, with a horrible feeling of suffocation. I finally fell asleep around 3.30 a.m., exhausted, frustrated, bored silly.

The next day was another scorcher, with no wind and no shade. The tent was like a sauna. Ian lay inside it, stripped down to his underrods, rubbing snow onto his skin to cool down. I could not bear it in there. I wandered around, photographing the camp, a multi-coloured squatters' camp set on the pristine snow. I watched climbers on the ridge up to camp 2, ant-like figures making agonisingly slow progress. That was tomorrow's mission.

Good and bad news was all around. Through the telephoto lens of my video camera I could see climbers on the final snow slope before the summit. What was stinking hot at camp 1 was perfect weather two kilometres higher. A total of sixteen climbers reached the top, the first to summit since the drama of the Polish and the Belgians.

Then over the rise into the camp came our Austrian neighbours from base camp, Wilfred and Sylvia. They collapsed at their tent, exhausted, and I took them cups of hot juice. Wilfred's voice had gone but he told me their story in an agonised whisper. They had left the top camp at 2 a.m. It was the third year they had attempted to climb Everest. But it had just got too chilly. They climbed without supplementary oxygen, which made them that much more vulnerable to cold. They had turned back - a third unsuccessful trip, but at least they were safely down.

As I plodded up the snow slope the next day I realised my rucksack was too heavy. Much of the weight was the video equipment and some of it was going to have to go. What had seemed so dinky and lightweight in Johannesburg was feeling remarkably heavy right now.

I focused on the next point where the rope was anchored and concentrated on climbing up to it without stopping. On arrival I doubled over, gasping for breath. The inadequate oxygen was painfully obvious in my slow climbing and frequent stops. Breathing was deep and fast. My pulse was hammering away.

Resting my arms on one bended knee, to get the weight of the rucksack off hips and shoulders for a few minutes, I watched the snowflakes landing gently on my black salopettes. We were lucky with the weather. We were climbing in cloud and gently falling snow, so the temperatures were reasonable. The snowflakes fell in absolute silence. Those that landed on the skin showing between my gloves and my sleeves melted instantly. Those on my clothing stayed awhile, slowly fading with my body heat, until they became completely transparent, and then disappeared. Most were six-sided stars, looking like white starfish. On a few I could see the delicate crystalline patterns of each arm.

As I neared camp 2 I began to be passed by the successful summiteers making their way back to ABC. They all had drawn faces and tired bodies. They moved with dreadful slowness, given that all they had to do was walk down a snow slope. Still, the camaraderie of the mountain shone through. Each time as we passed, stopping briefly to swap over safety slings on the fixed rope, I congratulated them and they wished me luck.

'It was hard, harder than I expected,' was a refrain I heard often.

Another 10 climbers reached the summit that day.

There was drama the next morning as we started out from camp 2 for camp 3. In the tent next to ours was Helge. Three Sherpas and three members from Russell's team, including Helge, had reached the summit the previous day. As we lay in our sleeping bags, trying to find the courage to get out into the cold, one of Russell's Sherpas floundered into her tent. He was snow blind and had spent the night stumbling down the ridge. The glare of the sun off the snow is so acute that, without sunglasses, it will burn the retinas, causing temporary but exceedingly painful blindness. The cure is to spend several days with the eyes in total darkness. He had lost his glasses while helping a Japanese climber. Not having experienced the condition before, he was terrified of losing his sight. Helge reassured him, while covering up his eyes to protect them from further damage. As we prepared to leave another Sherpa came up from camp 1, to lead his fellow climber down to safety.

Just for the sake of dropping his glasses, a big, strong climber had been reduced to a stumbling child. He had to have his crampons clipped on for him, have his safety sling attached to the rope, be guided step by step. That was the challenge of mountaineering. In normal life we make mistakes all the time. However, we hardly notice, because the consequences are so minor. On Everest those same mistakes can mean the difference between death and survival. The margin for error is so much narrower.

On the slope of the north face below camp 3 we were climbing at the top edge of a cloud blanket extending across Tibet. The cloud was typical of the two moods of the mountain.

❋ *Cathy on the lower section of the summit ridge, during the descent.*

❋❋ *Ian and Pemba on the ridge above the Third Step.*

❋❋❋ *Jangbu resting before the final rock climb to the top.*

❋❋❋❋ *Ian on the last few steps below the summit, with the Rongbuk glacier and Tibet below him.*

Sometimes it dipped below me, and became a beautiful silver-grey fluffy blanket bathed in sunshine. It blanketed the plains of Tibet, with the mountains west of us rising through it. I could see the smooth snow dome of Pumori, the jagged profile of Cho Oyu, and, closer to home, the scalloped ridge of Changste. Arching over it all was a sky of pristine blue, lit by a benign sun.

Sometimes the cloud rose up and enveloped me, and that lovely, fluffy blanket became grey, windy and full of wet snow. The icy wind howled round me, blowing mushy snowflakes into every available crack. They then melted against my skin and dribbled down the collar of my jacket.

As I climbed I was once more passed by successful summiteers on their way home. That day another 15 climbers reached the top, including most of the Tibetan team. I was also passed by those who had given up, finding it all too difficult. We never exchanged more than a few breathless sentences. Their passing was both sobering and exciting. We were the last team still making a way up the mountain. It could be done, but it would not be easy.

When the cloud dropped I saw above me the rock ridge that led up to the mountain's highest point. I could see the rock cliff, the First Step, where we had stopped the previous year. Beyond her lay the unknown territory that led to the summit. We should be there in the next 18 hours - maybe. In my confidence that I could climb this side of the mountain, that was the one uncertainty, the one unknown. What would the ridge be like?

❋❋❋ *Jangbu approaching the summit, which is visible beyond him.*

❋❋ *Jangbu on the summit, next to the portrait of the Dalai Lama.*

❋ *From left: Cathy, Pemba and Ian on the summit, 29 May.*

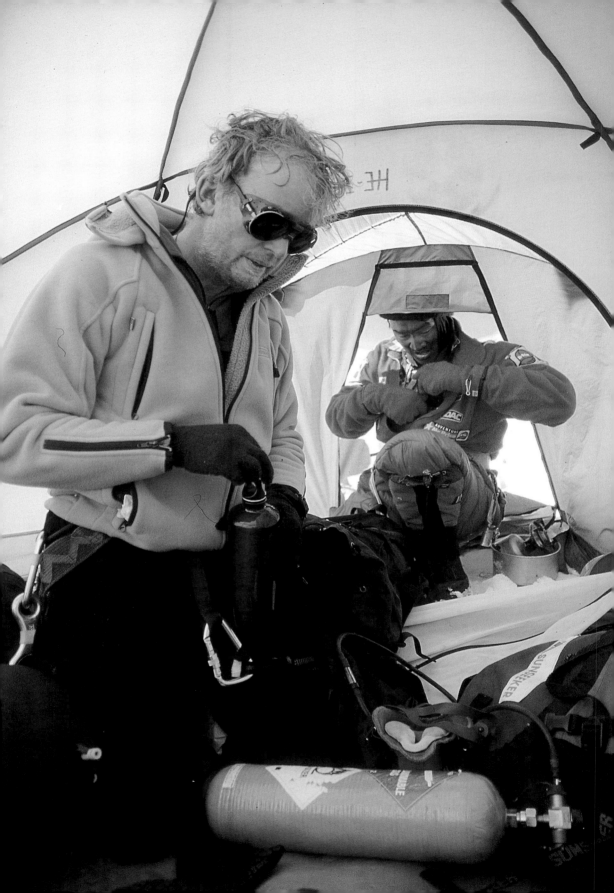

14

Highway in the sky

I lay staring into the velvet darkness. More than looking, I was listening, but the only sound was the subtle hiss of oxygen through my mask. Outside it was deeply, profoundly silent - Chomolungma's blessing, for it meant no wind, stable weather and relative warmth.

I pressed the light on my wristwatch and the tiny square of vivid green lit up, 11.15 p.m. Our summit bid would start in a few minutes. This would be the third time I had set out in the middle of the night for the summit of Everest, and as ever the emotions were mixed. I was warm, and relatively comfortable, deep in my sleeping bag, jammed between the food and bottles of oxygen. To get up, get out, go climbing through the dark icy hours of the early morning, when the human body is at its lowest ebb, seemed like a poor idea. And always there lurked the tension of the great unknown, the rocky ridge that stretched on from the First Step, virgin territory for us. But in the tension was excitement, challenge, anticipation. If all went well, we were less than 12 hours

Ian (left) and Pemba preparing to leave camp 3 for the summit later that night.

from the summit.

Ian's headlight went on, and he began to rustle around. The time for contemplation was over. The summit bid had started. I had had just four hours of sleep. I'd barely eaten since leaving camp 1. But I barely noticed either. Now was the time to run on reserves.

Dressing was a slow process - over the thermal underwear went a polartec top and fleece jacket. Then began the grovel to get into down salopettes, twisting awkwardly in a tent barely high enough to kneel in and crammed full of kit. Then I put the insulated inners into the hard plastic boot outers, before cramming my foot into the combination. Onto fingers went thinsulate inner gloves, a stretch fleece mid glove, with a fleece mitt over that.

Pemba was passing over thermos flasks full of hot drinks. We dressed slowly, stopping every so often to drink, to take a few puffs of oxygen. Then there was a check on everything in the rucksack: sunglasses, spare gloves, video camera, film, batteries, sponsors' flags, oxygen bottles and water bottles. My SLR camera went onto the rucksack waistbelt, the two compact cameras into pockets of the down jacket.

We were nearly ready to leave. Crampons went onto the boots, overgloves onto hands, a down jacket was the final piece of clothing. I struggled out of the tent to be greeted by a spectacular night. It was full moon. There were no clouds. Hundreds of snowy mountains were spread out below us and every one was glistening in the moonlight. I moved away from the tent, standing awkwardly on the snow slope, to allow Ian room to get out. My thermometer read -17°C, for Everest a very warm night. Looking out to the north, I could see just one sign of man, the glow of the lights of a town that I guessed must be New Tingri. There was no talking. As soon as we were all ready, around 12.30 a.m., we began to move up the steep slopes, first Jangbu, then me, then Ian, then Pemba. There had never been a better chance to go for the summit of the world.

Not that it felt like it for the first hour or two. Almost

immediately I felt badly overdressed. All the layers felt hugely awkward, and I was stiff and clumsy within them. Worse than that was the heat. Within minutes I was sweating heavily inside the clothing, the sweat then cooling against the skin, making me feel hot and cold simultaneously. I had never climbed this high in weather this warm. As always, starting out at night, I felt uncoordinated and unbalanced. Each time it seemed impossible that I could keep going like this hour after hour. Fretting about temperature and clumsiness got me up the steep snow slopes to the foot of the rock. I stopped and looked back out. The gleam of the moon on the snow was so strong we had no need of head-torches. The north face swept down below our feet, a swirling mixture of deep black and white-silver. The tents had already disappeared into the shadows.

I have always liked the look of mountains. The first real ones I ever saw were the French Alps. I remembered swinging across the Mer de Glace in the cable car, staring out at the dozens of rock pinnacles and snow slopes. Admittedly, at the age of eleven I was more worried about the cable car falling out of the sky than captivated by the mountain scenery. It was also the first time I had ever seen snow. Bundled up in my woolly jumper and mittens, I was affronted by women in bikinis sunbathing on the roof of the cable station. Snow was supposed to be cold. I knew that from books.

As a teenager I spent several December holidays at a summer camp in the Drakensberg. The camp staff were decidedly odd in retrospect, but they did allow us a lot of freedom. I explored the verdant mountain slopes on foot and on horseback. I loved the space, the grandeur of the peaks, the stillness of the valleys, the sheer expanses of open air. It felt like land without limits.

I turned back to the rock of the north face of Everest and switched on my torch to look for cracks. The climb up to the ridge consisted of intermittent small rock-faces, steep and loose, with diagonal snow runnels between them, up which we worked our way. With something technical to concentrate on, my discomfort

293

began to fade. I climbed close behind Jangbu. As the only one of the four of us who had climbed to the summit from the north before, he was in front. Ian and Pemba were shadowy figures below us. I drew some comfort from not being the slowest of the group, and kept on moving. The night was silent except for the crunch of snow under my feet and the rasp of breath through the oxygen mask.

I climbed up the last shale slopes to the top of the ridge, and stood by Jangbu. A hunt through the vast number of garments that covered my wrist (three gloves, four jacket sleeves) finally revealed my wristwatch - 2.30 a.m. Ian climbed up towards me slowly, and finally was gasping by my side. An icicle hung from the nose of his mask, the moist, warm air he was breathing out condensing and freezing immediately.

'What's my oxygen on?' he asked. I hunted for the spiky metal dial on the tube.

'About two-and-a-half,' I muttered past my own oxygen mask.

'Turn it up to four. I don't feel as if I'm getting any air to my chest at all.'

While I fiddled with Ian's oxygen Pemba pulled out a radio to see whom he could rouse at the foot of the mountain. Padam was clearly awake, answering quickly, sounding tense. Phuri was equally clearly sound asleep, ignoring all attempts to get a response from camp 1.

We started along the ridge. On our right the north face dropped away, with the plains of Tibet, and the western Himalaya visible. The ridge was corniced on our left, waves of snow hanging over the Kangshung face. We walked along the highest rock band. The cornice ceased for a few metres and we walked right on the edge. The Kangshung face dropped away vertically, with the glacier three-and-a-half kilometres below us. In the moonlight I could see Lhotse, Makalu. It was a breath-taking view. On the north side the lights of New Tingri had gone. It felt to me as if we were the only human beings left on earth.

The first mountaineering book I had ever read had been during my December vacation at the end of my first year at university. I was squatting with a group of rock-climbers in a flea-ridden flat in Fishhoek, to sample the delights of Western Cape climbing. To pass a rainy day, I raided the Fishhoek library and found a book about an all-woman expedition to Annapurna. I was fascinated by the concept of the challenge, and by the realisation that it was not just a man's world. Although not yet believing I could do such a thing myself, the first seed of my interest in mountaineering had been planted.

My first encounter with Everest had been a year or so later, when British mountaineer Stephen Venables came to my university in South Africa and told the story of his ascent of Everest, the first British ascent without oxygen. This caught my attention far more than any English lecture in the same venue ever had. However, it still didn't feel like something that I personally wanted to do.

The snow on the summit ridge had gone, and we were walking on rock. It was indeed a very dry season. I had remembered the ridge as flat, a straight line from where we emerged to where Fran lay. But it was both further and steeper than memory suggested. My head-torch was on now, to find a trail across the shattered rock. It provided a small pool of golden light, with everything else in pitch darkness. Suddenly my light pool illuminated a pair of green boots.

They were lime green, fitted with black crampons, lying right in my path. After a moment of complete shock I realised it was one of the three bodies Helge had warned me that we must pass on the summit ridge. It was probably the dead Ukrainian. I moved my torch away, stepped past him and kept moving. This was no time to loose concentration.

Ahead lay the squat, black mass of the First Step. In the back of my mind I knew Fran must be lying somewhere near by but I didn't swing my torch to look. I simply followed Jangbu as he grabbed the fixed ropes and began the steep ascent. If, a year previously, we had reached this step at this time of night we would not have seen Fran. We would have just climbed on past, and

The First Step looms on the left.

continued to the summit. Or so I thought at the time.

I found the First Step higher and steeper than I expected, and wasted little time on trying to climb it in style. I thrutched to the top, gasping for breath, pulse pounding. We had passed through the door from the known to the unknown. What followed from there would be the key to the success or failure of nearly two years of planning and attempting to climb Everest's north side.

What followed was spectacular, unnerving and unexpected. In the manic focus of both mountaineers and the public on the infamous Second Step, all else gets forgotten. The First Step gets a passing mention, but everything else is just preamble or epilogue to the Second Step. Russell had said the traverse between First and Second Step was dangerous, but the reality was an eye-opener.

We were not on top of the ridge, but traversing along its north side, big cliffs above us to the left, and a surprisingly sheer drop on the right. We were working our way along a system of ledges, many of them crumbling on the edges, and covered in loose scree. Occasionally a ledge would end, to resume half a metre higher, or lower, demanding a nasty little technical move over the gaping abyss of the north side. One particularly obnoxious little clifflet had me, face into the rock, stomach pressed against the cliff, tiptoeing (metaphorically speaking, given the massive boots and crampons) past a rotten bulge of rock, with hundreds of metres of fresh air below my heels.

The situation was not helped, but rather badly hindered, by the rotten ropes left lying from previous years. I had no confidence in the condition either of the ropes, or of their anchor points. Some lay loose on the rock and there was the constant danger of my getting them entangled around my crampons.

However, the climbing was interesting, and the exposure exhilarating. The great abyss fell away to the gleaming glacier. The full moon was hanging in majesty over Cho Oyu, and her massive neighbours. Climbing that high, over so much air, I felt more as if we belonged in the territory of the moon, than in that of the earth.

The ridge had eased for a short while, before presenting another cliff face, with a narrow ledge running round a corner into the unknown. Jangbu had already disappeared around it. It was the next challenge and I had just begun cautiously to negotiate it, when I heard Ian's voice. Although I was constantly aware of the shadowy figures climbing with me, they were like ghosts in the night. For one of them to speak, to break the sacred silence of this moonscape, was a shock.

Ian was calling to me.

'I'm not going on. This is not what I expected. I don't like this rock at all. I'll wait here.'

It took a moment for the implication of his words to sink in. The question is often asked how coherently you are thinking at these extreme altitudes. Looking back on this important moment of decision and communication, I know that I was thinking clearly, but more slowly than in normal life, and perhaps with less depth of future consideration. I just wanted to keep moving. I wasn't about to argue the decision with Ian, to try and persuade him otherwise. With excellent weather and approaching dawn, and no indication from him that this stemmed from anything more serious than his well-known dislike of rock-climbing, I was not concerned about leaving him.

'Are you sure,' I shouted.

'Yes.'

'Do you have enough oxygen?'

'Yes.'

'Okay.'

I turned round and moved on, believing Ian and Pemba could be trusted to sort out the issues themselves. I did wonder whether Pemba would turn back as well, and if so whether he was carrying any of the sponsors' flags I was supposed to photograph on the summit. However, climbing back to them to find out seemed far to much like hard work. Fate would sort it out.

I rounded the rock corner, out of their sight, and stepped down onto another ledge system. With my left foot down, my right foot jammed behind me, in mid step. Suddenly, instead of being fluid, mobile, in constant interaction with this rock challenge, I was awkwardly frozen, incapacitated, teetering on the edge of the sunless abyss. I suddenly realised what a rabbit must feel like when standing frozen in the glare of oncoming headlights.

I fumbled grimly behind me to find what had caught my foot. Although I twisted round, I could not see the offending appendage. I dare not twist too far, as the rucksack pushing against the cliff was forcing me off-balance. My thickly gloved fingers detected thin strands of rope wound round the toe bail and front points of my crampon. The worst of the loose rope was the kernmantle, where the mantle had frayed away. The kern consists of a number of fine strands of white rope, each in turn being made up of hundreds more strands. My crampon was caught in a nest of these fine, strong strands.

I heard Pemba's voice in the distance, apparently calling to me.

'Just wait, I'm stuck,' I shouted, the oxygen mask doubtless killing the sound immediately. I was tearing at the fine threads of rope, but the force was futile. In the end I had to slow down and concentrate, tracing the threads with my fingers, and then unlooping them one by one. Finally the foot came free. Once again I was on two feet, feeling stable. I edged back to the rock corner and looked round it, to see what had become of the others. Both Ian and Pemba were climbing towards me along the traverse. Assuming they had sorted themselves out, I moved on, looking out now for the infamous Second Step.

I was climbing into a magical moment. As we had moved along the summit ridge the moon had been slowly sinking in the west, while the sky in the east gradually lightened. The moon, burnished gold, was finally dropping into the low cloud in the west. The sun was just coming up, flaming orange, in the east. The narrow north-east ridge of Everest ran between the two, with nothing but empty air all around it. In the subdued pre-dawn light, it felt like a highway in the sky. It was a pathway to heaven, all the dross of the earth left thousands of metres below us. Such moments are unforgettable, unrepeatable. It was the priceless reward for all the effort involved in getting there.

And there, as if standing at the final guardpost on this road to heaven, loomed the Second Step. It was high, shadowy, a brooding mass facing east, the deep brown rock tinged pink by the rising sun. I took out the SLR for the first photograph of the day, the Step and then Jangbu climbing it. Its reputation is notorious and I was excited to finally be standing at its foot, to measure reality against the myth.

It comes in two sections, a fact, which I had not appreciated. The lower section was steep, awkward climbing up cracks. Then a ledge provided respite before the famous ladder, placed there on the second ascent by the Chinese in 1975. Given its fame, it turned out to be a surprisingly ordinary ladder, mustard-coloured, with

Ian rests just below the Chinese ladder set on the Second Step.
Cathy prepares to descend while Jangbu watches from above.

holes in the rungs, set on the right-hand side of an open book of rock.

The sheer verticality of the ladder was the first obstacle to overcome. The air might be thinner but gravity seemed stronger than ever, and with each step I seemed to be moving a tremendous load upwards. But worse was to come - the ladder ended, but the cliff didn't. The ladder stopped just below a bulge of rock, which was pushing my upper body out and back. To the right, up by a foot or two, was a narrow ledge backed by another, smaller rock-face. At the left-hand edge of the ledge was a solidly wedged little boulder, with loops of rope hanging from it. I teetered there for ages, unsure what to do, afraid to commit to the move. Finally I grabbed the loops with both hands, and edged up the ladder, to get my feet as high as I could. The only option seemed to be a desperate belly flop up and right. I was not impressed by the situation, feeling tired, heavy, and horribly overdressed for this kind of rock gymnastics. I flailed through the move, with all the grace of a fish out of water.

I grovelled across the ledge gasping for breath, irrationally tired. My oxygen mask seemed to be suffocating me, rather than helping. I hastily climbed the last steep steps, to reach the flatter, safer ground of the ridge above. Then I looked at my oxygen indicator. My bottle was empty. I was exposed to the full implications of trying to breath air that has only a third of the oxygen that is available at sea level. I cautiously took off my rucksack and transferred my mask from the now empty bottle to the full one next to it. Putting the mask back on, I once more got the sharp, tangy smell of the life-giving air.

The shadow thrown by the reputation of the Second Step is such that one tends to assume that the ascent is pretty much over once the Step has been climbed. That was to prove yet another myth in a morning full of surprises. Above the Step the ridge widened. The cornice dropped away on the left, providing the first uninterrupted view to the south. On the north side the ridge fell away gently. In our direction of travel it gained height slowly, moving towards the rock mass of the little-mentioned Third Step and the great snow slope, which is so clearly visible from base camp. With no technical difficulties for distraction, I suddenly felt terribly slow. I continued to move steadily, although I was stopping for a few breaths every eight or ten steps. At one such stop Ian caught up with me and suggested a vent stop. We were now bathed in sunshine. In contrast to the previous year, no wind had come with the dawn, the weather was clear and still. The temperature was probably only a little below freezing and we took off our down jackets. Nevertheless the water in our bottles was frozen close to solid. What little of it was liquid was teeth-jarringly cold.

I plodded on. Ian was right on my heels and this always made me feel too slow, worried that I was the one holding the team up. Now I was stopping to rest every few steps, bent over one knee, sucking air in to my depleted lungs. A growing depressing realisation was that the line of rope did not skirt round the Third Step, as I had always assumed, but climbed right through it. And then if this ridge was bad, how much worse was the steep snow slope going to be? As if to provide the final macabre touch to the dismal mood, a body was lying a little way down the slope on the right. His clothing was faded by years of harsh sun. He had obviously been there for a while. He looked so pathetic, a rag doll tossed aside, a tiny figure forgotten on the giant mountain slopes.

All along the ridge I had experienced sudden weird jolts of familiarity, as a scene appeared with which I felt uncannily familiar. In fact I was encountering scenes of which I had seen photographs, without having fully appreciated at the time what I had been looking at.

My first real encounter with icy peaks had been in 1990 when I went to the Ruwenzori mountains in Central Africa with a man I hardly knew. As we approached the mountain, concealed in cloud, the glaciers and rock peaks appeared suddenly out of the swirling mist, hovering in the sky like a divine revelation. I was hooked. Stephen Kelsey and I spent two weeks climbing every summit in the range, not seeing another person in all that time.

The following July vacation, for the second year running, I convinced the History Department to allow me to write delayed exams. I linked up with Stephen again and headed for Bolivia, for my first encounter with a real mountain range, the Andes, and with real altitude, up to 6 000 metres. I hared up the slopes, trying to keep up with the boys, and promptly went down with altitude sickness. I watched, I learnt, I got cold, tired and frightened and I loved every minute of it.

I swotted for the history exam on the plane back from South America. When I complained to one of my History professors that I never seemed to quite crack firsts, he told me dryly that if I could bring to my History the passion I expended on my climbing, I would have no problems.

Reaching the foot of the Third Step brought my mind back to the job at hand. It proved easy rock-climbing, and got Ian off my heels. The snow slope was not much worse. At least you had an obvious height gain with each step. In these last two seasons, I had watched many little figures tiptoe up this slope, visible from both base camp and ABC. I looked out, across and down the great basin of air held in the arms of the north and west ridges of Everest. From the glacial pool at the foot of the north face an ever thinner stream of ice wound its way north. And somewhere just beyond its end, at the beginning of the dusty plains of Tibet, lay base camp, invisible to the eye. There Padam would be anxiously watching our progress. Did anyone else even know we were up here? Camp 1 was closer and clearer, a tiny mass of faint colour on the snow below Changste and Everest. Phuri would be sitting in the doorway of the tent, watching. ABC was invisible on the rocks. Perhaps Russell was down there watching, waiting to see if the season would end peacefully, or in one final disaster he would be called on to sort out.

But if disaster struck us now, no one would be able to come to our aid. We were so high, trespassing on the edge of space, that we were beyond all human aid, except what we could offer each other. That, too, was severely limited.

Even now, the mountain never ceased to surprise. We did not simply climb up the snow slope onto a snowy summit ridge. Instead, we moved off to the right, onto yet another rocky traverse. Now we were directly above the centre of the north face, seemingly headed straight for the west ridge. We were crossing the very apex of an enormous pyramid. The face fell away and down, very distinctly down, for 3 600 metres. It was like standing on the summit of the highest mountain in South Africa, looking straight down at the sea. It was a hugely exhilarating place to be. The entire world lay at our feet, stretching out and away.

As a teenager even cable cars and glass-faced lifts frightened me. One classic epic in my second year of rock-climbing involved an overhanging jam crack with 45 metres of air below it. Terrified of swinging out into space if I fell off, I burrowed into the crack, refused to move in any direction, and burst into tears. The leader, with infinite patience, slowly coaxed me up, move by move. I rewarded that patience by finally clawing my way over the top of the cliff and absolutely refusing to do the 50 metre free abseil back into the gorge. To return to our campsite he and I were forced to walk cross country for five kilometres, without torches.

However, as I climbed more, my fear of heights lessened. I took to cleaning windows of high-rise buildings to earn money for my climbing trips. I would sit on abseil, rubbing away at the giant glass walls, listening to my English setworks on audio tape. Nauseated executives sometimes had to leave their offices rather than watch me hanging around outside their windows.

Fear of heights never goes completely. To lose that nervousness would be to become overconfident. However, one learns to control it, to distinguish between genuine danger and unhelpful psychological terror. From the moment we can crawl a voice from the heavens is telling us not to clamber up the stairs, or not to climb into that tree. We'll fall and hurt ourselves. The adults are right. We probably will. At the age of two I tried walking around the landing of my parent's staircase with a pink blanket over my head. It made sense at the time. I walked off the edge and was saved from nasty injury by bouncing off some cushions.

However, the fear can become so ingrained that it overwhelms our common sense, prevents us from doing what we would like to do with our lives. Despite having spent three seasons on Everest, the only time I have come close to killing myself was in the Swiss Alps. While abseiling off a rock route, I tried to reach an anchor point that was just too far from me. The end of the rope slipped through my hand. Unfortunately the ground was still 100 metres below me. It was an error born of carelessness and overconfidence. I had already abseiled hundreds of pitches that summer. As I fell, I managed to hook my elbow over a passing tree stump. I would live to climb another day.

Jangbu turned towards the rock and began a steep scramble up the final rocky slope. I followed up this unexpected final rock challenge. It was a straightforward but exposed set of diagonal scrambles. I pulled up onto the snow ridge at the top of the face and looked expectantly to my right. I saw Jangbu moving ahead with steady determination, a trail of footprints in the snow. No summit yet, and no indication of how much further it would be. There was nothing to do but keep climbing.

When I left university at the end of 1991 I had a degree in History, History of Art and Classical Civilisation. I'd had great fun getting it but had no idea what to do with it. I dithered between honours in History and a year climbing in Europe. Not a hard choice to make, I spent the British winter selling climbing equipment in London and the next summer camped in the French Alps. I linked up with a sweet traffic officer from Birmingham and talked him into trying a 16 pitch rock route. At the end of the first pitch he was looking pale and said I'd have to lead the whole route. I stared back at him. I had never done anything of this magnitude without a more experienced partner. As I hauled him up it, pitch by pitch, we watched avalanches come crashing off the Freney pillar. I was exhilarated by the situation and by the responsibility. He was very quiet and looked a little green. We reached the top of the rock pinnacle and then abseiled back down to the ground. He staggered back to camp and had a hernia.

I found other partners and kept climbing. We didn't do anything spectacular, just lots of it. Climbing with strangers, I had to take responsibility for us both, no matter what they claimed to have climbed before. Climbing is as much a mental game as a physical one. It is an intricate jigsaw puzzle of multi-faceted bits of challenge that need to be fitted together to create a harmonious whole. Mountaineering becomes a much larger extension of that. I now needed just one more piece to make my Everest jigsaw complete.

I crested a small rise and saw a series of little dips and rises, finally rising to a peak. On its left was a vertical drop down the Kangshung face. On its right it sloped away gently. A curved line of footprints, left by teams from the three previous days, ran like a confetti trail to the top. Jangbu pointed enthusiastically and shouted. I couldn't hear his words but I knew what he meant There was the final piece to my jigsaw. We were going to make it!

I turned and looked back. Ian and Pemba were at the top of the rock. We were all going to make it. I followed after Jangbu, finding the last section less tiring than I had anticipated. Finally the trail of footprints curved up and left to a marker - a photograph of the Dalai Lama, facing north over the plains of Tibet. A Sherpa had left it there three days previously. I stopped next to Jangbu, and looked at my watch. It was 8 a.m. We had made a fast ascent. It was 29 May 1999, three years and four days since our last summit, exactly 46 years since the mountain had first been climbed.

We were immediately hit by a cold wind from the south. Taking off my rucksack, I pulled my down jacket back on, and grabbed my camera. First I took the 360 degree panorama of the view from the top that we had not got in 1996. Then I took pictures of Ian and Pemba, little orange and yellow figures moving up the fluted snow ridge towards us. Then pictures of Jangbu as he posed on the very top.

Ian began to yell at us. The summit sits right on the edge of the Kangshung face, and is partly corniced over it. From his position on the ridge he could see we were straying onto the corniced section. We moved back to solid ground.

Looking around, we had a clear day with a little low cloud in the valleys. The portrait of the Dalai Lama was framed with prayer scarves and prayer flags lay on either side. The tripod that had marked the summit in 1996 was now about half a metre down on the south side. Footprints led off down the ridge towards the south.

Pemba joined us and immediately pulled out a radio to call down to Phuri and Padam. He was off in an excited chatter of Nepalese. He had finally achieved the summit that he had sacrificed the year before to accompany us down the mountain.

Ian came up after him.

'I don't like this,' he announced. 'I want to get out of here.'

We needed to get down to business. I pulled out the pile of sponsors' flags that needed to be photographed. Ian took the photographs. Pemba and I held the flags, with Jangbu standing behind. The lurking fear was that I would miss one, crumpled in some corner of the rucksack. I had to get this right, because there wouldn't be another chance.

Ian and Pemba got ready to leave. The wind was taking its toll. After eight hours of steady exertion, we all got cold quickly standing still. However good the weather, we could not under-estimate the danger of the descent. Four people had died on Everest this season, every one descending from the summit.

I saw two flags we had missed and said Jangbu and I would stay just a few minutes longer. I had hoped that this second time to the top of the world I would be able to sit down, just for a few minutes, and soak up the feeling of being there. Because there isn't going to be a third time. But in the end it was too cold. Having spent 45 minutes on the summit I turned to leave, the last of the four of us to go.

In some senses the summit was, perhaps inevitably, an anti-climax. The coldness of the wind and Ian's edginess both unsettled the experience. In some ways I was too busy taking pictures to just look at where I was. In fact it is impossible to freeze-frame a moment of your life, to put the emotions in a jar so they can be savoured for ever after.

There was less of the incoherent wonder of 1996, less of the incredible celebration at base camp and at home. Once I had left camp 3, just eight hours before, and seen how good the weather was, I had been basically confident of reaching the summit. But that had its own virtues. In place of wonder was confidence and experience. The 1996 expedition had dropped out of the sky, a miraculous gift. This one had been my expedition from first conception to this summit. This was the culmination of two years of work, of planning, of training, of climbing, of just keeping on trying. That was a greater summit than the pile of snow that lay on top of the mountain.

Cathy on the summit on 29 May 1999, the first woman to have climbed Everest from both its south and north sides.

Epilogue

Climbing down the ridge was spectacularly beautiful. We were once more out of the wind, moving in idyllic conditions. I got to photograph everything I had missed in the dark on the way up. Ian and Pemba were ahead, providing two figures, yellow and orange, to pose against the dramatic swirls of the corniced ridge. As one film ended it got pulled out and stuffed in the pocket of my jacket. Another canister was pulled open with my teeth and jammed into the SLR.

Sometimes I had to remind myself just to stop and look, rather than photograph, to appreciate the moment, rather than always trying to record it for future appreciation. And sometimes I had to remember to forget the photography and concentrate on the climbing. One error and all this could yet end in disaster.

With the confidence that comes of returning home, rather than venturing into the unknown, I enjoyed the rock traverses, revelling in their exposed positions. The Second Step was as unhelpful in the descent as it had been in the ascent, but the rest was simply great fun.

Crossing the traverse in full daylight, I could now appreciate just how exposed and narrow it was. Somewhere, several hundred feet below me lay the body of George Mallory, who had fallen to his death 75 years previously, and been discovered by the Americans a few weeks before. There, too, lay the bodies of many others. I could now see why. With the route narrow and loose, the chance for error was considerable. An able climber, tired, moving quickly and unroped, had only to make one slight mistake, to slip, to stumble, to find himself tumbling down those steep slopes. A fall might not be immediately fatal but anything that left one basically immobile was a virtual death sentence this high on Everest.

The dreams of many mountaineers had come to an abrupt end on these summit slopes. I stood on the top of the First Step, and looked down onto Fran, lying at its bottom. She had slumped down from the sitting position we had left her in, but otherwise she was just the same. And now she would be there for eternity. What for us was a beautiful descent had been for her an ever growing nightmare.

Yet as I walked on along the ridge I wondered at the turn fate had dealt us. Ian and I had always assumed that, if we had not encountered Fran on 24 May 1998, we would have climbed on and reached the summit. We would have been spared another year of waiting, another entire expedition to fund, organise, and climb on. But now I was not so sure. We had climbed this year in supremely good conditions, no wind, high temperatures. The previous year had been different. Even as I had approached the foot of the First Step the wind, the cold had been slowly eating away at my reserves. I knew now, and Ian was later to agree with me, that we had underestimated the difficulty of the climb from the First Step to the summit. Last year, given our uncertain start, the poor weather, our misjudgement of the route, would we in fact have reached the summit, if Fran had not stopped us? I began to doubt it. I think we might have ground to a halt, too cold, too disconcerted by the difficulties, and have turned back. And had we turned back in such circumstances, it was most unlikely that we would ever have bothered to return. In a strange way, it had all turned out for the best.

We were back at camp 3 by 1 p.m. I was now thoroughly tired. We had been on the move for over 12 hours. Ian and I collapsed into our tent and drank warm juice while slowly beginning to pack up. However, 'slowly' was not in the vocabulary of Pemba and Jangbu. For them it was time to go home, right now. The tent was more or less taken down round us, the sleeping mats rolled up from under our backsides. We piled our rucksacks high, and then set off down the mountain. This was less like fun. I was deeply tired, running on too little food, too little water, and carrying too much kit. My back hurt, my feet hurt. And just after that the spell of good weather that had seen teams summit every day for the previous four days, ended. Abruptly. The season was over. We had made it by a mere six hours.

First it began to snow lightly. That was almost a pleasure, as once again I was feeling overdressed in a full down suit. Then the grey clouds closed in around us, and the wind began to blow. The temperature was falling rapidly. My shoulders were aching from the weight. With a down suit and a climbing harness in the way, it was almost impossible to get the weight of the rucksack onto my hips. We plodded stoically down the snowy slopes.

Phuri had climbed up from camp 1 and met us at 7 900 metres. The other two headed on down while he gave us some hot juice and took some of our load. We took our crampons off and prepared to descend the rock ridge to camp 2. This was where conditions became truly unpleasant. The snow had stopped but the wind began to howl. The scree of the rock ridge had formed an icy skin over ground damp from the earlier snowfall. The surface was desperately slippery. The safety rope was also frozen, at times with a rind of ice on its windward side thicker than the rope itself. Time and again my foot would hit an ice patch and I would slip, crashing onto my butt. The rucksack would swing wildly across my back, pinning me under its weight. Tired, miserable, generally cross, I would sit in a huff, trying to find the energy to pull myself together and keep moving.

I would struggle onto my knees only to be knocked sideways by a brutal gust. The exposed north ridge left us open to the full fury of the west wind. More than once I turned my back to it, and huddled down to wait out the spell. Seeking sympathy for my misery, I pulled out my wind metre to confirm that conditions were as bad as they felt. They were. Winds were gusting up to 86 kilometres per hour, and the wind-chill temperature was -40°C.

My greatest worry was whether the camp 2 tent was still there, not blown away in the wind.

The agony seemed endless, an unmitigated nightmare. The ridge stretched on forever. We were the only people alive in an icy hell, without beginning, without end. Just as I was about to drown in my own drama, the ridge grudgingly came to an end. I sat down in the lee of a big boulder to put crampons back on. The tent, which was mercifully still there, was only some 10 metres away, but with my load and my exhaustion, I was not about to risk a slip on the icy snow.

I finally collapsed in the camp 2 tent at 6 p.m., frozen, drained, the nasty end to 18 hours of climbing. Ian stumbled in a while later. His voice was almost totally gone. He lay unmoving across the tent floor, a cold, heavy heap.

I found a spare bottle of oxygen, put my mask onto it, and pushed it towards him.

'What's this?' he mumbled.

'Oxygen. Just take it. It'll help'.

'I can't breath,' he whispered. 'My chest has closed up. I can't get any air.'

Four hours of climbing into the icy cold wind had proved the final straw for Ian's lingering chest infection. I bullied him out of his outer clothes and boots, and into his sleeping bag. Then I turned to the problem of liquid. Both stoves were frozen solid. The lighters could barely raise a spark. And there was no snow in the tent bell clean enough to risk melting for drinking. Ian was dead to the world. I simply was not going outside again to fetch snow.

I slumped down on my sleeping bag. Tears of exhaustion trickled down my cheeks. Ian took over the role of bully long enough to get me to give up on the stoves, and get into my sleeping bag. Enough was enough. The day was over. We both slept like the dead.

We woke to howling wind. The clouds had cleared and the sun was shining. However, the wind wailed on and temperatures were low. I would have given a lot not to have to climb on down that day, but that is the nature of mountaineering. You always have to have enough left to get back to the bottom. We dressed, packed and prepared to leave. I ate half a packet of Super Cs. The stoves were still refusing to work. The water in our bottles was mostly frozen, leaving only a few trickles to pour down our throats. I noticed that the urine in my pee bottle was totally opaque and dark orange. I was badly dehydrated, but felt neither thirsty nor hungry. I was now digging deep into my reserves.

Ian was ready first and set off into the wind, leaving me putting crampons on and sorting my outer gloves. When I stood up outside, it was totally still. I put my Goretex overmitts and camera on top of the bell of Russell's tent, which still stood next to ours. A gust came up, grabbing one of the gloves. I watched it tumble down the snow slope, straight over the edge of the ridge towards the glacier. We were not out of it yet.

A few hours later we were 500 metres further down, sitting at camp 1. The great ice cliff that protected the campsite sheltered us from the wind. I felt warm again for the first time in 18 hours. Pemba and Jangbu had stripped camp 1 and were waiting for Phuri to bring down the last of camp 2. They had a stove going and I was pouring hot juice and coffee down my throat. My hunger was back with a vengeance. I hadn't eaten for 90 hours and had lost four or five kilograms in that time. Now I was stuffing my face - whole-wheat digestives, Melrose cheese wedges, Koo fruit, biltong - all the pleasures of home.

I felt that it was now finally 'over', that the expedition could be called safe and successful. But Ian refused to agree. We had to reach the glacier first, had to be off all the mountain slopes. There were still the steep ice slopes below camp 1 to negotiate, with a final challenge. The general high temperatures were melting the top layer of ice. The anchors, generally icescrews, which secured the safety ropes were all coming loose. We needed to descend with particular care.

It was a slow process as we let our tiredness set the pace. There was no need to push now. At the top of the abseil, where once the

Tibetans had poured over me, the Sherpas caught up with us. We stood aside to let them pass, and they descended one by one. Their style said so much about the character of each of them.

Pemba came swinging past with a cheerful greeting: 'Okay, Bara sahib, okay, Didi?' With little preamble he swung himself over the edge, with solid, purposeful gestures. His feet hit hard into the ice wall, assured, deliberate. There was no sign of the shy young man of the 1996 expedition. He had grown to be a superb mountaineer, confident and competent. He was more than that, though. He had a sense of responsibility for others, a care for their welfare that made him an excellent sirdar. Although our team of Sherpas was a group of equals, Pemba's voice was the one heard most often.

Phuri went down second. Jangbu checked his abseil set-up for him, for he was still new to these more technical matters. He dropped over the edge with a worried frown and a huge grin. He flailed all over the place as he descended, still technically amateur but yet with an ingrained confidence in this vast mountain environment. Next year he hoped to get a place as a summit Sherpa on an Everest team. Sadly, it would not be one of ours, but it had been a pleasure to watch the ABC cook gradually transformed into a summit climber.

Jangbu went last, his movements small and precise, his face composed, his emotions unreadable. He floated down the wall, each crampon meticulously placed, just the frontpoints grazing the ice. He had reached the summit of Everest four times, three times on our expeditions. He was now a married man. New challenges spread out in front of him

These men, with their enormous physical strength, capacity for endurance and balanced temperaments, had allowed us to complete these expeditions. We could not have done it without their aid. I used to think their physical ability was simply the result of their environment. Where we grew up behind school desks and travelling in cars, they walked the precipitous slopes of the Himalayan, breathing the thin mountain air. But now, particularly having watched Phuri so rapidly extend his mountain experience, it felt to me as if it was something more intangible than that. Some of the Sherpas seemed to have a psychological affinity for the mountains, a capacity for belonging that we would never have. Russell, with his vast Everest experience, perhaps came closest to it. We would always be aliens, trespassing where we should not go.

In the years that I had been associated with Everest, the Sherpas had increasingly been asserting their own identity as superb high-altitude mountaineers, rather than living in the shadow of the foreigners. Earlier in the season Babu Tshering Sherpa had climbed to the summit from the south side and had camped there for over 21 hours, without oxygen. The previous season, in October 1998, Kaji Sherpa had climbed from south side base camp to the summit in 20 hours and 24 minutes, the fastest ascent ever. Ang Rita Sherpa and Apa Sherpa were tied for the most ascents of Everest, with 10 summits each. The profile of Sherpas such as these is high in their home country. The rest of the world is also beginning to wake up to their ability, and to their contribution to Everest ascents.

I could not have made my ascents of the mountain without their assistance. I could also not have got the same enjoyment out of those ascents without their company, their even temperaments, their gentle humour. They were the people to whom these mountains truly belonged.

Two days later we were all back at base camp, with all our equipment. We received an emotional welcome from Padam, who had spent two long and lonely weeks trying to stop yak herders liberating our equipment at every opportunity. Padam did not speak the Sherpa language, and so could not talk to the Tibetans. The herders would open tent zips and look under flaps, whether the tents were occupied or not. If caught, they simply backed off with a huge grin and nipped round the back to try again.

Already the mountain was moving into our past, our eyes were refocusing on the future. We had spoken to family and the media back home. I had washed off five weeks of dirt in Russell's hot shower. The results were heavenly - clean, fragrant skin and hair

The Chomolungma
Castle party:

Top from left:
Padam and Jangbu.

Bottom from left:
Ian and Phuri.

that was not stuck together all the time. The trucks would be arriving in two days time to take us away, back to the lowlands, to greenery and people. I was ready to go. I wanted warmth and no wind, no coughing and normal food. I wanted to move on.

But first came the party, one last celebration of the mountain and its people. We joined with Russell's team, who had got six to the summit. Helge had done up one of his tents as the 'Chomolungma Castle', complete with party hats, streamers, balloons and prayer flags. Russell appeared in a jacket, made out of goatskin, and a tie, made of the carry rope for the water bottles. He brought out the French champagne, and team members, Sherpas, and support staff crowded into the tent to celebrate. The Tibetan Mountaineering Association officials appeared to hand out silver-white prayer scarves, so long they almost reached the ground. Later we danced to ABBA, while the Sherpas ran around outside firing rockets into the air.

We drove out of base camp at 5 a.m., two days later. The mountain was partly obscured by pink cloud but the summit was clear and the very first rays of sun were catching the ridge. The summit hung above the cloud, a golden jewel suspended in the sky. At last the pressure was off, the expedition was over and highly successful. We had done all we had set out to do. During the hard days of climbing high on the mountain there had been little time to reflect over what we had achieved. The focus was always on the immediate moment, and on that to follow it. But now, at last, things were beginning to sink in.

I had made it.

By the end of the spring season of 1996 there had been 835 ascents of Everest and I had been the 39th woman ever to have reached the summit. By the time we drove away in 1999 there had been 1 173 ascents and 52 women had reached the highest point in the world. But the summit of Everest from both the south and the north - I was first woman ever to achieve that. It was not bad for a girl from a land of sun and beaches, at the southern tip of the African continent, who just three-and-a-half years earlier had

Cathy and Ian happy to be at the end of four years of Everest.

looked at the Sunday Times and wondered if she should send in an application for an Everest expedition led by some man she had never heard of.

I had sent in that application because I loved the mountains, and because I didn't want to spend to rest of my life merely wondering what would have happened if I had applied. Perhaps somewhere in a parallel universe is another me who didn't apply and now lives a totally different life. I wouldn't swap places with her. Although I waded through many kinds of difficulty, nothing even began to outweigh the joy of experience that I gained.

The record as the first woman was something special, something fun to have achieved, but it occurred almost by accident. What I have that I cherish most is three-and-a-half years of life lived to the full, of memories, of experiences, of knowledge of the world and of myself. I remember sunrises, special vistas, moments of laughter, more clearly than I do the summits.

Why climb Everest at all? And why on earth climb it twice?

Just for the love of it.